WEAVING WITH FOOT-POWER LOOMS

WEAVING WITH FOOT-POWER LOOMS

EDWARD F. WORST

DOVER PUBLICATIONS, INC.

NEW YORK

Published in Canada by General Publishing Company, Ltd., 30 Lesmill Road, Don Mills, Toronto, Ontario.

Published in the United Kingdom by Constable and Company, Ltd., 10 Orange Street, London WC 2.

This Dover edition, first published in 1974, is an unabridged and unaltered republication of the sixth (1924) edition of the work originally published by The Bruce Publishing Company, Milwaukee, in 1918. The work was formerly titled *Foot-Power Loom Weaving*.

International Standard Book Number: 0-486-23064-3
Library of Congress Catalog Card Number: 74-75270

Manufactured in the United States of America
Dover Publications, Inc.
180 Varick Street
New York, N.Y. 10014

INTRODUCTION

THE suggestions offered in this manual are for those who believe that the more advanced weaving should be pursued as a most wholesome occupation and that it should again, in the near future, find a place not only in the school but also in the home. Few lines of occupation furnish more excellent opportunity for color combination and design than does the craft of weaving.

Girls taking the various household-arts courses will find weaving a great aid in understanding the structure of a piece of cloth.

The work is so full of possibilities and the results obtained have such a wonderful effect on the character of the worker that these alone afford ample reasons why weaving should be carried on in both school and community.

Double weaving as it was done in the early days is such a mystery to the home weavers of today that it was thought advisable to add a chapter on this branch of the work in the present edition.

The scarcity of linen at the present time suggested to the author the addition of a few good linen weaves. Flax is so easily cultivated and prepared for use that those interested will find little difficulty in preparing the flax from the seed to the finished piece of cloth.

The descriptions given are for the amateur weaver who will find them more easily understood than those given in the more technical books on the subject.

It is hoped that those interested will find help through the suggestions offered in this manual.

EDWARD F. WORST.

TABLE OF CONTENTS

TABLE OF CONTENTS—Concluded

CHAPTER I
The Loom, Warping and Threading

Loom Weaving

Notwithstanding the introduction of the power loom and all its wonderful possibilities, the hand loom still survives and seems likely to continue in use since numerous schools and handicraft societies as well as many independent art workers are becoming interested. This gives hope that at some time in the near future the domestic occupations of weaving and spinning in both flax and wool will again find a place, not only in the home but also in the studio and in the industrial school. The appreciation of handwork has, during the past decade, increased in the estimation of the public.

In various European countries, as well as in India, China and Japan, hand loom weaving still continues. In Norway and Sweden a very successful line of home industry is carried on to great advantage to many women who find it necessary to aid in the family support. This may also be said of the women in the Orkney and Shetland Islands.

Of late much has been written of the beautiful hand-weaving done by the women in the mountains of Kentucky and Tennessee. So attractive is this work that little difficulty is experienced in disposing of the articles woven.

Since the introduction of machine spinning and weaving, no home industry which approaches them in usefulness or interest has taken their place. It is true that there are many lines of weaving now produced by the machine, too intricate to be attempted on the hand loom, but the weaving of linen, cotton, woolen and the coarser silk threads into materials of strength and beauty for home use, can quite well be carried on in the studio and even by the home-maker who has other household occupations.

There is no doubt as to the superiority of a well made, hand-woven article. This is plainly shown if the hand-made and the machine-made articles are compared. Hand loom weaving, too, is superior to machine weaving if judged by the effect it is likely to have on the worker. The hand weaver is employed in a pleasant, ingenious occupation which exercises all his faculties, while the attendant on a power loom is engaged in a monotonous toil in which no quality but intense watchfulness is required.

The object of this manual on weaving is to give to the amateur weaver the benefit of the author's experience in preparing the fibers, the warping and the threading of the loom for plain weaving, as well as learning to interpret and to execute various pattern drafts used in our own and other countries.

Through the exercises given it is hoped the weaver may be led to invent and to work out many interesting and original designs.

The Construction of Plain Cloth

If a piece of plain cloth is examined, it will be found to consist of a number of longitudinal threads placed side by side and interlaced by a continuous single thread. The latter thread passes alternately above and below or before and behind the longitudinal threads. Fig. 1 shows the arrangement of the longitudinal threads and the continuous thread crossing and intersecting them.

The longitudinal threads of a piece of woven material are always called the warp. They are so named, because, in order to allow their being intersected conveniently by the continuous crossing thread, they have to be warped, that is, tightly strained in position on some kind of frame prepared for the purpose. The continuous crossing thread has several names, such as weft, woof, or shoot (shute).

If the warp threads are carefully examined they will be found to consist of several fine threads twisted together. This is done to give added strength. The weft may be single and the thread only slightly twisted, as this makes

Fig. 1—A Piece of Plain Cloth

it soft so the warp and weft are easily pressed together into a firm material.

The weaving of mats and baskets from local materials and from raffia, reed and willow may be done without any special appliance for holding or stretching the material while it is being woven.

When fine thread is to be woven the problem is very different, and it becomes absolutely necessary to devise some kind of frame to hold and stretch the warp upon, so that the weft may be readily interlaced with it. The more elaborate frame constructed for this purpose has by universal consent been called a loom.

The Essential Parts of a Loom

In all the ancient pictures of looms the stretched warp threads are shown and the insertion of the weft threads is suggested; but the lease, the one universal and indispensable contrivance used in weaving, has been omitted. While not shown, it must have been there, for no loom could be operated without it.

Fig. 2 illustrates the three steps in the construction of a simple loom. The construction is similar to the looms made by the pupils of the lower grades.

Fig. 2, "A" shows the loom without the thread.

"B" shows the warp threads wound upon it lengthwise.

"C" shows the strings on the board intersected by two rods, "D," in such a way that alternate strings go over and under each rod. In the space between the rods the alter-

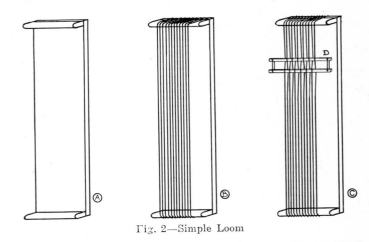

Fig. 2—Simple Loom

nate strings cross each other in regular succession. While the rods "D" are kept in their position in the warp it is impossible for the threads to get out of place or to get hopelessly entangled, as they certainly would if any great number of threads were used.

This cross is called the lease and is really the one indispensable part of the loom. No two looms may be alike in any other respect but in the case of the lease. One cannot dispense with this simple yet perfect contrivance for keeping the warped threads in order when a long warp made up of hundreds of threads is required.

Preparing a Long Warp

A warp longer than the loom cannot be made upon the loom shown in A, B, C, Fig. 2.

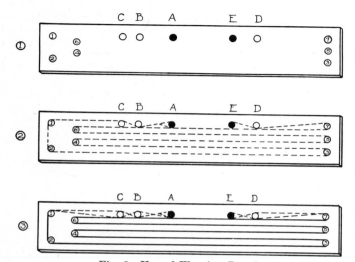

Fig. 3—Use of Warping Board

This being true, some sort of apparatus must be constructed on which to build up a series of threads of exactly the required length and number of threads. These threads must be held in exactly the same tension so that, when transferred to the loom and stretched between its front and back beams, they shall give the weaver as little trouble as possible with loose threads.

This process of preparing the threads is called *warping.* There are several ways of doing the warping.

Construction of Warping Board

Fig. 3 shows the construction of a warping board. On this board may be warped a moderate number of threads, such as would be required for a foot-power loom.

The board shown in Fig. 3 (1, 2 and 3) is six feet long by one foot wide. It is made to hang firmly on a wall at such a height from the ground that the operator can reach to any part of it without difficulty.

A thread ten yards in length may be warped on a board of the given size. A longer length may be warped either by increasing the length of the board, or by increasing its width, and adding to the number of pegs. The pegs should be made of hard wood not less than six inches long and one inch in diameter.

The pegs marked A and E must be movable, perfectly smooth and have nicely rounded ends. The space between A and B should not be less than one foot, and the space between B and C, six inches. The space between D and E should also be one foot.   (No. 1, Fig. 3).

The Board in Use

Let the problem at hand be to make a warp of thirty threads ten yards long.

Place a spool of ordinary four-ply carpet warp on end in a receptacle of some kind in order that the thread may freely unwind. If a spool rack is at hand, the spool may be slipped on to one of the rounds of the rack. Tie the free end of the warp to the movable peg A, No. 2, Fig. 3. Guide the thread *under* peg B and *over* peg C. Then follow the dotted line, as shown in No. 2, Fig. 3, by allowing the thread to pass outside the pegs 1, 2, 3, back to 4, then to pegs 5, 6 and 7. Then carry the thread under peg D, over and around peg E, and then begin its return by carrying the thread over D, No. 3, Fig. 3, on to peg 7 (see dotted lines) and so back in the same course, until we again reach peg 1. It must now be taken below C, over B, and below A (see dotted lines). This completes one course. The warping board should now look like No. 3, Fig. 3, with the threads crossed between pegs B and C, and D and E. Two threads have now been warped, having a length of ten yards between the crosses.

The second thread having been carried around and over peg A, pass it under B and then follow exactly the course of the first thread until it reaches E. Then, following the second thread back it reaches A, goes under and over the peg, and four threads out of the thirty are warped. By the time fifteen forward and fifteen backward journeys are made the warp of thirty threads is finished and may be taken from the board as soon as the crosses have been made secure.

One can readily understand from the foregoing explanation, that a great amount of time would be consumed in making a warp by handling one thread at a time. Since four-ply carpet warp is to be used for the first warping, four spools may be placed on the spool rack, the four ends tied to the proper peg at one time and then the course pursued with the four threads, as was described for only one thread. This causes four threads to pass under and over the pegs instead of one. On account of the coarseness of the warp there is little or no danger of the threads becoming tangled. A more detailed explanation of running more than four threads will be given later. The above, however, works very successfully.

Securing the Crosses

The important matter of securing the crosses is easily done, but if forgotten the warp will be spoiled when it is removed from the board.

Fig. 4 shows clearly the way it is done. The letters indicate the pegs of the warping board; the heavy lines are the threads of a warp, which may consist of any number of threads.

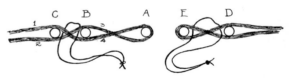

Fig. 4—Securing the Crosses

The important crosses are shown between C and B and between D and E. A thin, pliable cord about two yards long is drawn in at each cross from the back to the front, through the openings in front of the pegs. Tie the ends of the cord as shown in Fig. 4. By this means the crosses are perfectly secured.

It will be observed that there is another cross in the warp between B and A. This is not so important. A short cord may be drawn through the loop at peg A, and the threads may be tied all together.

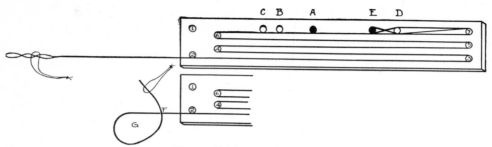

Fig. 5—Taking off the **Warp**

The warp may now be removed from the board and made into what is called a chain.

Taking Off the Warp

The warp is taken off the warping board for convenience in transferring it from the board to the warp beam of the loom.

The crosses having been made secure, the warp is ready to be removed from the board. The long strings between the crosses may be wrapped around the warp to prevent them from hanging in the way.

First remove the peg A, Fig. 5. Allow the warp to slip from the other pegs, B and C, and also No. 1, Fig. 5. Hold the warp with the left hand about two feet from the end. While it is thus held with the left hand, throw the free end over the rest of the warp with the right hand, as shown at F, Fig. 5.

This makes a kind of loop. With the left hand still holding the warp, the right hand is put through the loop at G, Fig. 5. The warp is grasped and drawn through the loop far enough to make a second loop, held by the right hand. The left hand is now free and is put through the new loop held by the right hand. The warp is grasped and drawn through the new loop thus making a third loop held this time by the left hand. The right hand being free is put up through the third loop, the warp is grasped and

Fig. 6—Chain Made with Warp from Warping Board

13

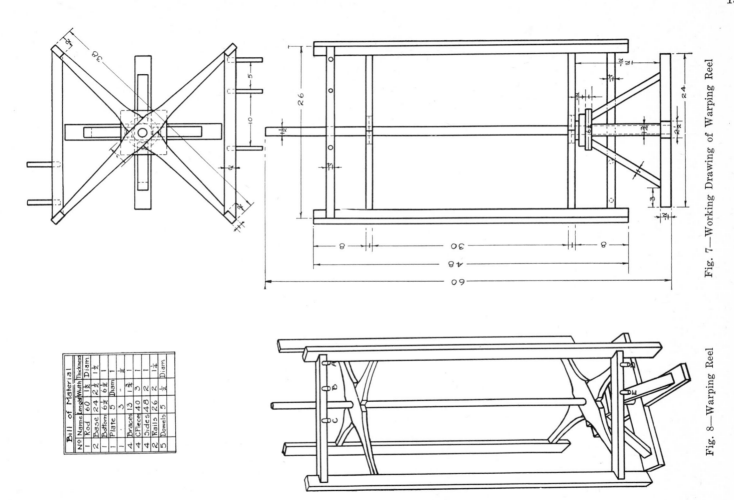

Bill of Material

No	Name	Length	Width	Thickness
1	Rod	60	1½	Diam
2	Base	24	2½	1½
1	Bottom	6½	6½	1
1	Plate	5	Diam	1
1	"	3	"	½
4	Braces	13	1¾	1
4	C.Pieces	40	3	1
4	Sides	48	2	1
2	Rails	26	2	1¼
5	Dowels	5	½	Diam

Fig. 7.—Working Drawing of Warping Reel

Fig. 8.—Warping Reel

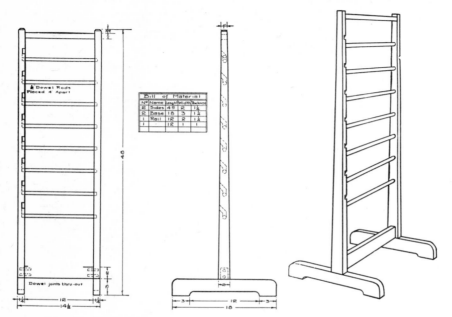

Bill of Material

Nº	Name	Length	Width	Thickness
2	Sides	45	2	1½
2	Base	18	3	1¼
1	Rail	12	2	1¼
1		12	1	1

Fig. 9—Working Drawing of Spool Rack   Fig. 10—Spool Rack

Fig. 11—Method of Starting Threads

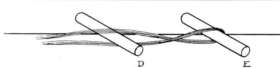

Fig. 12—Threads Passed over Lower Pegs

Fig. 13—Another Method of Starting Threads

drawn through the loop. This is continued until the entire warp has been removed from the board.

The process of taking off the warp will be recognized as the same as making a chain stitch in crocheting, the hands doing the work instead of a hook. See Fig. 6.

Before placing the warp, which may now be called a chain, on the warp beam of the loom, another method of warping will be considered.

The Warping Reel

The use of the warping reel, sometimes called the warping mill, somewhat simplifies the process of warping. Fig. 7 shows a working drawing of a warping reel, and Fig. 8 shows the finished reel.

It will be observed that the pegs appear on the cross bars of the finished reel marked A, B, C, and D, E, the same as on the warping board. The distance between the upright posts of the reel is 27 inches. The spools of warp are placed as when the warping board was used. Some sort of a spool rack is almost indispensable. Yet any convenient way of arranging the spools so the thread will freely unwind, will answer the purpose. Fig. 9 shows the working drawing of the spool rack and Fig. 10 shows the finished rack.

Supposing that four threads are to be warped at one time. The four ends are all tied at one time to peg A, Fig. 11. They are carried under B and over C and then start on their way around the reel, the threads being guided on their way to pegs D and E by the left hand while the reel is turned by the right hand. The person performing the work remains stationary. On reaching peg D the group of four threads is carried over it, under and around E and back under D, as shown in Fig. 12. From here the threads start back toward pegs A, B and C, passing under C, over B, under and around A, and then back again, passing under B, over C, and so on as in the beginning.

The reel measures 27 inches between posts. Passing around the reel once is equal to three yards of warp. Knowing this, makes it an easy matter to measure off any number of yards.

Another Way to Begin With Four Threads

The four threads may be tied together and slipped on to peg A, two threads being on top of the peg and the other two below. Bring the two threads which are below A, over B, and the two above A, below B. Allow the two below B to pass over C and bring the two above B so that they pass below C, Fig. 13. From this point the four threads are guided around the reel just as above described. The four threads pass over and under D and E, as shown in Fig. 12. On their return to peg A the four threads pass under the pegs the two went over, and over the pegs the two went under, and the warping proceeds in the same manner as when using the warping board.

Keeping Account of the Number of Threads Warped

As soon as the threads have crossed a few times between pegs D and E, it will be found difficult to remember how many threads are gathered together on the pegs. It becomes necessary to use some device for keeping count in order to know when the warp is completed.

This account can be easily kept if a piece of cord or tape is used.

After the group of four threads passes between pegs D and E five times, draw one end of the cord or tape

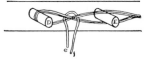

Fig. 14—Keeping Account of Threads Warped

through the opening next to peg D, and the other end through the opening next to E, as shown in Fig. 14.

The warping continues until five more groups have been warped, or reeled, as the process is sometimes called. The end of the colored cord or tape marked "f," Fig. 14,

Fig. 15—Removing the Warp from the Reel

is then passed through the opening next to peg D, and the end of the cord or tape marked "e" passes through the opening next to peg E, thus making a cross in the cord or tape between the first group of five and the second group of five. As there are twenty threads in each group the worker knows that the warp contains forty threads. This is continued until the required number of threads has been reeled.

The cross at the beginning and the one at the end of the warp are now secured in the same way as when the warp is made on the warping board.

Removing the Warp from the Reel

Peg A is removed and the warp is slipped from pegs B and C. A chain is made the same as when removing a warp from the warping board. See Fig. 15.

To Warp a Number of Threads at Once

If only four or six threads are warped at a time these may easily be carried and placed over and under the pegs in a group. It will be learned a little later that, when the lease rods are placed, either four or six threads, according to the number warped at a time, will pass over and under the rods at one time.

When eight, ten, twelve, or sixteen threads are warped at a time the problem is somewhat more complicated and should be done in such a way as to bring alternate threads over and under the lease rods. This arrangement of the threads makes the threading of the loom easy and keeps the threads from becoming snarled or twisted one with another. Arrange the spools on the spool rack, as shown in Fig. 16.

A paddle-shaped piece of ¼″ or 3/16″ basswood is cut as shown in Fig. 17, to serve as a guide. Any number of holes may be bored. Sixteen is usually the greatest num-

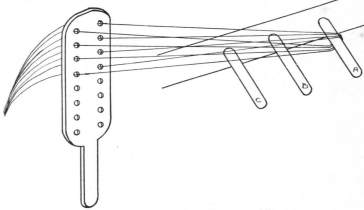

Fig. 17A—Method of Using Paddle

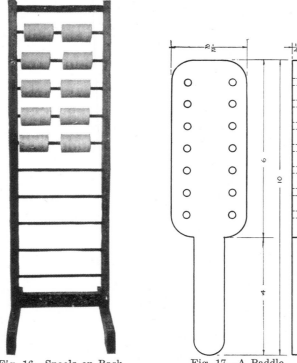

Fig. 16—Spools on Rack   Fig. 17—A Paddle

ber for the amateur. The ends of the threads coming from the spools on the left side of the rack and all unwinding in the same direction are threaded through the holes in the left side of the guide, Fig. 17A, and the ends coming from the spools on the right side of the rack are threaded through the holes in the right side of the guide, 17A. The ends are now all gathered together and tied in one knot and slipped over peg A of the warping reel, half of the threads being on top and half of them below the peg, as is shown in Fig. 17A. The guide is held in the left hand in an upright position so the threads are well separated. With the first finger and thumb of the right hand the threads (warp) must be crossed. This is done by placing the first finger of the right hand on the lowest thread on the right side of the guide

Fig. 17B—Reeling Eight Threads with Paddle

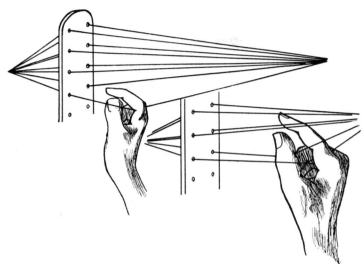

Fig. 18—First Thread Pulled
Down

Fig. 19—Second Thread Pulled
Down

and pressing it downward, Fig. 18. The thread just pressed down passes under the finger and over the thumb. With the thumb press down the lowest thread on the left side of the guide, Fig. 19. This thread passes under the thumb and over the finger. Allow the finger to press down the second thread on the right side of the guide. This thread now passes under the finger and over the thumb. With the thumb press down the second thread on the left side of the guide, Fig. 18. This is continued until all the threads are crossed on the finger and thumb of the right hand. This cross is transferred to the pegs. When placed on the pegs B and C, it will be found that there is a crossing of alternate threads. The eight threads are now held in one group and carried around the warping reel until the pegs at the other end are reached. The group of threads is carried over and under the pegs the same as was described with the warping board when only one or four threads at a time were warped.

Turning On, or Beaming

At the present time the warp is in a long chain ready to be placed on the loom in such a way as to make it possible for the weaver to produce a piece of cloth. To do this the ends at E must be attached to a roller, (in this case the warp beam) and spread out and wound evenly and tightly upon it. The warp beam fits into the back of the loom frame, as shown in Fig. 20.

As an example, suppose that the cloth to be woven is 22 inches wide and there are to be 24 threads to each inch. The warp then contains 528 threads, and this number is made up of 66 groups of eight threads each. It will be remembered that count was kept of the groups by means of the cord or tape between the pegs D and E while the warping was in progress.

The Warp Spreader (Raddle)

Fig. 21 shows a working drawing of the spreader, also called raddle.

Fig. 22 shows the drawing of the finished spreader with the top removed.

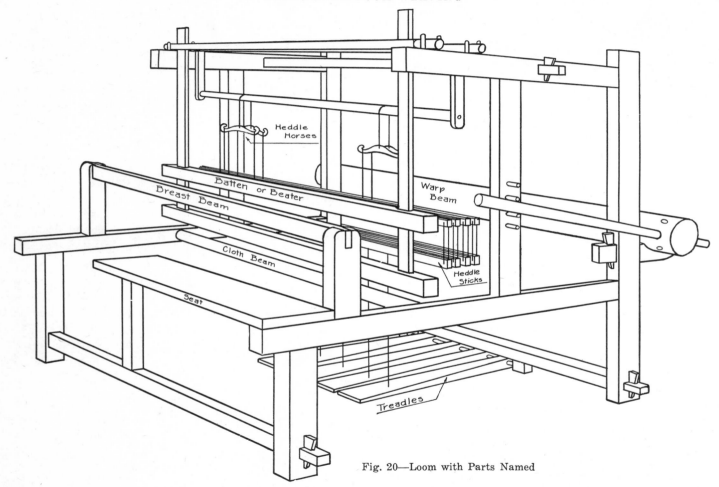

Fig. 20—Loom with Parts Named

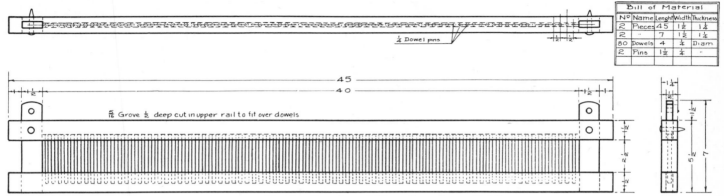

Bill of Material				
Nº	Name	Lenght	Width	Thickness
2	Pieces	45	1½	1¼
2	"	7	1½	1¼
80	Dowels	4	¼	Diam
2	Pins	1½	¼	"

¼ Dowel pins

45
40
⁵⁄₁₆ Grove ½ deep cut in upper rail to fit over dowels

Fig. 21—Working Drawing of Warp Spreader or Raddle

The spreader is most simply described as a comb, with a movable cap to cover the ends of the teeth. The frame is made of wood. The teeth may be made of dowel rods or hard wire. Nails have sometimes been used.

The cap is deeply grooved above the teeth and has holes near the ends. Through these holes the sides of the frame pass in order to fix it on, as shown in Fig. 22.

A loom fully equipped has in the equipment a couple of rods, one to be used in placing the warp on the beam.

With the chain of warp at hand, and taking the end

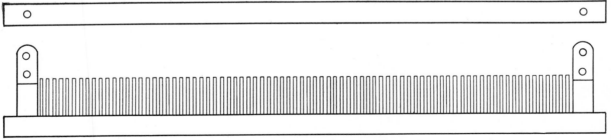

Fig. 22—Warp Spreader with Cap Removed

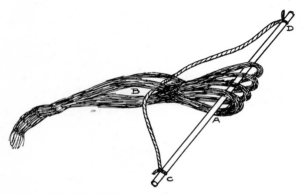

Fig. 23—Method of Keeping the Cross

doing the cross is retained. The rod may now be tied to the warp beam. A provision is always made for this tying. In the old colonial looms, holes are bored; the same is true of the Swedish type, while the Danish looms have a groove ploughed in the beam from end to end into which a smooth wooden or metal stick is placed to hold the warp to the beam.

From the front of the loom remove the beater, sometimes called the batten, the breast beam and the harness, Fig. 20. This makes a free opening from the front to the warp beam.

Tie the rod shown in Fig. 23 to the warp beam with No. 12 blocking twine. This fastens the warp chain to the beam, but in order that it may be placed on the beam evenly the groups of thread must be distributed in the warp spreader. Place the spreader under the chain and on a level with the warping beam. To hold the spreader in this position it may be tied to the upright parts of the loom, or

which, when on the reel was between D and E, push a rod through the opening marked "A," Fig. 23. Untie the cord which held the cross but allow it to remain on the other side of the crossed threads, as shown in B, Fig. 23. Tie the ends of the cord to the ends of the rod, at C and D. By so

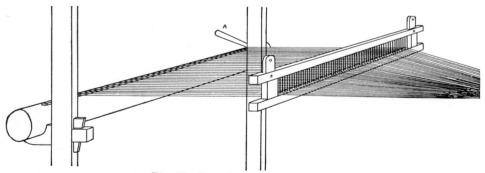

Fig. 24—Spreader in Place on Loom

it may be held by two persons, one at each side of the loom. Fig. 24 shows the spreader in place. With the top of the spreader removed the groups of thread may now be distributed in their regular order. Since there are 528 threads in all and eight threads in each group, there will be exactly 66 groups. There are to be 24 threads to each inch. This means that three groups of eight threads must be placed to the inch. This will occupy three spaces on the spreader.

By means of the cross the groups of thread may be used in their regular order and placed in the spaces of the spreader. When this is completed the cap is placed and fastened, and the warp is ready to be beamed.

One person holds the chain and the other turns the beam, by placing a peg into one of the holes at the end of the beam, as shown at A, Fig. 24.

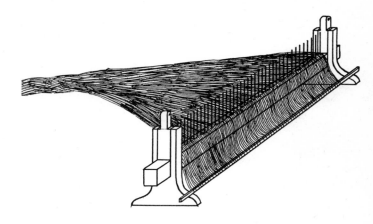

Fig. 26—Warp Distributed

Laying in Sticks

As the warp is being wound on to the beam, thin strips of wood about 3/16″ in thickness are laid on the beam for the warp to wind on. This prevents the warp from becoming tangled and also keeps the warp even across the entire beam. Strips such as are used in the bottom of shades are good for this purpose. After four or five yards of warp are wound on to the beam, lay in more strips.

A stand may be made to hold the spreader, as shown in Fig. 25. Fig. 26 shows the warp distributed. After the warp is distributed the spreader cap is put on, thus holding the groups of threads securely in their proper spaces. The spreader, warp, and all may now be trans-

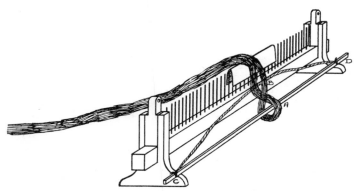

Fig. 25—Stand to Hold Spreader

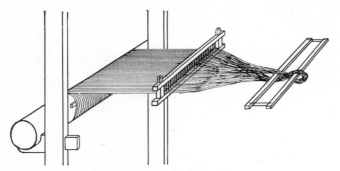

Fig. 27—Lease Rods in Place

ferred to the loom, and the rod with the warp may be fastened to the warp beam as described before.

The beam is then turned until the other end of the chain of warp is reached. Care should be taken to hold the warp firmly while the winding is done. The chain unravels as it is wound on to the beam. When the opposite end is reached, the cross which was so carefully guarded at the pegs A, B and C is also reached. Into the openings of this cross, the lease rods are placed, as shown in Fig. 27.

The warp spreader may now be removed.

Later the loops are cut, causing the ends to hang instead of the loop, as shown in Fig. 28. These ends may be tied in bunches in a loose knot, thus preventing them from losing their places in passing under and over the lease rods, Fig. 31.

Knotting the Heddles

After the warp has been placed on the beam, it becomes necessary to consider the knotting of the heddles or leashes, as they are sometimes called. In order that each heddle may be of exactly the same size, a heddle frame is constructed about 12 inches by 1½ inches by 3 inches, shown in Fig. 29. The pegs are numbered a, b, c and d. About 1½″ from each end a peg is placed and in the center two pegs are placed one inch apart, Fig. 30. The pegs should be rounded at the top and well sanded to make them perfectly smooth, thus causing the heddles to slip off easily.

The ordinary four-ply carpet thread is a fairly good material to be used in heddles. Sometimes linen thread is used and sometimes a hard twisted cotton, called seine twine, used in fish nets, is utilized. The twine is cut long enough in order that it may be looped around a, Fig. 30. Tie a knot at b and another as shown in c. The ends are then tied at "d." From 25 to 50 may be tied before removing them from the pegs. There must be as many heddles

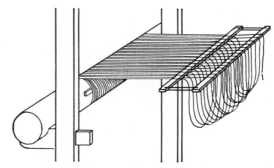

Fig. 28—Loops Hanging Over Lease Rods

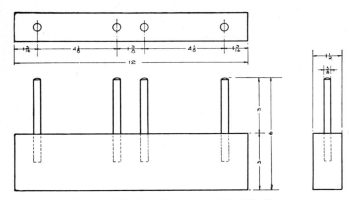

Fig. 29—Working Drawing of Heddle Frame

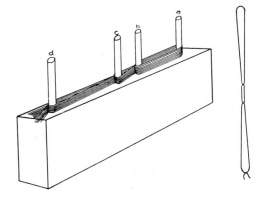

Fig. 30—Method of Tying Heddles

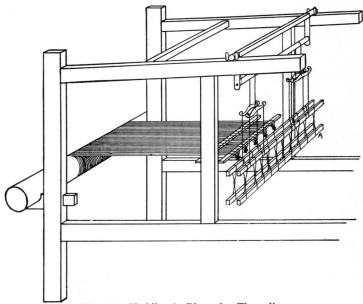

Fig. 31—Heddles in Place for Threading

as there are threads in the warp. Heddles found in the market are made of wire. These may be successfully used.

Heddle Sticks

In most foot-power looms the heddle sticks are used instead of the heddle frames. Fig. 31 shows, at A, heddles on the sticks. The harness, which consists of the various heddle sticks on which the heddles have been placed, is

Fig. 32—Threading the Heddles

the two ends of the cord are passed, Fig. 40.   Fig. 37, A, B, C, and D show in the successive steps the way the knot is made.

A shows simply the loop and ends.

B shows the ends drawn through the loop.

C shows the ends drawn through the loop and a single knot started with them.

D shows the single knot tied and drawn down to the loop.

By using the above method for tying, the cords may be shortened or lengthened, as the case may be. By pulling the two ends of the single knot the latter is drawn close to the loop. It will be found that the knot will not give way no matter what the weight of the pull may be. If the cord is to be lengthened the knot is loosened and the cord is adjusted.

Fig. 40—Two Ends of Cord Placed in Loop

The harness, which is made up of the heddles and heddle sticks, hangs just behind the beater and is suspended by tying the heddle sticks to the heddle horses.

The heddle horses are tied one to one end of a piece of No. 16 blocking cord and one to the other.   Fig. 41 is the drawing of a heddle horse.   The rope is thrown over the roller just above, allowing one horse to hang to one side and one to the other.   Two other heddle horses are tied

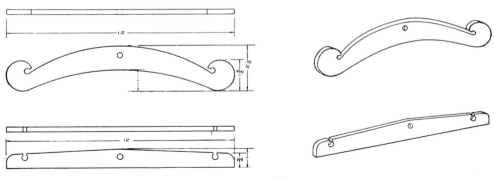

Fig. 41—Heddle Horses

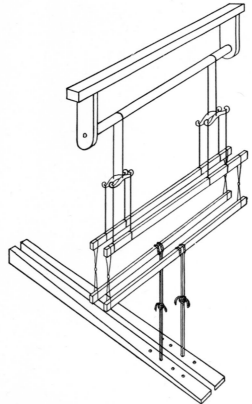

Fig. 42—Method of Tying Heddle Sticks to Treadles

and hung in the same way at the other end of the roller. Fig. 20 shows heddle sticks hung in the finished loom.

Cords are tied from the ends of the heddle horses to the top heddle sticks. From the center of each lower heddle stick a loop of No. 12 blocking cord is tied. The ends of the cord extending from the treadles slip into the loop, extending from the heddle sticks, as shown in Fig. 42. When pressure (in this case the foot) is applied to a treadle the part of the harness tied to that particular treadle draws the threads downward. Upon releasing this treadle and applying the pressure to the other treadle the other half of the threads is drawn downward.

The Cloth Beam

The ends drawn through the reed are now hanging loosely or tied in bunches in the front of the reed. These

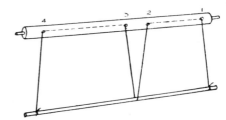

Fig. 43—Method of Preparing Cloth Beam

ends must in some way be connected with the cloth beam (Fig. 20). Holes have been bored through the cloth beam. Through these holes the No. 12 blocking cord is drawn.

Beginning at the right of the cloth beam draw one end of the cord through the first opening. The other end is tied to the end of a rod, which is as long as the reed.

(These rods were mentioned earlier in the process of warping. One was used in fastening the warp to the beam.)

The cord is now threaded through the next hole, which is No. 2 in the cloth beam, and then through hole No. 3.

A long loop is left between No. 2 and No. 3 and the rod is pushed through it. The cord is now threaded through hole No. 4 and tied to the other end of the rod, as shown in Fig. 43.

The cord is cut long enough to allow the rod to be brought up and over the breast beam up to the reed. The ratchet which is connected with the cloth beam is now turned, rolling on the cord until the rod is about 8 or 10 inches from the reed. The ends now hanging in bunches are untied. About 30 threads are held in one group. The group is divided, allowing one-half of the group to pass under the rod and the other to pass over the rod. With the ends of the groups tie a single bow knot over the rod. Take up another group, divide it, and tie the same way. Continue until all have been tied to the rod, as shown in Fig. 44.

The Shed

After the loom is "tied up" and the right treadle is pressed downward, all the threads which pass through the eyes of the heddles on the front heddle sticks are pressed downward, thus causing a space between the threads passing through the front heddle eyes and those passing through the back heddle eyes.

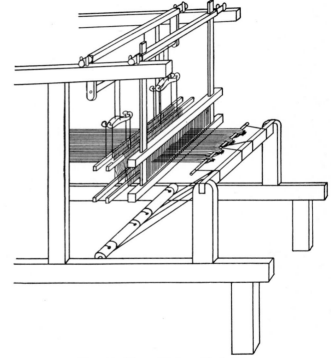

Fig. 44—Warp Tied to Cloth Beam

This space comes just in front of the reed when the beater is swung back, as shown in Fig. 45.

This space is called the "Shed," and it is through this opening that the woof is passed. The woof once in place, and the treadle released, the beater is swung to the front, thus by means of the reed the woof is pressed in place. The left treadle is now pressed downward, and the woof again passes through the shed from the left, the beater and reed pressing it into place the same as in the first thread.

If rags or similarly heavy materials are used, they are wound on what is called a shuttle which in this case is simply a piece of quarter-inch bass, poplar, or pine, cut as shown in Fig. 47. If finer materials such as mercerized cottons are used, a shuttle similar to the one shown in Fig. 46 is used.

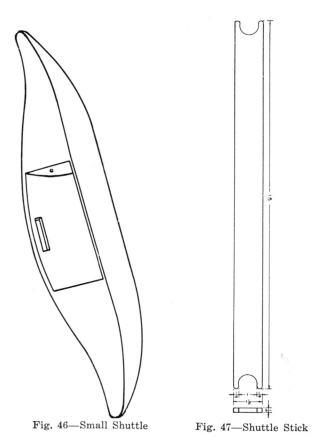

Fig. 46—Small Shuttle   Fig. 47—Shuttle Stick

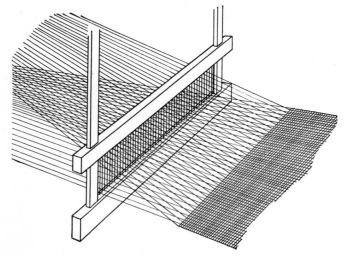

Fig. 45—The Shed

The Small Shuttle

The beginner will, no doubt, use principally the coarser

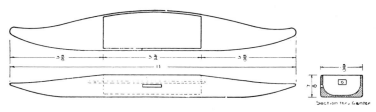

Fig. 46a—Working Drawing of Small Shuttle

materials for the woof and will, therefore, use the shuttle as shown in Fig. 47.

The shuttle shown in Figs. 46 and 46a is so constructed as to admit of a piece of 10 or 12-gauge wire. This wire extends lengthwise across the inside of the opening, the ends being forced into two little holes, one in each end of the opening. In one of the holes, a small spring is concealed and the wire is put in place very much as a bobbin is placed into the shuttle of a sewing machine. Fig. 47 shows a shuttle stick.

Fig. 48—Bobbin Winder

Fig. 49—Spinning Wheel Used for Bobbin Winder

Bobbin Winder

Fig. 48 shows a bobbin winder extensively used in Norway and Sweden. Small wooden spools are slipped on to the shaft of the winder, or a piece of paper may be tightly wrapped around the shaft. The end of the thread to be wound is caught in the wrapping of the paper. By means of the small crank the wheel is turned and the thread is wound on the spool or paper. The bobbin is made in this way. If the bobbin winder as shown above is not

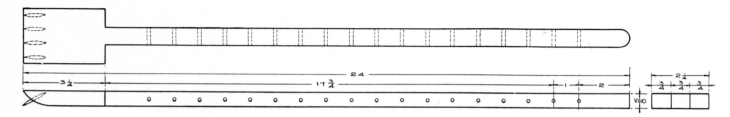

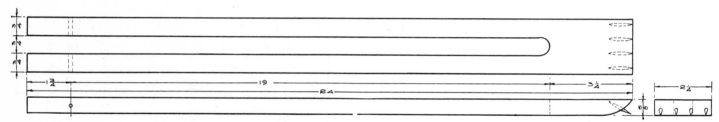

Fig. 50—Working Drawing for Temple

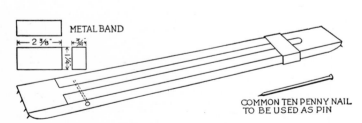

METAL BAND

COMMON TEN PENNY NAIL
TO BE USED AS PIN

Fig. 51—Temple Closed

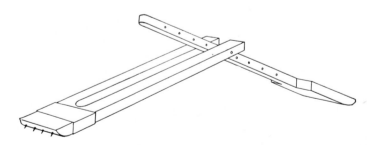

Fig. 52—Temple Opened

available, a spinning wheel may be equipped to do the work. A plug with an extension may be forced into the spindle, as shown in Fig. 49. The spool or the paper may be wrapped around this extension, and the wheel may be turned just as when spinning.

The Temple

As the weaving continues, it will be found that there is a tendency in the fabric to "draw in" narrower than the entering of the warp in the reed. When this "drawing in" becomes noticeable, it may be corrected by using the temple.

The temple is very simple in its construction. Fig. 50 shows the working drawing. At the broad ends of each of the parts, 1½" 16-gauge brads are driven in and the heads are filed off. For heavier material, the brads should be of 12 or 14-gauge.

The parts when joined together are for the purpose of holding out the edges of the material being woven, to the required width. The means of adjusting the length of the temple are shown in Fig. 51 and Fig. 52. The parts are held together by a wire nail or wooden pin, which is forced into the holes bored through the two parts.

The pin is first inserted and the temple placed on the cloth a short distance from the reed, with the filed points of the brads catching the edges of the material, as shown in Fig. 52. When the temple is pressed down in this position, it will force out the edges of the cloth. The small

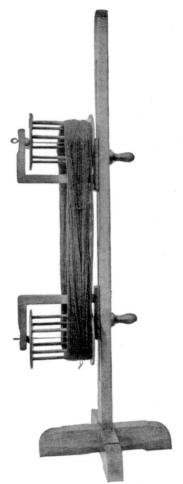

Fig. 53—Floor Swift

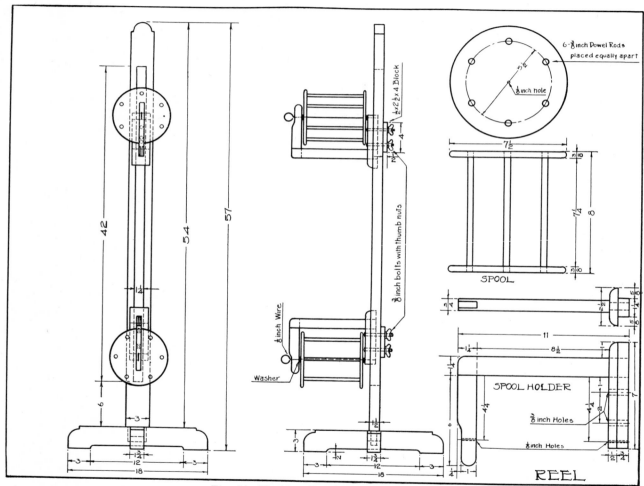

Fig. 54—Working Drawing of Floor Swift

metal band which fits closely, is moved along so it holds the two parts together.   After weaving from four to six inches, the temple is moved so it again is a few inches from the reed.

To move, slip the metal band so the parts may swing on the pin and proceed as described before.

Floor Swift

A great many of the different threads used in weaving must be purchased in skeins.   This fact makes the Floor Swift almost indispensable, in order that the skeins may conveniently be made into bobbins.

Fig. 53 shows a floor swift consisting of a pair of reels, mounted on a stand in such a manner that the distance between them can be regulated.   Fig. 54 shows the working drawing of the floor swift.   It will be observed that the upright of the stand has a slot cut in it for the greater part of its length.   The reels revolve on elongated axles, and may be fixed in the slot at any height, by means of a screw and collar.   This makes it possible to adjust them to different-sized skeins.

Fig. 55 shows another kind of swift which may be fastened to a table.   It opens like an umbrella and may be adjusted to skeins of various sizes.   The small skein allows only a partial opening of the swift.   The skein is placed over the swift while closed.

Fig. 55—A Table Swift

CHAPTER II

Plain Weaving

Rag Rugs

In weaving rag rugs the loom is usually threaded with a four-ply carpet warp, ten or twelve threads to the inch. This calls for a number 10 or 12 reed. Since the process of preparing the loom has already been described in detail, the description of the weaving may begin at once.

Any number of most interesting striped rugs may be woven. The width and color of the stripes being varied as shown in Figs. 56 and 57.

Figs. 58 and 59 show what may be done by laying straight pieces of cloth about one and one-fourth inches wide and any desired length right over the strip used in the body part of the rug. To do this the strip used in the body part of the rug is passed through the shed and beaten. It is again pushed out into the shed. The strip used in the design is then placed in the same shed and wrapped around the foundation material which has been pressed together through the beating above mentioned. In this way most interesting straight line designs as shown in Figs. 58 and 59 may be woven into our ordinary bath and bed room rugs. The straight line design need not be limited to those shown

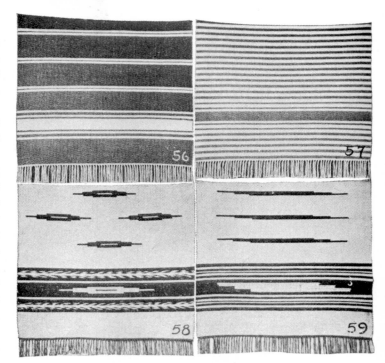

Figs. 56, 57, 58, 59—Woven Rag Rugs

in Figs. 58 and 59 but may be carried into flower designs, animals, etc. Designs of this character should be first designed on square paper similar to the way cross stitch designs are made. The rug shown in Fig. 56 is made of Dutch blue calico and unbleached muslin. The material used in Figs. 58 and 59 is unbleached muslin while the borders and figures are of dark blue outing flannel. Fig. 60 shows a rug woven on a two harness loom threaded by placing three threads through each eye of the heddles. Use a No. 12 reed and draw one thread through each dent. When weaving the threads are raised and lowered in groups of three.

Fig. 60—Rug

Fig. 61—Plaids

Fig. 62—Automobile Scarf

Plaids

Fig. 61 gives an idea of what may be woven on a two harness loom in the way of plaids. In all plaids the various stripings are brought about by placing the various colors in the warp. For example: When making the chain a very interesting plaid is made by warping the

colors in the following order: 20 white, 5 black, 20 white, 20 black, 5 white, 20 black, 16 white, 5 black, 28 white, 5 black, 16 white, etc. In weaving the plaid above suggested the same number of woof threads of a color are woven as there are threads of the same color in the warp. In this particular plaid there are first 20 white threads in the warp so there must be 20 white threads in the woof. Next there are 5 black threads in the warp so there must be 5 black threads in the woof. Twenty white next follow in the warp so twenty white woof threads are woven, etc.

Automobile Scarf

Germantown yarn for both warp and woof make most practical automobile scarves. With yarn of this weight, use a No. 9 reed and do not beat too hard when weaving. With Shetland floss use a No. 12 reed being careful not to beat too hard. Very often the finished product is greatly improved by washing and pressing. If not washed, a damp cloth should be placed over the finished article and well pressed with a hot iron. No article should ever be considered finished without a thorough pressing. Fig. 62 shows finished scarf.

Luncheon Set

Fig. 63 shows one of the napkins of a simple luncheon set woven on a two harness loom. The lunch cloth is woven on a two harness loom, as large as the loom will permit. The same narrow bands of blue are warped into the lunch cloth as are found in the napkins. After the

Fig. 63—Napkin

two threads are drawn through each of 15 dents. Fifteen dents are then left vacant. Then two threads are again drawn through each of 15 dents, and so on until the entire reed is threaded. When weaving, 15 threads are woven back and forth. A space equal to the strip woven is skipped and again 15 threads are woven back and forth. To assist in getting the vacant spaces all the same size, a piece of reed of the desired thickness may be laid in the

cloth and napkins are removed from the loom they must be thoroughly boiled in a strong solution of soap and water. This softens the material and brings out the beautiful gloss, linen should have when pressed.

Curtains

Fig. 64 shows a curtain material woven of 2-ply cotton warp or of mercerized machine twist. The loom is threaded the same as any other two harness loom. The threads are drawn through the dents of the reed in groups. A very fine thread requires a No. 30 reed and two threads to each dent. To bring about the effect shown in Fig. 64

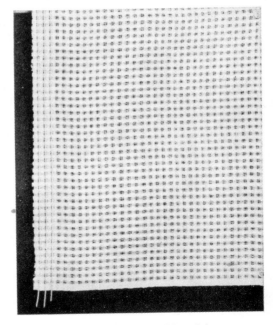

Fig. 64--Curtain Material

shed and then the weaving with the thread continued. The strip of reed may now be pulled out and again placed in the shed. Several pieces of reed may be used as shown in Fig. 64. This may be continued indefinitely. After a little practice the reed will not be necessary as the weaver's eye can judge the space to be left. If a coarser thread than the machine twist is used, a No. 20 reed with two threads to each dent, threaded as above described, will make the material fine enough.

Checked Curtains

Very interesting checked curtains as shown in Fig. 65 may be woven on a two harness loom. These curtains are warped so that there are 40 threads of green, and then 40 threads of white, and the weaving is done in the same way, that is, by using first 40 green threads and then 40 white.

Fig. 66—Interior

Fig. 65—Green and White Checked

Use a No. 20 reed, two threads to each dent. Fig. 66 illustrates the way in which the green and white checked curtains may be used with the open mesh white curtains as described in Fig. 64.

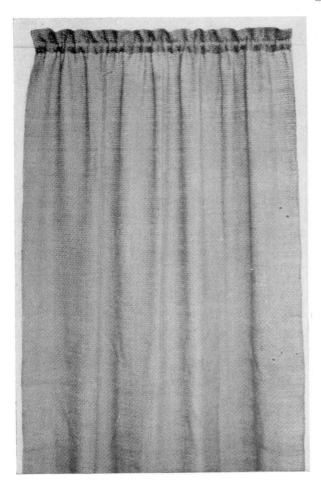

Fig. 67—Shows the Finished Material

Other Curtains

Fig. 67 illustrates how a heavy and a fine thread may be used in curtains. One thread is a No. 5 mercerized cotton and the other a "OO" (double O) mercerized machine twist. In making the warp the spools or balls are so arranged that there are two fine threads and then one coarse one.

When threading the heddles, thread one coarse thread and then two fine ones, remembering to draw only one thread through each eye of the heddles.

Use a No. 12 reed. Draw two fine threads through a dent and then one coarse thread through the next dent

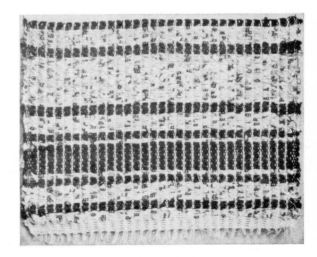

Fig. 68—Silk Rags

Fig. 69—Rug of Gray and White Warp

Alternate in this way throughout the entire threading of the reed. When weaving use the threads in the same order as above mentioned. First two fine threads and then a coarse one. Care should be exercised in not beating the woof too hard. Fig. 67 shows the finished material.

Silk Rags

There are several ways in which silk rags may be woven. When weaving silk rags into portiers it is well to make the warp of a rather fine mercerized cotton. The threading through the heddles is the same as for any two harness loom. Use a No. 12 reed. When threading the reed draw six or eight threads through a dent. Then skip three dents or possibly four and draw another group of six or eight threads through a dent. This order of threading is continued throughout the entire threading. The silk rags are now woven the same as when weaving a rug. The open spaces allow the finished material to hang more gracefully than it could if threaded one thread to each dent. Fig. 68 shows finished material. When making couch covers of silk rags the weaving should be done the same as when weaving the ordinary rag rug. This weaving adds strength, which the wear and tear on the finished product in this case needs.

Another Rug

Another interesting two harness weave is shown in Fig. 69. In the particular rug shown the warp is of a gray and white alternating. In reeling the warp, the spools may be so arranged that every other one is gray. To make the dark band along the edges only gray warp is reeled; about 30 threads along each edge. The threading is done so that 30 white threads come on the front harness and 30 gray on the back as shown in Fig. 70.

Basket Weave

A very effective plain weave may be had by reeling the warp in the usual way. When threading the loom thread two heddles on the back heddle sticks and then two on the front heddle stick. Continue to thread in this way until all the warp threads have been used. When threading the reed draw only one thread through each dent. After the loom is tied up it will be found that the threads are raised and lowered in pairs.

When weaving use two shuttles, passing first one and then the other through the same shed. By using two shuttles as above described a twist in the woof is avoided.

Pattern Weaving

To the casual observer of hand-woven articles, many of the complicated patterns woven on the ordinary foot-power loom seem quite impossible. To those who have done weaving, however, the work does not seem so wonderful, for the amateur quickly grasps the idea of pattern weaving.

In all that has gone before, nothing but plain weaving has been suggested; in other words, only two sets of heddles have been used and only two treadles.

To do pattern weaving, it will be necessary to use four sets of heddles and four treadles. In Fig. 20 may be seen the four sets of heddle sticks just behind the beater. Heddles are placed on each pair of the sticks. They are hung for threading just as the two sets are hung in Fig. 32.

The warp is reeled and placed on the warp beam just the same for pattern weaving as for plain weaving. Assume that the pattern shown in Fig. 71 is to be woven. This pattern is known as the Monk's Belt. The name, no doubt, comes from its use in weaving the belts used by the early monks.

Let the material to be used be a four-ply white or gray carpet warp just the same as was used in the rug weaving.

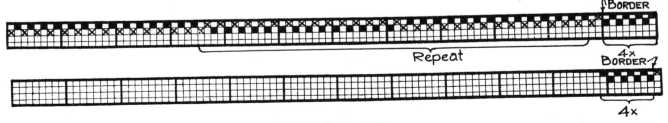

Fig. 70—Draft of Rug

In the rug work only twelve threads to the inch were used. For this pattern twenty threads to the inch will be used.

If the article to be woven is to be about 22 inches wide, and if there are to be 18 threads to the inch, it will require 412 threads to be reeled, if 16 threads are allowed for the selvages. If four threads are reeled at a time, it will require 103 groups of four threads to make the required number. The length depends upon the weaver.

Having placed the heddles on the heddle sticks and the warp on the beam, the worker is ready to do the threading. Seated as shown in Fig. 32, with the pattern as shown in Fig. 71 at hand, the work of threading is begun.

It must be remembered that the sets of heddles are numbered from the front to the back. That is, the heddle stick just in front of the worker is number 1, the next number 2, the next number 3, and the farthest number 4. The row of squares in the pattern marked No. 1 indicates that all the threads in this row must be threaded in their order through the heddles on heddle stick No. 1. The squares in the pattern in row No. 2 indicate that these threads are threaded in their order through the heddles on the second pair of heddle sticks. Three and four follow in the same manner.

Beginning to Thread

Beginning at the right of the pattern, the first thread of the selvage is indicated by a dark square in the fourth row. This means that the first thread passes through the eye of the first heddle on the back or fourth row of heddles.

This heddle threaded, it is pushed along and the next thread is taken care of. The next thread is on the third row and is passed through the eye of the first heddle on the third pair of heddle sticks. This heddle is now pushed along and the third thread is cared for. The third thread passes through the first heddle on the second pair of heddle sticks and is pushed along. The fourth thread passes through the eye of the first heddle on the first pair of heddle sticks and is pushed along. The fifth thread passes through the eye of the second heddle on the fourth row. This is continued until the part of the pattern marked selvage is completed. The selvage is threaded but once, at the beginning and at the end, unless otherwise indicatd.

The threading of the real pattern begins after the selvage has been threaded. Upon investigation it will be found that 36 threads make one repeat of the pattern, Fig. 71. If there are 412 threads in all and 16 are used for the two selvages 396 threads remain. If it requires 36 threads to thread the pattern once, 396 threads will repeat the pattern eleven times.

The first thread of the pattern appears on the fourth or back row of heddles; the second thread is on the third row, etc. Continue until each thread indicated by the dark squares is threaded. When this is done, the pattern has been repeated once. Go back to the beginning, which is the first thread on the fourth row after the selvage. In this way thread the pattern eleven times. When this is done, there are still eight threads left for the selvage,

Fig. 71—Monk's Belt. Draft of Pattern

which is threaded the same as the selvage at the right or beginning.

Fig. 72 shows another way of expressing the pattern shown in Fig. 71. There are several other ways of writing patterns, all of which will be given in order that the weaver may understand and make use of patterns found in various books on the subject.

Fig. 71, however, shows the way patterns are written in textile schools.

Threading the Reed

The threads having been drawn through the heddles in the order indicated by the pattern are now ready to be drawn through the dents of the reed. A No. 18 reed is hung as shown in Fig. 34. With a reed hook, as shown in

Fig. 35, the threads are drawn through the reed in their regular order as before described.

To make the selvage, two threads of the selvage are drawn through each of the first four dents. This uses the eight threads of the selvage as shown in the pattern.

If the number 18 reed is used, each thread of the pattern passes through a dent until the selvage is again reached, when two threads pass through each dent.

If a No. 18 reed cannot be had, a No. 9 reed may be used by placing two threads of the selvage through each dent of the selvage and two threads of the pattern through each of the pattern dents.

Very often the reed has many more dents than is required for the number of threads used in a particular pattern. In such case care must be taken to draw the threads

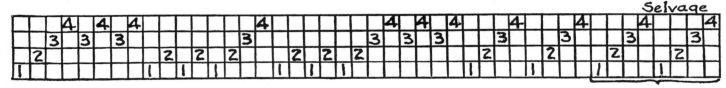

Fig. 72—Monk's Belt. Another Way of Drafting Pattern

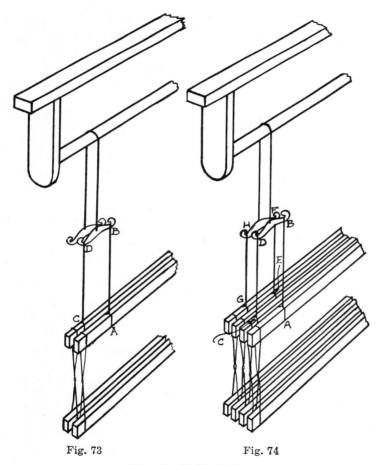

Fig. 73   Fig. 74

Tying the Heddle Sticks

through such dents as will bring the weaving in the center of the reed. For example, if the finished work is to be 22 inches wide and the reed through which the threads are drawn is 28 inches long, it is of the greatest importance that the first thread is drawn through the dent three inches from the right end of the reed. After all the threads have been drawn through the dents, three inches are left at the left end of the reed. The ends now are tied to the rod which leads to the cloth beam, the same as in Fig. 36.

Tying the Heddle Sticks

Fig. 20 shows the position of the heddle horses. Two heddle horses are tied together with a piece of No. 12 blocking cord. The cord is thrown over the roller or the pulley above, leaving one heddle horse at one side and one at the other, as shown in Fig. 20.

The upper heddle sticks are tied to the scroll-like ends of the heddle horses, one to each. To do this take four heddles the same as were used on the heddle sticks. These are looped all at one time over one end of the first heddle stick. This is done by placing one loop at the end of the heddle to one side of the heddle stick, as shown at A, Fig. 73. The other ends of the heddles are placed through this loop and are drawn tightly over the heddle stick. With the thumb and finger, make a loop in the other end of the heddles similar to the loop in Figs. 38 and 39. Slip this loop over the scroll-like end of the heddle horse as shown at B, Fig. 73. Take four other heddles and loop one end over the second heddle stick far enough from the end so that it is directly under the other scroll-like end of the same heddle horse, as shown at C, Fig. 73.

With the finger and thumb, make a loop in the other end of the heddles and slip this loop over the other end of the heddle horse, as shown at D, Fig. 73. Heddle sticks 1 and 2 are now tied to the one heddle horse; see Fig. 73. Take four other heddles and loop them over the third heddle stick the same distance from the end as the first was looped at E, Fig. 74. Loop the other ends of the heddles over the scroll-like end of the second heddle horse, as shown at F, Fig. 74. The fourth heddle stick is tied in the same way and the same distance from the end as the second one, as shown at G and H, Fig. 74. This finishes the tying at one end. Tie heddle sticks at the other end to the heddle horses in the same way. Heddles are used to tie the heddle sticks to the heddle horses because they are all exactly the same length. This is of great importance.

Tying Heddle Sticks to Treadles

To keep the heddle sticks even and all together, tie them together at each upper end. From the center of each lower heddle stick, tie a loop of No. 12 blocking cord as shown at A, Fig. 37.

From each treadle allow two ends of No. 12 blocking cord to extend upward. Beginning at the right, tie the first treadle to the first lower heddle stick; the second treadle to the second heddle stick. In the same way tie 3 and 4. This numbers the treadles from right to left 1, 2, 3, 4. The loom is now ready for work.

Weaving the Pattern

Before beginning to weave the pattern, experiment by pressing down certain treadles. Press down treadles 1 and 2 at the same time. Press down 3 and 4. Press down 1 and 3 by placing one foot on 1 and the other on 3. Press down 2 and 4. It will be found that 1 and 2, when pressed down, make one part of the pattern, as shown at A, Fig. 75.

By pressing down treadles 3 and 4, the part of the pattern shown at B, Fig. 75 is made.

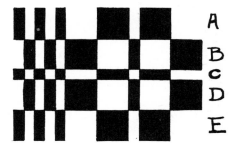

Fig. 75—Pattern Woven

These two changes are all that are found in Fig. 75. C, Fig. 75, is the same as A, only there are fewer threads used in weaving C. D, Fig. 75, is the same as B; and E, Fig. 75, is the same as A.

It was found that when treadles 1 and 3 were pressed down exactly one-half of the threads were drawn down. When 2 and 4 were pressed down the other half of the threads were drawn down.

Any amount of plain weaving may be done by pressing down alternately 1 and 3 at the same time, and 2 and 4 at the same time. This being true, it is possible to place pattern borders with as much plain weaving in between as is desired.

When doing pattern weaving the thread used in the pattern should be at least as heavy as the warp.

For every pattern thread that is placed in the weaving there must be what is called a binding thread or binder. The binding threads are always put in while the feet press down treadles 1 and 3, and 2 and 4. It will be remembered that it is these two sets of treadles that make the plain or tabby weave.

Let us suppose that everything is ready to begin the actual weaving. Treadles 1 and 3 are pressed down at the same time and the shuttle is passed from the right through the shed to the left.

Treadles 2 and 4 are next pressed down and the shuttle is passed through the shed from the left to the right. In this way as much plain weaving may be done as is desired.

If a table runner is to be made, about five inches of plain weaving in the beginning are sufficient before introducing the pattern.

To Make the Border as Shown in Fig. 75

When weaving a pattern there must always be a binder woven in every time a pattern thread is woven. It is this binder that holds the pattern thread in place. It is always well to have the binder of finer thread than that used in the plain weave, or than that used in the pattern, as the pattern threads may be more closely beaten together.

The shuttle containing the thread to be used for the binder is now at the right.

Treadles 1 and 2 are pressed down at the same time and a pattern thread passed through the shed. When this is beaten in place, treadles 1 and 3 are pressed down and a binder thread is passed through the shed. Treadles 1 and 2 are again pressed down and a pattern thread passed through the shed. Treadles 2 and 4 are now pressed down and a binder passes through the shed. Press 1 and 2 again for the pattern thread and 1 and 3 for the binder. Press 1 and 2 again, and 2 and 4 for the binder.

The weaver has, no doubt, discovered by this time that the pattern thread may enter the shed from either the right or left while care must be taken to enter the binder from the side it should be entered in order to make the plain weave. With the amateur it might be well to give the following direction concerning the weaving in of the binder.

When the first and third treadles are pressed down the binder must always enter from the right, and when the second and fourth treadles are pressed down the binder enters from the left. The beginner when returning to the work often finds it difficult to know which treadles to press down for the first binder thread. This may be decided by the position of the shuttle. If the thread from the shuttle is to the right then treadles 1 and 3 are pressed down for the binder. If the thread is at the left then 2 and 4 are pressed down. In other words, when the right foot presses

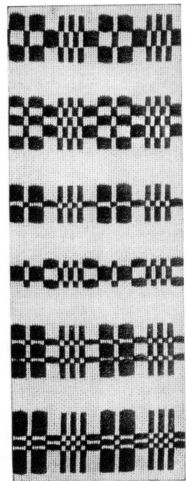

Fig. 76—Borders

down one of the outside treadles the shuttle must enter the shed from the right side and when the left foot presses down an outside treadle the shuttle enters the shed from the left side. This will aid the beginner in keeping track of the binding thread.

Second Change in Pattern

The second change in the pattern is shown at B, Fig. 75. To weave in the pattern threads for this change, treadles 3 and 4 are pressed down each time. Three and four are pressed down and the shuttle containing the pattern thread is thrown through the shed.

The shuttle containing the binder is at the right, therefore treadles 1 and 3 are pressed down. The shuttle at the right means that the right foot pressed down the right treadle. If it had been at the left, then 2 and 4 would have been pressed down, the left foot pressing down the left treadle which is the outside treadle to the left.

C, Fig. 75 is the same as A; and D is the same as B. E is the same as A.

Checked Paper

After the pupils have worked out the design shown in Fig. 75, pass to them checked paper and have them work out as many different combinations taken from Fig. 75 as possible.

When this is done the different combinations may be woven on the loom.

Figs. 76 and 77 show a few such combinations.

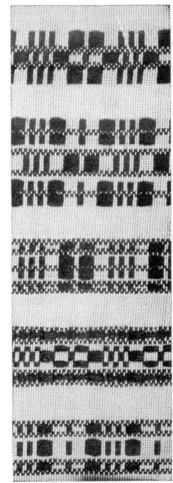

Fig. 77—Borders

Adaptations

There is very little value in asking pupils to design in textiles if they known nothing about the real working of a loom. At first thought one is very likely to look upon loom weaving as a very mechanical line of work because of the fact that the loom is threaded for a certain pattern. This work may be made so, if the teacher cannot see beyond the one little pattern for which the loom is threaded. If, however, the instructor will use the checked paper freely and have the pupils make as many different combinations of the changes as shown in Fig. 75 as possible, a great deal of good may be derived from the standpoint of design and color. Attention has already been called to the combinations shown in Figs. 76 and 77. These interesting borders may be woven into table-runner borders, bags of various kinds, pillow tops, curtains, etc.

In Fig. 78 is shown a bag for fancy work. The material for the plain part is of Ecru Jap Six No. 20. Twenty threads to the inch were used, two threads passing through each dent. The border is of a No. 5 mercerized cotton.

Fig. 79 shows a knitting bag in which the Monk's Belt threading is used. This bag was woven on the same loom as was the fancy work bag. The change in design is due to a change in colors and the order of treadling for the stripes. The Jap silk is the same.

When one begins really to work, the possibilities begin to dawn.

Fig. 80 shows a pair of curtains woven of Egyptian twine. A number 20 reed is used, one thread passing

Fig. 78—Fancy Work Bag

through each dent. A No. 3 mercerized cotton is used for the border, which is another adaptation of the Monk's Belt. The binder is Egyptian twine.

Fig. 79—Knitting Bag

Numerous all-over designs may be produced by using the threading draft shown in Fig. 71.

The Rose Path

Fig. 81 shows the threading for the pattern called the Rose Path. It is one of the most interesting of all the simple threadings and may be worked out by beginners in a great variety of ways and colors.

When threading any pattern always begin at the right and work toward the left.

Threading for the Rose Path

Thread first the selvage. There are but eight threads in a single repeat of the pattern. The material to be woven is 20 inches wide plus the width of the selvages.

If there are to be 20 threads to the inch, it will require 400 threads plus sixteen threads for the selvages, making in all 416 threads.

If four threads are reeled at a time, it will be necessary to reel 104 groups.

Since 400 threads are used for the pattern and there are eight threads to each repeat, the pattern may be repeated 50 times.

The selvage is threaded the same for the Rose Path as was threaded for the Monk's Belt.

The first thread of the pattern is drawn through the eye of the first heddle on the back row.

The second thread goes through the eye of the first heddle on the third heddle sticks.

The third thread passes through the eye of the first heddle on the second heddle sticks.

The fourth thread passes through the eye of the first heddle on the first heddle sticks. From here the threading runs back to the fourth heddle sticks.

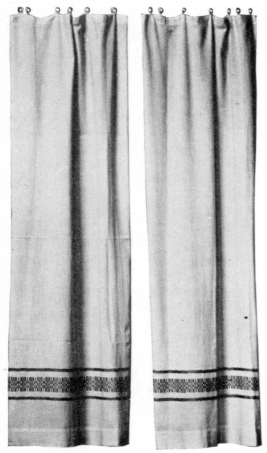

Fig. 80—A Pair of Woven Curtains

The eighth thread of the pattern passes through the eye of the second heddle on the first heddle sticks. This finishes one repeat. All the other repeats are simply a repetition of the first.

The left selvage is the same as the right.

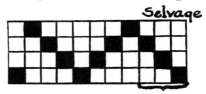

Fig. 81—Rose Path. Draft of Pattern

If a number 20 reed is used, two threads of the selvage are drawn through each of the first six dents and then one thread through each dent until the left selvage is reached, when two are again drawn through each of four dents.

If a number 10 reed is used two threads of the selvage are drawn through a dent at a time and then two threads through each dent until the left selvage is reached.

The upper heddle sticks are tied to the heddle horses the same as for the Monk's Belt.

The lower heddle sticks are also tied to the treadles the same as in the Monk's Belt.

Weaving the Pattern

It must be remembered that the treadles are always numbered from right to left. By pressing down treadles 1 and 3, one-half the threads are drawn down. Treadles 2 and 4 draw down the other half.

With the shuttles containing both the pattern thread

and the binder at the right, press down treadles 1 and 2 and pass the pattern thread through the shed.

Press down treadles 1 and 3 and through the shed pass the binder. Press 1 and 2 down again and through the shed pass the pattern thread.

Press down 2 and 4 and pass the binder through the shed.

Press down the treadles in the following order:

1 and 2	2 and 3	1 and 4
1 and 3 Binder	2 and 4 Binder	1 and 3 Binder
1 and 2	3 and 4	1 and 4
2 and 4 Binder	1 and 3 Binder	2 and 4 Binder
2 and 3	3 and 4	
1 and 3 Binder	2 and 4 Binder	

When the above has been completed all the changes possible in this threading are shown.

On ruled paper have the pupils make as many combinations of the above changes as possible.

Figures 82 and 83 show a few of the combinations woven into borders.

The Rose Path is full of interesting combinations which may be used in borders for curtains, bags, table runners and pillow tops.

Finer Threads Used For Warp

It is not necessary to confine the warp used to the ordinary four-ply carpet warp. It must be remembered, however, that the finer the warp the more threads there must be to the inch.

For extra fine work the mercerized cotton may be

Fig. 82—Borders

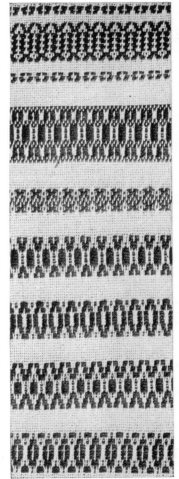

Fig. 83—Borders

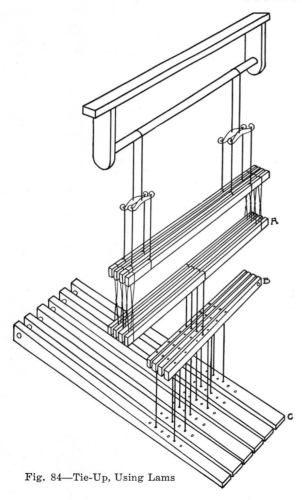

Fig. 84—Tie-Up, Using Lams

used. This is obtainable in various sizes. Numbers 3 and 5 are most commonly used. Jap silk No. 20 makes a very good warp for finer articles. Glo silk is also good. To the one interested there is an unlimited variety to be had.

The Lams

In the pattern weaving up to this time the loom has been tied up in such a way that it has been necessary to use both feet in pressing down the treadles to bring about the desired changes in the pattern.

Fig. 84 shows the drawing of such parts of the loom as are concerned in pattern making. At A, Fig. 84, are shown the heddle sticks without the heddles.

At B are shown the lams. The lams are new and no reference up to this time has been made to them. C, Fig. 84 illustrates six treadles instead of four as shown and described in previous drawings.

The lams are held in place at one end by brackets screwed to the inner right side of the loom. See B, Fig. 84. By the use of the lams, the loom may be so tied up that one foot will press down the desired number of heddle sticks at one time.

The tying of the upper heddle sticks to the heddle horses is the same as shown at A and as previously described.

On examination of B it will be found that instead of the treadles being tied directly to the lower heddle sticks, it is the lams which are tied, one to each lower heddle stick.

This tying of the lams is done exactly the same as if the treadle were being tied.

After the lams are tied to the lower heddle sticks, attention will be given to the treadles. There are six treadles in all.

The two center treadles are used in drawing down the heddles that will do the plain weaving. The other four, two at each side of the center, are used to make the pattern. These are numbered from right to left, 1, 2. Skip the two center ones and number the last two, 3 and 4.

If the first change in the pattern indicates that heddle sticks 1 and 4 are to be drawn down, then the lams 1 and 4 are tied to the first treadle, as shown in Fig. 84. Then if treadle No. 1 is pressed down, it draws down lams 1 and 4, and since lams 1 and 4 are tied to the lower heddle sticks 1 and 4, the pressure must draw down these heddles.

If the next change in the pattern indicates that heddles 2 and 3 are to be drawn down, then lams 2 and 3 are tied to treadle No. 2 as above described.

This is continued until all treadles have been tied to draw down the right heddles. The heddles doing the plain weaving are tied to the two center treadles. The knot used in the tying has been fully described in Figs. 37, 38, 39 and 40.

Fig. 85 shows an adaptation of the Rose Path to a border which may be used in curtains. A number 9 reed is used; one thread to each dent. The woof and warp are of the same material. Care is taken not to beat the woof too hard. This material resembles a coarse scrim. A number 3 mercerized cotton is used in the border and a 2-ply thread is used for the binder.

Fig. 85—Curtain Boarder. Adaptation from Rose Path

CHAPTER III

Colonial Patterns

Many of the patterns used by amateur weavers of to-day are simply the old Colonial patterns which have been handed down from one generation to another.

It is difficult to know just where they originated. The names often suggest the country from which the original pattern might have come. Such names as the Olive Leaf and Bonaparte's March may have come from France; the Queen's Delight and the Governor's Garden may have come from England; while the Whig Rose may have originated in our country as late as the time when the Whig Party sprung into existence. One of the interesting features of this work, to the amateur weaver of today, is not to accept the patterns just as they have been handed down, but to make such changes as will enable the finished products to find an appropriate place in the house furnishings of today.

The patterns which follow are given as they were originally woven, together with such changes as make them desirable at this time.

Reading a Draft

"Draft" is the term usually applied to a threading as shown in Figs. 86 and 87. This, when properly followed, produces the pattern as shown in Figs. 88 and 89. Fig. 88 shows the upper or right side and 89 shows the under side of the finished weaving. "The Big Diamond" is the particular name of this pattern.

The following is a detailed description of the pattern:

First: In threading a pattern always begin to read at the right. When the first part is finished begin at the right of the second, etc.

Second: The pattern begins with the first thread after the right selvage and ends with the last thread just before the left selvage.

Third: Find the number of threads to make one repeat. All threads within a brace are to be repeated the number of times indicated. For example, 4X means to repeat the threading four times. The actual number of threads in this pattern is 154.

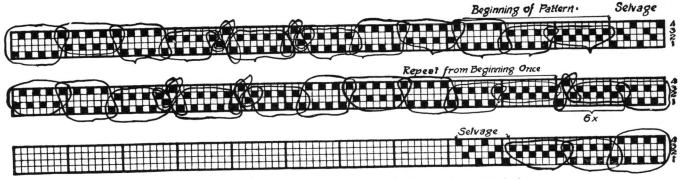

Fig. 86—The Big Diamond. Draft of Pattern with each Group Marked

Thread the pattern up to the place where it states "Repeat once from beginning."

In repeating, go back to the beginning and thread through the entire draft.

The number of threads to produce the piece of cloth shown in Fig. 88 is as follows:

Selvage 8 threads. From the beginning of the pattern to the placed marked, "repeat from the beginning" is 154

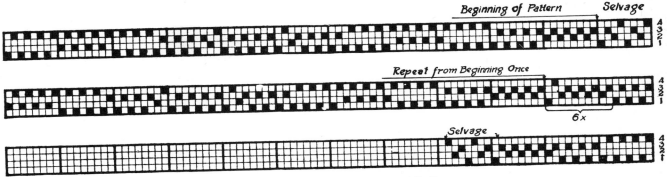

Fig. 87—The Big Diamond. Draft of Pattern

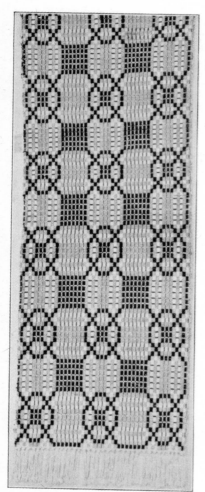

threads. Repeating from beginning makes 154 more threads. Then repeat to the end 103 threads. Selvage 8 threads. In all there are 427 threads. The use of a four-ply carpet warp and a No. 10 reed and two threads to the dent makes a table runner about 21 inches wide while in the loom.

After the warp has been reeled and placed on the beam, the threading may begin.

Fourth: Threading—The selvage is threaded as before described.

Beginning with the real pattern the first thread passes through the eye of a heddle on the third heddle sticks. The second thread passes through the eye of a heddle on the second heddle sticks.

The draft shows that this combination is repeated four times; this is indicated by the brackets drawn around this group. The next group is made up of the combination of 3 and 1, indicated by brackets.

The next threads run in the combination of 4 and 1, and the next 4 and 2, as indicated by brackets. The threading is continued until the left selvage is reached, the brackets indicating the grouping.

The draft is usually written as shown in Fig. 87.

Fifth: The threading completed, the threads are drawn through the reed, two to each dent. Care must be taken to draw the threads through the dents so the threading is in the middle of the reed. This has been explained previously.

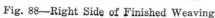
Fig. 88—Right Side of Finished Weaving

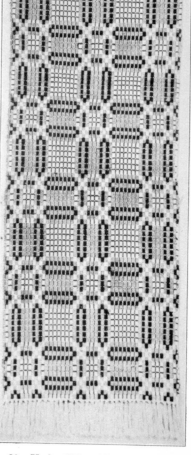
Fig. 89—Under Side of Finished Weaving

The Tie-Up

The upper heddle sticks are tied to the heddle horses as before described.

The lower heddle sticks are tied, one to each of the lams instead of directly to the treadles.

The treadles are tied to the lams in the order indicated by the draft.

The first combination in the threading is 2 and 3, therefore lams 2 and 3 are tied to the first treadle. The next combination is 1 and 3, then 1 and 3 are tied to the second treadle.

The third change in the pattern is 1 and 4. It is tied to the fifth treadle which is next to the last, skipping the two center ones.

The fourth combination is 4 and 2 which is tied to the last treadle.

The plain weaving for this pattern is done by pressing down heddle sticks 1 and 2 at one time, and 3 and 4 the next. This means that lams 1 and 2 are tied to the right middle treadle, and 3 and 4 are tied to the left middle treadle.

Weaving the Pattern

Before beginning the real pattern about one-half inch of plain weaving is done. This is done by pressing down first one and then the other of the two middle treadles.

With the shuttle at the right, press down the first treadle which draws down heddle sticks 2 and 3. Through the shed pass the first pattern thread.

For the binder press down the middle treadle to the right. For the second pattern thread press down the first treadle again. The thread for the plain weaving is at the left, so the left treadle is pressed down and the binder is sent from the left to the right.

For the third pattern thread press down the first treadle again. The binder is now at the right, so the right middle treadle is pressed down. This is continued until the first treadle is pressed down as many times as there are threads indicated in the first combination. In this case there are eight, and the binder is used after each pattern thread. If eight times makes too large a color spot, press down the first treadle only six or even four times. The weaver must be the judge.

The second change in the pattern is 1 and 3 in the threading, therefore the second treadle which draws down 1 and 3 is pressed down 4, 6 or 8 times, just as the weaver desires.

The third change is 1 and 4, so the fourth or next to the last treadle is pressed down 4, 6 or 8 times. The fourth change is 2 and 4, so the last treadle is pressed down 4, 6 or 8 times.

It will be observed that the threads all come in combinations. Sometimes the combination consists of only two threads. Fig. 86. When this is true then only two pattern threads are run across.

The draft shown at Fig. 87 tells all that must be known about a pattern to produce the finished piece of cloth.

The Treadling Draft

It is not necessary to make a "treadling draft" for each pattern.

Attention has already been called to the fact that the threading is done in groups, each small square representing a thread. If the combination 3-2 is used four times in succession, making eight threads, it means that the treadle pulling down the combination 3-2 is pressed down eight times and a pattern thread carried across each time with a binder after each. Any group of threads within a brace is repeated in the treadling as many times as is indicated by the figure below. In this way the threading draft becomes the treadling draft.

The weaver has no doubt learned by this time that all horizontal spacing is determined by the number of times a certain combination is threaded and cannot be changed after the pattern is threaded. The vertical spacing is controlled by the weaver and may be changed at any time. For example—if the threading draft calls for the combination 3-4 four times it means that eight threads are drawn through the heddle eyes; in weaving the pattern it means that eight pattern or woof threads are passed through the shed made by drawing down the combination 3-4. If the weaver desires only 4 woof threads the combination 3-4 is drawn down only four times or it may be drawn down only once, thus changing the vertical spacing each time, but leaving the horizontal the same.

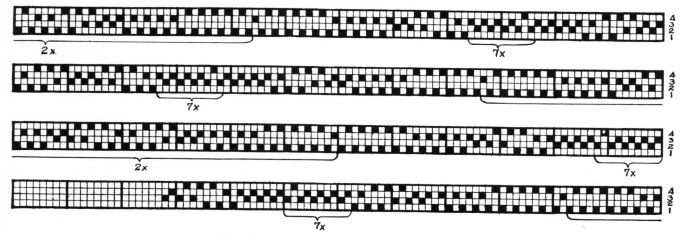

Fig. 90—Double Snow Ball. Draft of Pattern

From the foregoing it is plain that the threading draft frequently can also be used as the treadling draft.

It is only when the treadling is irregular that a separate draft is necessary.

The drafts are all written so that the pattern begins and ends in a convenient place, making it possible to sew two strips together. If the draft is that for a table runner or pillow top the entire draft is given, showing both borders.

There is little or no difficulty in finding the parts of a draft that will produce certain parts of the finished pattern, by comparing the threading draft with the finished pattern. The repeats marked 7X, etc., leads one at once to what the Kentucky women call the "Table" in the finished pattern. Locating any one part of the design is a guide to all the other parts.

It must be remembered that the pattern may be woven by using only four treadles, one tied to each heddle stick as described in the Monk's Belt and the Rose Path.

In case each heddle stick is tied to a treadle, the pat-

Fig. 91—Finished Weaving Using Double Snowball Pattern

tern is produced by pressing down treadles 2 and 3 as many times as desired. Then 1 and 3 as many times as desired, 1 and 4 and then 2 and 4.

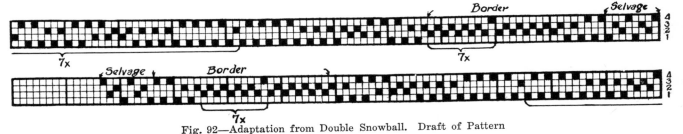

Fig. 92—Adaptation from Double Snowball. Draft of Pattern

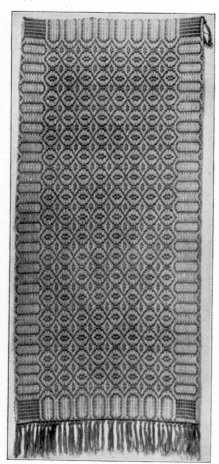

Fig. 93—Right Side of Table Runner

The plain weaving is done by pressing down treadles 1 and 2 at one time, and treadles 3 and 4 at another.

The patterns which follow will be described in as brief a way as possible, because all tying and treadling are read in the draft as above described.

Fig. 90 shows the original draft for the Double Snowball, and Fig. 91 shows the woven pattern when the draft shown in Fig. 90 is followed. The draft is so written that the two widths may be sewed together.

Where to Begin

Owing to the width of looms it is necessary to weave counterpanes and couch covers in two strips, to be sewed together. In all drafts care is taken to begin the threading so two edges may be sewed together to make one complete pattern, just the same as figured carpets are woven and sewed.

The tie-up for the double snowball pattern shown in Fig. 90, is as follows: Each lower heddle stick is tied to a lam and the lams are then tied as follows:

1 and 4 to the first treadle.
1 and 3 to the second treadle.
2 and 3 to the third treadle.
2 and 4 to the fourth treadle.
The plain weave is done by tying lams.
1 and 2 to the right middle treadle.
3 and 4 to the left middle treadle.

Figure 93 shows an adaptation of the Double Snowball. It is not difficult to find the part of the pattern used in the original pattern. This particular part when used alone as in Fig. 92 is often called the Dogwood Blossom.

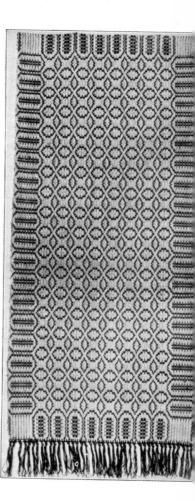

Fig. 94—Under Side of Table Runner

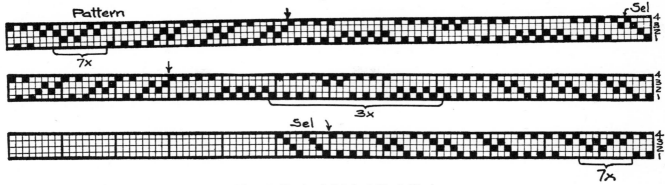

Fig. 95—Draft of Original Block Work

Figure 92 shows the draft for the adaptation and is read as follows:

First: 615 threads required for the entire pattern.
Second: Each lower heddle stick is tied to a lam.
Third: The lams are tied as follows:
1 and 4 to the first treadle.
1 and 3 to the second treadle.

2 and 3 to the third treadle.
2 and 4 to the fourth treadle.
The plain weave is done by tying lams.
1 and 2 to the right middle treadle, and
3 and 4 to the left middle treadle.
The material is a two-ply unbleached cotton warp.
Use a No. 15 reed, placing two threads to a dent.

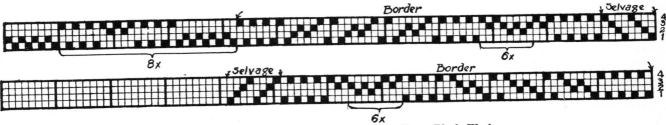

Fig. 96—The Draft of Table Runner Taken From Block Work

The material used in the pattern may be a colored four-ply carpet warp or a No. 3 mercerized cotton. The two-ply carpet warp may be used for the binder or a fine mercerized thread may be used.

When weaving the pattern, the part within the brace is woven as many times as is indicated by the figure. For example, the brace marked 7X means all within the brace is woven seven times before proceeding with the remainder of the pattern.

Figure 91 shows the original pattern, while Figs. 93 and 94 show a table runner taken from Fig. 91.

This pattern is often used for pillow tops. In such a case a square is woven.

Fig. 95 shows a draft of what is known as Block Work, the original of which is shown in Fig. 97. This design, as well as many of the old Colonial patterns, is full of suggestions for pillow tops, table runners and even counterpanes.

Figure 98 shows a pillow top taken from Fig. 96.

There will be no difficulty in locating Fig. 98 in Fig. 97.

Figure 99 shows a table runner taken from Fig. 97.

Figure 99 was woven on the same loom, with the same threading as the pillow top shown in Fig. 98.

Reading of the Draft, Fig. 96

No. 10 reed, two threads to a dent.

421 threads four-ply carpet warp required.

Each lower heddle stick is tied to a lam.

The lams are tied as follows:

1 and 4 to the first treadle.

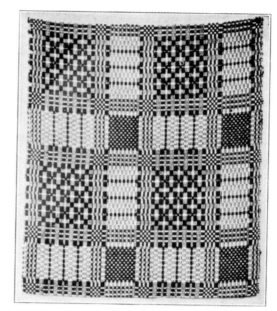

Fig. 97—Finished Weaving of Block Work

3 and 4 to the second treadle.

2 and 3 to the third treadle.

1 and 2 to the fourth treadle.

For plain weave tie:

1 and 3 to the right middle treadle.

2 and 4 to the left middle treadle.

The part of the draft that is repeated is set off by small arrows and the word PATTERN printed between these arrows.

Fig. 98—Finished Pillow Top

Chariot Wheel

Figure 100 shows a draft taken from what is known as the Chariot Wheel pattern.

Figure 101 shows a pillow top woven on a loom threaded for Fig. 100.

Fig. 102 shows the under side of Fig. 101.

Very often the under side of the weaving is more attractive than the upper or right side. The design of the under side is usually more broken, thus making it many times more desirable from an art standpoint.

When making a pillow, let one side of the pillow show the right side and the other the under side of the weaving.

Figure 103 shows a counterpane, using the draft shown in Fig. 100.

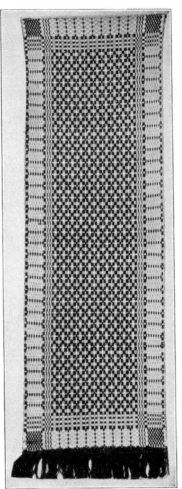

Fig. 99—Table Runner Woven from
Block Work

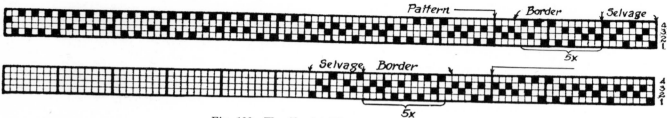

Fig. 100—The Chariot Wheel. Draft of Pattern

Reading the Draft, Fig. 100

Material: A two-ply unbleached carpet warp.

Number 15 reed, placing two threads to a dent.

Woof: Any color of wool, four-ply carpet warp or No. 3 mercerized cotton; 672 threads required to complete the threading.

The lower heddle sticks are tied one to each lam.

Fig. 101—Pillow Top Woven from Chariot Wheel Pattern

The lams are tied as follows:

1 and 3 to the first treadle.

2 and 3 to the second treadle.

2 and 4 to the third treadle.

1 and 4 to the fourth treadle.

For the plain weave:

1 and 2 tie to the right middle treadle.

3 and 4 tie to the left middle treadle.

When threading the draft as shown in Fig. 100, thread the right selvage first and then the border, repeating the threads within the brace the number of times indicated. The real pattern begins just after the right border. This part of the draft is threaded four times before threading the left border and the left selvage.

Figure 104 shows a pair of curtains, the border of which is an adaptation of the "Chariot Wheel."

To the one truly interested there is no limitation of adaptations. Whole bedroom sets may be woven, carrying the "Chariot Wheel" into the various borders. Such a set

Fig. 102—Under Side of Pillow

includes the counterpane, curtains, dressing table mat, valence and even the rug for the floor, which may be woven of coarse materials, carrying out the unity of design.

This particular pair of curtains is woven of Egyptian twine. The border is of two shades of blue No. 3 mercerized cotton.

The loom was threaded 30 ends to the inch. A number 15 reed was used, drawing two threads through each dent. This does not give the scrim weave as shown in the

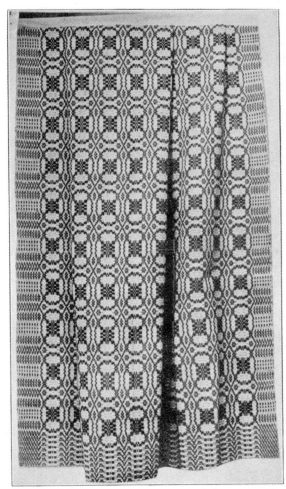

Fig. 103—Counterpane Woven from Chariot Wheel Pattern

curtains, Figs. 80 and 85, but more of a marquisette weave, which is very pleasing.

When weaving the border use only the treadles which will raise and lower the sets of thread that will produce the one row of wheels. It is well, however, to weave in a narrow stripe below and above the principal border stripe, which in this case is the row of wheels. If the narrow bands are to be used across the top great care must be exercised to get the separate bands exactly the same distance from the top and at the same time make the borders at the bottom come together. If the bands across the top are omitted the weaving of curtains is greatly simplified. It is not necessary to be limited to materials, as almost any threads may be woven into most attractive fabrics.

In weaving curtains it is always well to make a liberal allowance for shrinkage. Almost all materials whether of wool, cotton or linen will shrink.

The Orange Peel

Attention has not been called to the fact that in many cases the original woven pattern appears without the draft for the same. Fig. 105 shows the original pattern of the Orange Peel, while Fig. 106 shows the draft for Fig. 107 and Fig. 108. Should a counterpane of this pattern be desired the threading is done the same as shown in Fig. 106, omitting the left border each time. The number of times the pattern is repeated depends upon the width of the loom and also the width of the couch cover or counter-

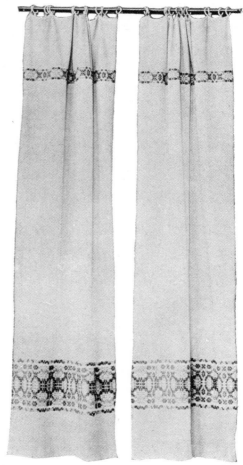

Fig. 104—Curtain Woven with Border from Chariot Wheel

pane desired. It must be remembered that the strips are sewed together and must be made to match.

The weaver will have gained by this time sufficient experience to make the changes to meet the demands. Originality is one of the chief requirements to be developed, for this work.

The draft reads as follows:

Material: Two-ply unbleached carpet warp.

Reed number 15, placing two threads to a dent.

The material used in the pattern (the woof) may be any of the three following materials:

Wool, four-ply carpet warp, or No. 3 mercerized cotton.

Use a finer thread for the binder.

739 threads repeating the pattern six times.

Each lower heddle stick is tied to a lams.

The lams are tied as follows:

2 and 4 to the first treadle.

2 and 3 to the second treadle.

1 and 3 to the third treadle.

Fig. 105—Original Pattern from Orange Peel

1 and 4 to the fourth treadle.

For the plain weave tie:

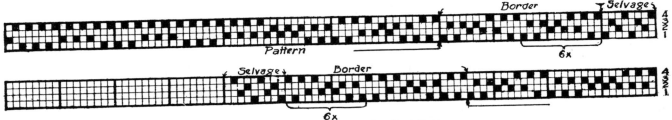

Fig. 106—The Orange Peel. Draft of Pattern

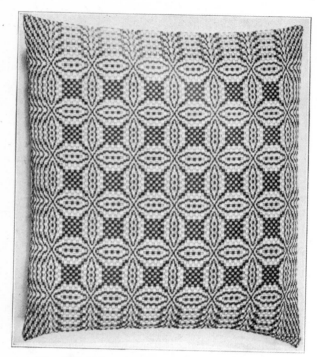

Fig. 107—Pillow Top Woven from Orange Peel

Figure 107 shows the "Orange Peel" worked out in a sofa pillow top.   The draft shown at Fig. 106 will make this pillow top.

Figure 108 shows the under side of Fig. 107.

Governor's Garden

Figure 109 is the draft for the Original pattern of "Governor's Garden" shown in Fig. 111.

Fig. 108—Under Side of Pillow shown in Fig. 107

1 and 2 to the right middle treadle.

3 and 4 to the left middle treadle.

It will be observed that the right and left edges are not the same, only half the pattern showing on the right edge and almost a complete pattern on the left edge.

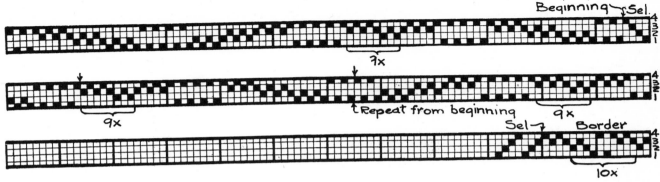

Fig. 109—The Governor's Garden. Draft of Original Pattern

Figure 110 gives the draft for the pillow tops shown in Fig. 112 and Fig. 113.

It is difficult to recognize Figs. 112 and 113 as having been taken from Fig. 111.

It is quite wonderful what even the amateur weaver will be able to do after a somewhat limited experience in actual work with the loom.

Any draft is full of suggestions for borders, curtains, table runners, complete couch covers, pillow tops, counterpanes, etc.

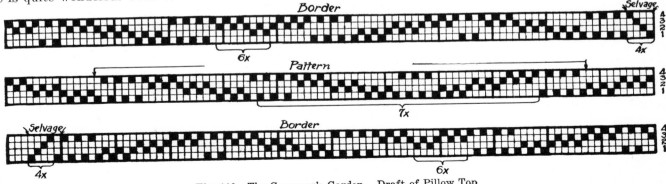

Fig. 110—The Governor's Garden. Draft of Pillow Top

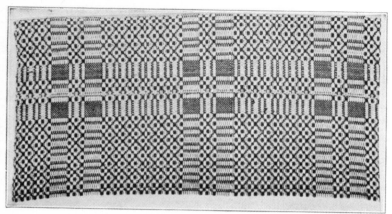

Fig. 111—Original Pattern of Governor's Garden

The "Governor's Garden" is the longest of the drafts and is threaded just as given in Fig. 110.

The draft reads as follows:

Materials: Two-ply unbleached carpet warp.

Reed: Number 15, placing two threads to a dent.

The material in the pattern (woof) may be any of the materials before mentioned.

Use 641 threads for the complete pattern. Each lower heddle stick is tied to a lam.

The lams are tied as follows:

1 and 4 to the first treadle.
1 and 2 to the second treadle.
2 and 3 to the third treadle.
3 and 4 to the fourth treadle.

For the plain weave tie:

1 and 3 to the right middle treadle.
2 and 4 to the left middle treadle.

Figure 112 shows the right side of the finished weaving, while Fig. 113 shows the under side.

Fig. 112—Pillow Top Woven from Governor's Garden

The border on the front and back edges of any weaving is always taken care of by weaving the repeat of the border as many times as is suggested in the draft.

Bonaparte's March

Figure 115 shows the woven sample of Bonaparte's March. It was woven by following the draft shown at Fig. 114. In weaving the old-time counterpanes it was necessary to weave them in two strips because of the width of the looms at that time. In order that the two strips might be sewed together, the pattern was begun in the center of some particular figure found in the pattern.

Only four threads were used in the selvage along the left edge. The border was usually placed on the right edge.

Borders

Borders are made by repeating certain sets of threads a number of times. Any one at all familiar with pattern weaving can readily understand the making of borders.

Figure 116 shows a draft taken from draft 114. It is that part of the draft that will make an interesting pillow top.

Figure 114 reads as follows:

Count the number of threads in the pattern.

Each lower heddle stick is tied to a lam.

The lams are tied as follows:

1 and 4 to the first treadle.

2 and 3 to the second treadle.

1 and 3 to the third treadle.

It will be observed that only three treadles are necessary to weave the pattern.

Fig. 113—Under Side of Pillow Shown in **Fig. 112**

The plain weave is done by tying lams:

1 and 2 to the right middle treadle.

3 and 4 to the left middle treadle.

The material may be any of the material before mentioned.

Figure 116 may be read and the treadles tied the same as described in Fig. 114.

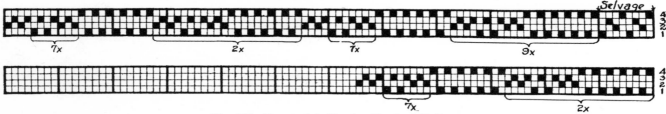

Fig. 114—Bonaparte's March. Draft of Pattern

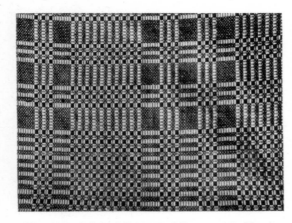

Fig. 115—Original Pattern of Bonaparte's March

Snail's Trail

Figure 117 shows the draft for the pattern shown in

Fig. 118.   This pattern is often called the "Snail's Trail" and "Cat's Paw."

Each lower heddle stick is tied to a lam.

The lams are tied as follows:

1 and 4 to the first treadle.

2 and 4 to the second treadle.

2 and 3 to the third treadle.

1 and 3 to the fourth treadle.

The plain weave is done by tying lams:

1 and 2 to the right middle treadle.

3 and 4 to the left middle treadle.

Press the treadles in the order indicated by the draft and as before described.

The Blooming Flower

"The Blooming Flower" is a pattern often used for

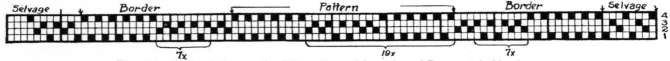

Fig. 116—Draft of Pattern for Pillow Top. Adaptation of Bonaparte's March

counterpanes. Fig. 119 shows the draft while Fig. 120 shows the pattern woven by following the draft, Fig. 119. Only four threads are suggested in the selvage. This will permit of the sewing together of the two strips.

The material is usually a two-ply carpet warp for the warp and wool for the woof. Each lower heddle stick is tied to a lam.

For the pattern the lams are tied as follows:

1 and 4 to the first treadle.

1 and 3 to the second treadle.

2 and 3 to the third treadle.

2 and 4 to the fourth treadle.

The plain weaving is done by tying lams.

1 and 2 to the right middle treadle.

2 and 4 to the left middle treadle.

Pine Knot

Fig. 121 shows the draft for "The Pine Knot" and

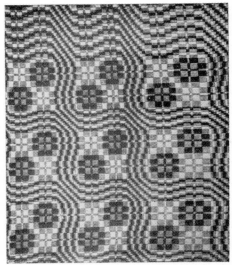

Fig. 118—Original Pattern, Snail's Trail and Cat's Paw

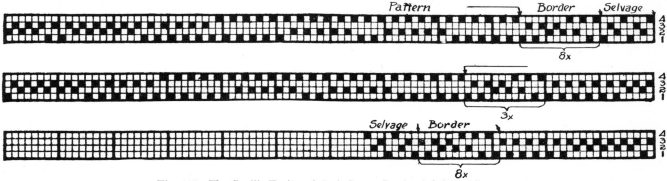

Fig. 117—The Snail's Trail and Cat's Paw. Draft of Original Pattern

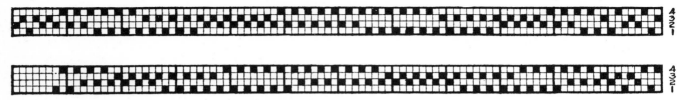

Fig. 119—The Blooming Flower.   Draft of Pattern

Fig. 122 shows the woven sample. This pattern lends itself to several interesting combinations.

If the weaver has read what has gone before there will be no difficulty by this time to select such parts of the pattern as are desired.

The draft reads as follows:

Fig. 120—Original Pattern, Blooming Flower

Tie each lower heddle stick to a lam. The lams are tied as follows:

2 and 3 to the first treadle.

2 and 4 to the second treadle.

1 and 4 to the third treadle.

1 and 3 to the fourth treadle.

The plain weave is done by tying lams:

1 and 2 to the right middle treadle.

3 and 4 to the left middle treadle.

It must not be forgotten that the lams are not absolutely necessary. Each treadle may be tied directly to the lower heddle stick. In such a case only four treadles are used but two are pressed down each time a thread is passed through the shed. This has already been described.

Federal Knot

Fig. 123 shows the draft for the "Federal Knot" and Fig. 124 shows the woven sample. This pattern, the same as those previously described, is full of suggestions.

Any of the materials before mentioned may be used in this pattern.

The draft reads as follows:

Tie each lower heddle stick to a lam.

Fig. 121—Pine Knot. Draft of Pattern

Fig. 122—Original Pattern, Pine Knot

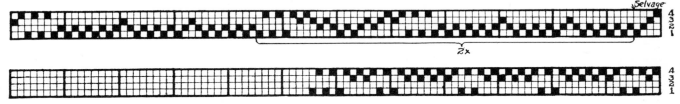

Fig. 123—Federal Knot. Draft of Pattern

The lams are tied as follows:
1 and 4 to the first treadle.
3 and 4 to the second treadle.
1 and 2 to the third treadle.
2 and 3 to the fourth treadle.

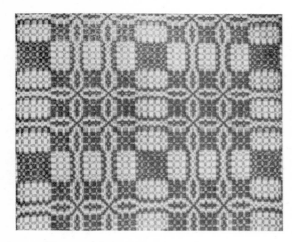

Fig. 124—Original Pattern, Federal Knot

The plain weave is done by tying lams:
1 and 3 to the right middle treadle.
2 and 4 to the left middle treadle.

Wheel of Fortune

Figure 125 shows the draft for what is known as the "Wheel of Fortune," sometimes called the "Wheel of Time."

The draft reads as follows: Material 2, 3, or 4-ply unbleached carpet warp for the warp.

The material used in the pattern (the woof) may be any one of the materials already mentioned.

For 2-ply carpet warp use a No. 15 reed, for 3-ply use a No. 12 reed, for 4-ply use a No. 10 reed.

It requires 232 threads for one repeat of the pattern. The selvage requires seven threads; and the border for a counterpane, 120 threads. If a pillow top is to be made the border should be made narrower and on both edges.

Fig. 126—Wheel of Fortune. Original Pattern

Tie-up: Each lower heddle stick is tied to a lam.
The lams are tied as follows:
2 and 4 to the first treadle.
2 and 3 to the second treadle.
1 and 3 to the third treadle.
1 and 4 to the fourth treadle.
For the plain weave tie:
1 and 2 to the right middle treadle.

3 and 4 to the left middle treadle.

The weaver must always remember that a great deal of judgment must be exercised when doing the weaving.

Four treadles may be used, one tied to each lower treadle stick. In such a case two treadles must be pressed down at the same time. Almost any kind of material may be used for the work. When the material is coarse there must be fewer threads to the inch.

Figure 126 shows the finished weaving.

Irish Chain

The "Irish Chain," sometimes called the "Nine Wheels," and sometimes the "Nine Snow Balls," is shown in Fig. 128.

The draft for the "Irish Chain" is shown in Fig. 127.

The draft reads as follows:

Material: Two-ply unbleached warp. The material used in the pattern (woof) may be any one of the materials already mentioned.

Number 15 reed, placing two threads to a dent, 288 threads required to complete one repeat of the pattern.

The Tie-Up

The lower heddle sticks are tied one to each lam.

The lams are tied as follows.

2 and 3 to the first treadle.

2 and 4 to the second treadle.

1 and 4 to the third treadle.

1 and 3 to the fourth treadle.

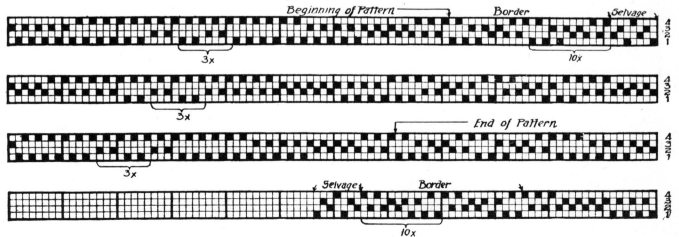

Fig. 125—Wheel of Fortune. Draft of Pattern

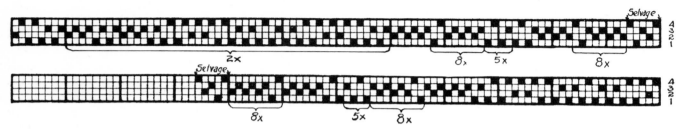

Fig. 127—The Irish Chain.   Draft of Pattern

For the plain weave:
1 and 2 to the right middle treadle.
2 and 4 to the left middle treadle.
Figure 130 shows the original pattern woven by fol-

lowing the draft shown in Fig. 129 without the border.   A counterpane or couch cover is not quite complete if left without a border.   Fig. 131 shows a counterpane with border.   Fig. 129 shows the complete draft for the same.

Fig. 128—Irish Chain.   Original Pattern

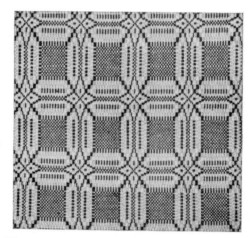

Fig. 130—Rings and Chains.   Original Pattern

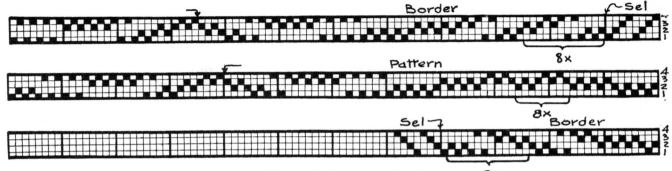

Fig. 129—Rings and Chains. Draft of Pattern **8x**

The same draft may be used for a pillow top or table runner by threading the border fewer times and repeating it and the selvage along the left side.

The amateur weaver has no doubt discovered by this time that any border consists only of a certain number of threads of each combination repeated a number of times, the number of repeats depending entirely upon the width of the border desired.

The front border is always produced by following the draft shown within the brace marked "border," repeating the weaving as many times as is indicated.

Upon examination it is found that to produce the finished piece of cloth the pattern treadles are tied as follows:

The lower heddle sticks are tied one to each lam.

Treadles 1 and 2 are tied to the first lam.

Treadles 1 and 4 are tied to the second lam.

Treadles 3 and 4 are tied to the third lam.

Treadles 2 and 3 are tied to the fourth lam.

Plain weave:

Treadles 1 and 3 are tied to the right middle treadle.

Treadles 2 and 4 are tied to the left middle treadle.

The materials used are similar to those previously suggested for other patterns.

Figure 132 shows a pair of curtains woven of Egyptian twine. The border is an adaptation of "Rings and Chains." The part used in the border may easily be found in the completed counterpane. Fig. 131. The threading for the border in the curtains is the same as shown in Fig. 129. In weaving only the treadles are used that will produce the borders shown in the curtains.

Old Quilt Pattern

The finished counterpane shown in Fig. 133 was woven by following the draft shown in Fig. 134.

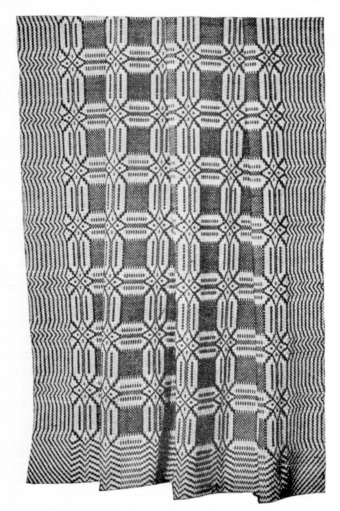

The name of this particular pattern is unknown to the author. The draft was taken from an old counterpane belonging to Miss Elizabeth Gauger, of Joliet, Ill.

Each lower heddle stick is tied to a lam.

The treadles are tied as follows:

Treadles 1 and 2 are tied to the first lam.

Treadles 2 and 3 are tied to the second lam.

Treadles 3 and 4 are tied to the third lam.

Treadles 1 and 4 are tied to the fourth lam.

Plain weave:

Lams 1 and 3 are tied to the right middle treadle.

Lams 2 and 4 are tied to the left middle treadle.

Other Patterns

The amateur weaver has, no doubt, learned by this time just how to read each draft. It has already been stated that the draft tells the whole story.

The lams are always tied one to each lower heddle stick.

The treadles are then tied to the lams. Fig. 86 suggests the way the draft may be divided in order easily to read the various changes and make the "tie-up" stand out.

It is better to figure out the "tie-up" for the pattern first. The plain weave "tie-up" cannot be the same as any one of the pattern combinations.

It is only possible to have six combinations in all. This makes the plain "tie-up" very apparent, as it must be either 1 and 2, 3 and 4, or 1 and 3, 2 and 4.

Very rarely does it appear in any other combination.

Fig. 131—Counterpane Woven from Rings and Chains

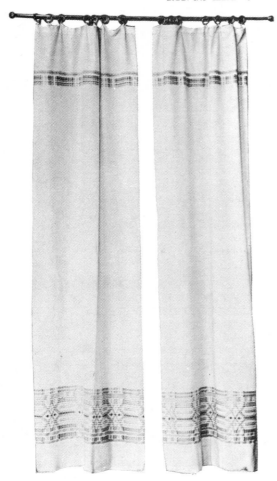

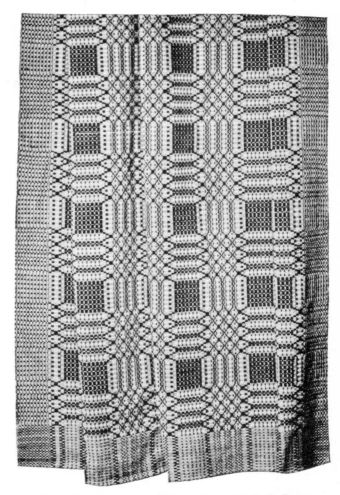

Fig. 132—Curtains with Border from Rings and Chains

Fig. 133—Counterpane Woven from Old Quilt Pattern

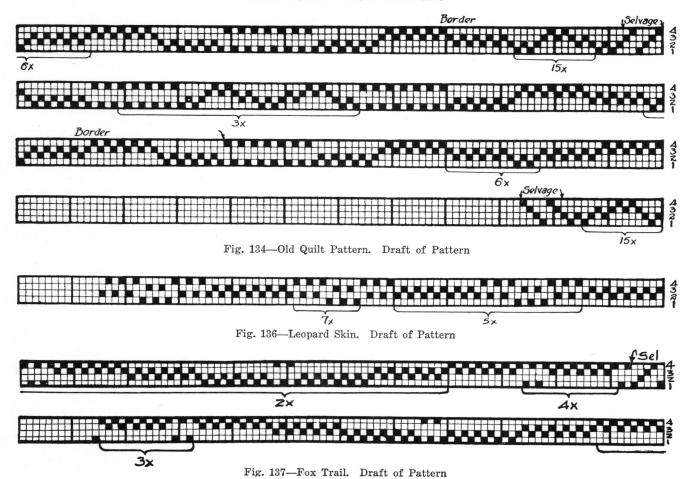

Fig. 134—Old Quilt Pattern.   Draft of Pattern

Fig. 136—Leopard Skin.   Draft of Pattern

Fig. 137—Fox Trail.   Draft of Pattern

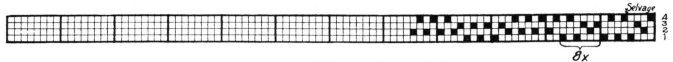

Fig. 140—Doors and Windows.   Draft of Pattern

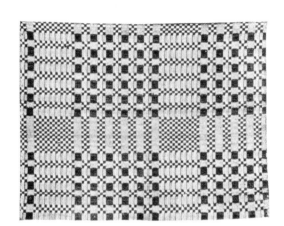

Fig. 135—Leopard Skin.   Original Pattern

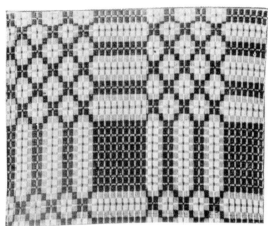

Fig. 138—Fox Trail.   Original Pattern

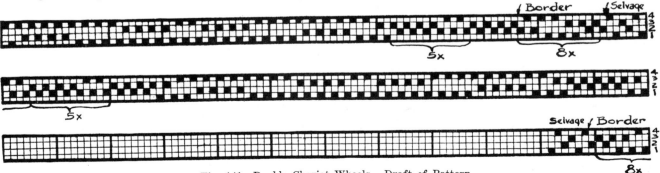

Fig. 141—Double Chariot Wheels.   Draft of Pattern

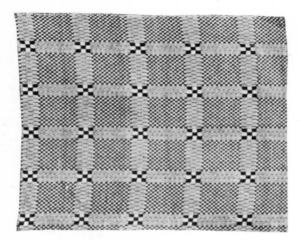

Fig. 139—Doors and Windows.   Original Pattern

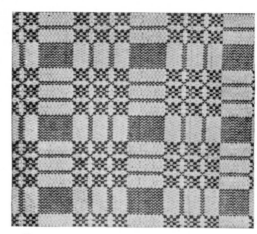

Fig. 143—Scarlet Balls.   Original Pattern

Fig. 142—Double Chariot Wheels.   Original Pattern

Fig. 146—Sea Star.   Original Pattern

Fig. 144—Scarlet Balls. Draft of Pattern

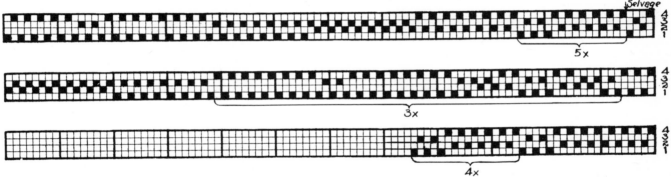

Fig. 145—Sea Star. Draft of Pattern

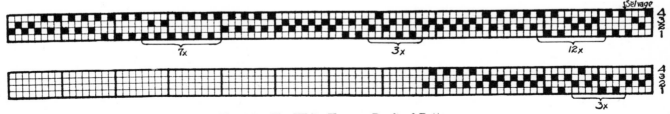

Fig. 148—The White House. Draft of Pattern

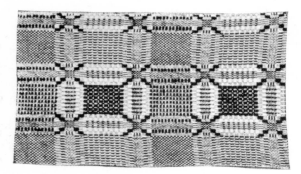

Fig. 147—The White House. Original Pattern

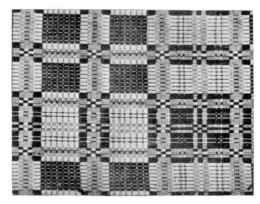

Fig. 150—The Indiana Frame Rose. Original Pattern

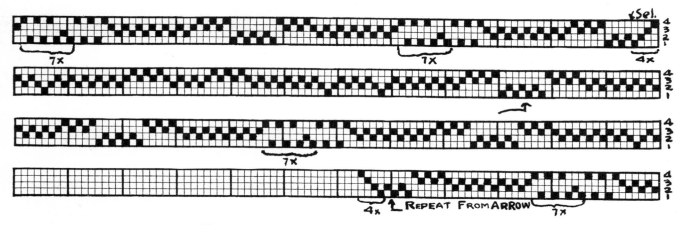

Fig. 149—The Indiana Frame Rose. Draft of Pattern

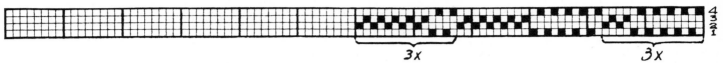

3x   3x

Fig. 152—Window Sash. Draft of Pattern

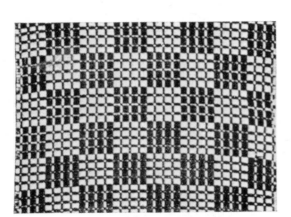

Fig. 151—Window Sash. Original Pattern

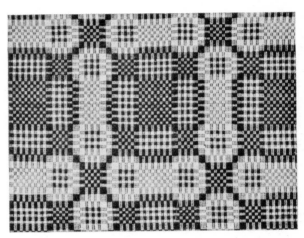

Fig. 154—Parson's Beauty. Original Pattern

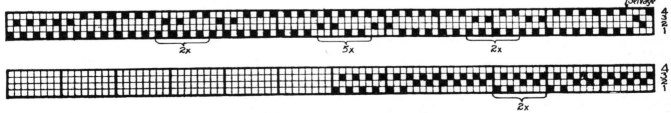

2x   5x   2x

2x

Fig. 153—Parson's Beauty. Draft of Pattern

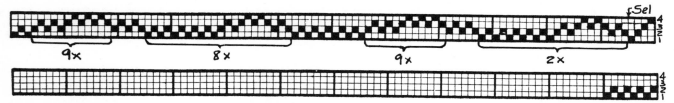

Fig. 156—Braddock's Defeat. Draft of Pattern

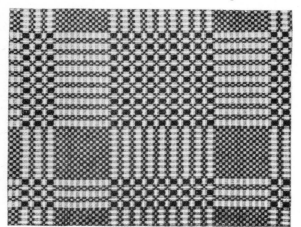

Fig. 155—Braddock's Defeat. Original Pattern

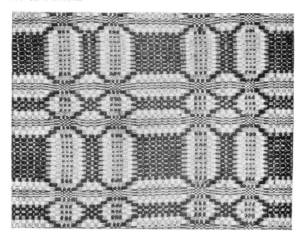

Fig. 158—The King's Flower. Original Pattern

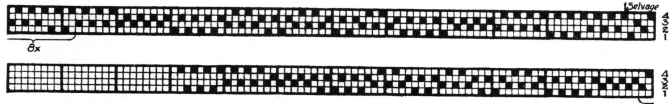

Fig. 157—The King's Flower. Draft of Pattern

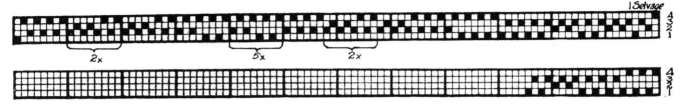

Fig. 160—Queen's Delight.   Draft of Pattern

Fig. 159—Queen's Delight.   Original Pattern

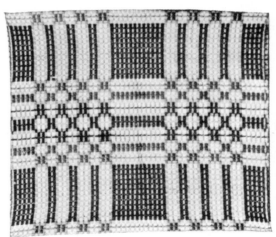

Fig. 162—Old Irish Quilt Pattern.   Original Pattern

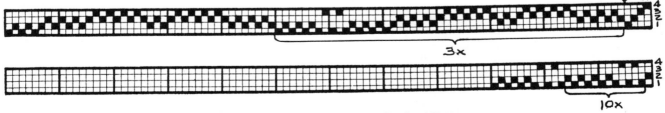

Fig. 161—Old Irish Quilt Pattern.   Draft of Pattern

Fig. 163—The Cross. Original Pattern

Fig. 166—Double Bow Knot. Original Pattern

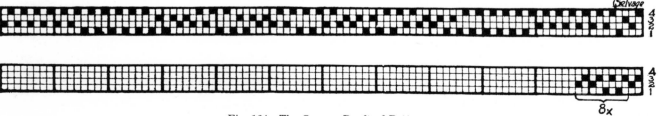

Fig. 164—The Cross. Draft of Pattern

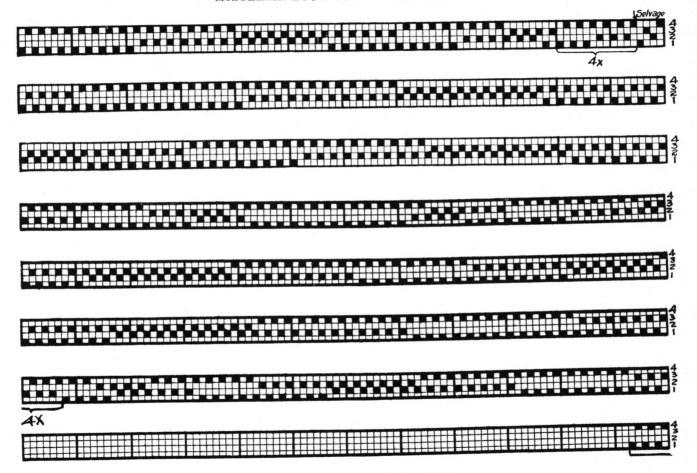

Fig. 165—Double Bow Knot.   Draft of Pattern

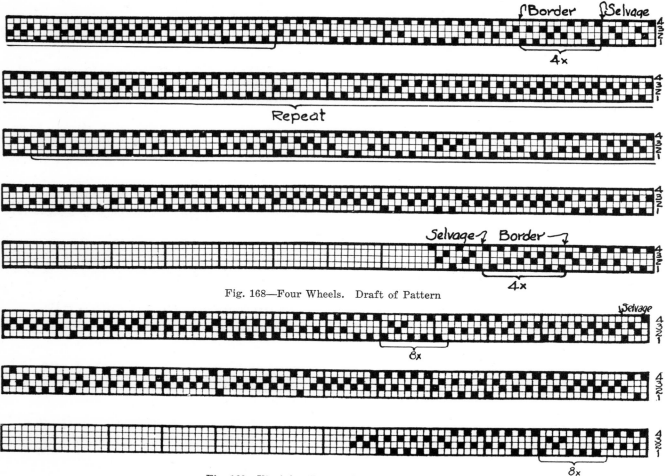

Fig. 168—Four Wheels. Draft of Pattern

Fig. 169—Virginian Snow Ball. Draft of Pattern

Fig. 167—Four Wheels.   Original Pattern

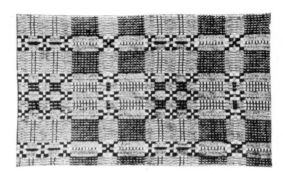

Fig. 170—Virginian Snow Ball.   Original Pattern

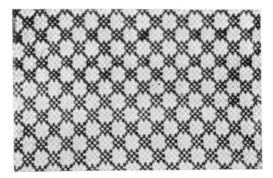

Fig. 171—Dog Tracks.   Original Pattern

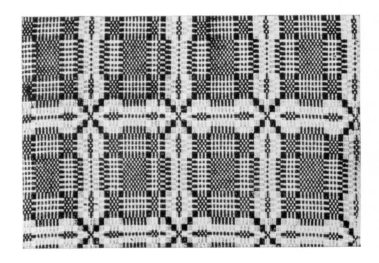

Fig. 174—The Platform.   Original Pattern

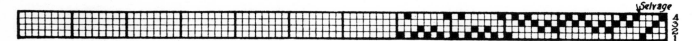

Fig. 172—Dog Tracks.   Draft of Pattern

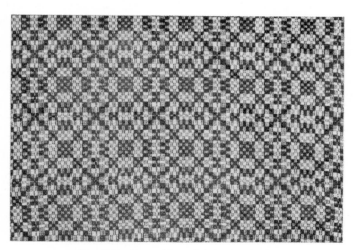

Fig. 175—Guess Me.   Original Pattern

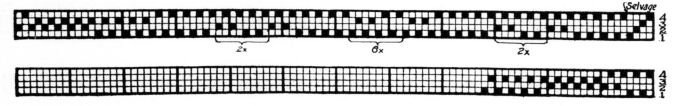

Fig. 173—The Platform.   Draft of Pattern

Fig. 176—Guess Me. Draft of Pattern

There are other ways for the amateur weaver to determine this, but for the present the one given is sufficient.

With the knowledge previously gained the "tie-up" for each of the following drafts may easily be determined.

Wind Flower

The "Wind Flower," Fig. 178, is a good example of a counterpane in which two drafts are used; one to be followed in the threading, and the other to be followed in using the treadles.

Figure 177 shows exactly the way the loom should be threaded to produce the pattern shown in Fig. 178. After the threading is completed there is no further use for Fig. 177. The lams and treadles are tied the same as in previous patterns:

2 and 3 to the first treadles.

1 and 2 to the second.

1 and 4 to the third.

3 and 4 to the fourth.

For the plain weave, 2 and 4 are tied together, and 1 and 3.

Instead of following the draft shown in Figure 177 for the weaving of the fabric, a treadling draft follows in which the harnesses to be drawn down are written out in their regular order to produce the pattern shown in Figure 178.

The one operating the loom must understand that the treadling draft as given deals with the harnesses and not the treadles. For example: The first harnesses to be drawn down are 1 and 2. To draw these two harnesses down, the operator must press the treadle to which these harnesses have been tied, no matter which one it may be.

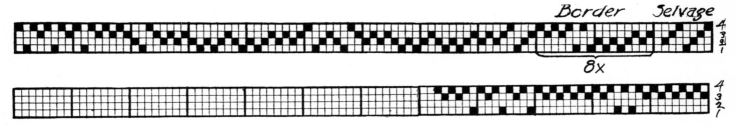

Fig. 177—Wind Flower. Draft of Pattern

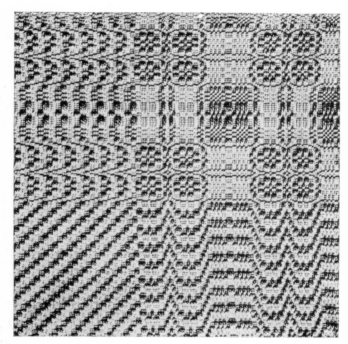

Fig. 178—Original Pattern and Border Woven from The Wind Flower
Pattern

Fig. 179—The Whig Rose. Original Pattern

The entire treadling draft is followed in the way above mentioned. According to the "tie-up" given, harnesses 1 and 2 are tied to the second treadle from the right, therefore if the second treadle is pressed downward, it will carry with it harnesses 1 and 2.

Treadling Draft of Wind Flower

1 and 2—once ⎫
2 and 3—once ⎪
3 and 4—once ⎬ Selvage.
1 and 4—once ⎭

1 and 2—4 times ⎫
2 and 3—4 times ⎪ 8 Times,
3 and 4—4 times ⎬ Border.
1 and 4—4 times ⎭

Beginning of Pattern.

1 and 2—once ⎫
2 and 3—once ⎪
3 and 4—once ⎪
1 and 4—once ⎪
1 and 2—4 times ⎪
2 and 3—4 times ⎪
1 and 2—2 times ⎪
2 and 3—4 times ⎬ Repeat as many times as desired.
1 and 2—4 times ⎪
1 and 4 once ⎪
3 and 4—once ⎪
2 and 3—once ⎪
1 and 2—2 times ⎪
2 and 3—once ⎪
3 and 4—once ⎭

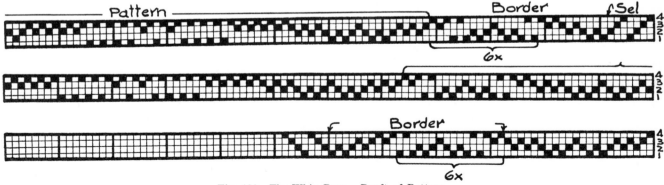

Fig. 180—The Whig Rose. Draft of Pattern

1 and 4—once ⎫
1 and 2—4 times
2 and 3—4 times
1 and 2—2 times
2 and 3—4 times
1 and 2—4 times
1 and 4—once
3 and 4—once
2 and 3—once
1 and 2—once
1 and 4—4 times
3 and 4—2 times
1 and 4—2 times ⎬ Repeat as many times as desired
3 and 4—2 times
1 and 4—2 times
3 and 4—2 times
1 and 4—4 times
3 and 4—2 times
1 and 4—2 times
3 and 4—2 times
1 and 4—2 times
3 and 4—2 times
1 and 4—4 times ⎭

1 and 2—once
2 and 3—once
3 and 4—once
1 and 4—once
1 and 2—4 times

2 and 3—4 times
1 and 2—2 times
2 and 3—4 times
1 and 2—4 times
1 and 4—once
3 and 4—once
2 and 3—once
1 and 2—2 times
2 and 3—once
3 and 4—once
1 and 4—once
1 and 2—4 times
2 and 3—4 times
1 and 2—2 times
2 and 3—4 times
1 and 2—4 times
1 and 4—once
3 and 4—once
2 and 3—once
1 and 2—once

1 and 4—4 times ⎫
3 and 4—4 times ⎬ 8 Times,
2 and 3—4 times   Border.
1 and 2—4 times ⎭

1 and 4—once ⎫
3 and 4—once ⎬ Selvage.
2 and 3—once
1 and 2—once ⎭

Whig Rose

Figure 179 shows the finished cloth for what is known as the Whig Rose. Fig. 180 shows the threading draft for the Whig Rose. The harnesses are tied 1 and 2 to the first treadle, 2 and 3 to the second, 3 and 4 to the third, 1 and 4 to the fourth.

The plain weave is done by tying 1 and 3 to the right middle treadle, and 2 and 4 to the left middle treadle.

After the threading has been completed there is no further use for Fig. 180.

The treadle draft for the Whig Rose is followed the same as was described in the weaving of the Wind Flower. The operator must remember that the drafts as written, deal with harnesses and not with treadles.

1 and 2—once ⎫
2 and 3—once ⎬ Selvage.
3 and 4—once ⎪
1 and 4—once ⎭

1 and 2—2 times
2 and 3—4 times
1 and 2—4 times
1 and 4—4 times

3 and 4—4 times ⎫
2 and 3—4 times ⎪
1 and 2—4 times ⎬ 6 Times
2 and 3—4 times ⎪ Border.
3 and 4—4 times ⎪
1 and 4—4 times ⎭

Beginning of Pattern.

1 and 2—6 times
2 and 3—4 times
1 and 2—2 times
2 and 3—4 times
1 and 2—6 times
1 and 4—8 times
3 and 4—8 times
1 and 4—4 times
3 and 4—4 times
1 and 4—4 times
3 and 4—8 times
1 and 4—8 times

Repeat from beginning.

1 and 2—6 times
2 and 3—4 times
1 and 2—2 times
2 and 3—4 times
1 and 2—6 times
1 and 4—8 times
3 and 4—8 times
1 and 4—4 times
3 and 4—4 times

1 and 4—4 times ⎫
3 and 4—4 times ⎪
2 and 3—4 times ⎬ 6 Times
1 and 2—4 times ⎪ Border.
2 and 3—4 times ⎪
3 and 4—4 times ⎭

1 and 2—6 times
2 and 3—4 times
1 and 2—2 times
2 and 3—4 times
1 and 2—6 times
1 and 4—4 times
3 and 4—4 times
2 and 3—4 times
1 and 2—4 times
2 and 3—4 times
3 and 4—4 times
1 and 4—4 times

1 and 4—4 times
3 and 4—8 times
1 and 4—8 times
1 and 2—6 times
2 and 3—4 times
1 and 2—2 times
2 and 3—4 times
1 and 2—6 times

1 and 4—4 times
1 and 2—4 times
2 and 3—4 times
1 and 2—2 times
1 and 4—once ⎫
3 and 4—once ⎬ Selvage.
2 and 3—once ⎪
1 and 2—once ⎭
Repeat from beginning of pattern.

Sun, Moon and Stars

Figure 181 shows the draft for what is known as the Sun, Moon and Stars.

After the threading has been completed, there will be no further use for the draft, as the treadling draft is written out in such a way that it may be followed the same as for the Wind Flower and the Whig Rose.

The harnesses are tied as follows:

1 and 2 to the first treadle,

2 and 3 to the second treadle,
3 and 4 to the third, and
1 and 4 to the fourth treadle.

For plain weave, tie harnesses 1 and 3 to the right middle treadle, and 2 and 4 to the left middle treadle.

The halftone, Fig. 182, shows the finished pattern, as it is used at Berea, Kentucky.

The Warp is a two-ply-twenty (2/20) cotton thread.
The woof is of wool.

There are 30 threads to the inch, threaded through the dents of a No. 30 reed, one thread to the dent, or a No. 15 reed, two threads to the dent.

Treadling Draft

1 and 2—once ⎫
2 and 3—once ⎬ Selvage
3 and 4—once ⎪
1 and 4—once ⎭

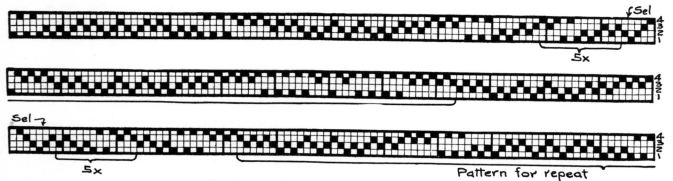

Fig. 181—Sun, Moon and Stars. Draft of Pattern

1 and 2—4 times ⎫
2 and 3—4 times ⎪ Border
3 and 4—4 times ⎬ 5 times
1 and 4—4 times ⎭
1 and 2—4 times
2 and 3—4 times　　　1 and 2—2 times
3 and 4—6 times　　　2 and 3—2 times
1 and 4—6 times　　　1 and 2—4 times
2 and 3—6 times　　　2 and 3—6 times
1 and 2—4 times　　　1 and 4—8 times
2 and 3—2 times　　　3 and 4—8 times
1 and 2—2 times　　　1 and 4—2 times
2 and 3—2 times　　　3 and 4—2 times
1 and 2—4 times　　　1 and 4—2 times
2 and 3—6 times　　　3 and 4—8 times
1 and 4—6 times　　　1 and 4—8 times
3 and 4—6 times　　　2 and 3—6 times
1 and 2—6 times　　　1 and 2—4 times
2 and 3—4 times　　　2 and 3—2 times ⎫ Repeat
1 and 2—2 times　　　1 and 2—2 times ⎬ as often
2 and 3—2 times　　　2 and 3—2 times ⎭ as needed
1 and 2—2 times　　　1 and 2—4 times
2 and 3—4 times　　　2 and 3—6 times
1 and 2—6 times　　　1 and 4—6 times
3 and 4—6 times　　　3 and 4—6 times
1 and 4—6 times　　　1 and 2—6 times
2 and 3—6 times　　　2 and 3—4 times
1 and 2—4 times　　　1 and 2—2 times
2 and 3—2 times　　　2 and 3—2 times
　　　　　　　　　　　1 and 2—2 times

2 and 3—4 times ⎫
1 and 2—6 times ⎪
3 and 4—6 times ⎪
1 and 4—6 times ⎪
2 and 3—6 times ⎬
1 and 2—4 times ⎪
2 and 3—2 times ⎪
1 and 2—2 times ⎪
2 and 3—2 times ⎪
1 and 2—4 times ⎪
2 and 3—6 times ⎭
1 and 4—6 times
3 and 4—6 times
2 and 3—4 times
1 and 2—4 times
1 and 4—4 times ⎫
3 and 4—4 times ⎬ Border
2 and 3—4 times ⎪ 5 times
1 and 2—4 times ⎭
1 and 4—once ⎫
3 and 4—once ⎬ Selvage
2 and 3—once ⎪
1 and 2—once ⎭

Pine Cone Bloom

Figure 183 shows the draft for what is known as the Pine Cone Bloom.

As in other drafts, the whole story of threading tie-up, and treadling is found in the draft itself.　Use a 2/20

Fig. 182—Finished Cloth.　Adaptation of the Pine Cone Bloom

cotton for warp and a No. 30 or 15 reed, 30 threads to the inch.

The Pine Cone Bloom is a favorite draft throughout the South, especially in Kentucky. It is one of the drafts extensively used at Berea. The weaving from which the half-tone, Fig. 184, was taken came from Berea, the draft having been made from the finished piece of work.

Lily of the Valley

Figure 185 shows the draft of what is known as The Lily of the Valley. The photograph shown in the half-tone, Fig. 186, was taken from a counterpane found in Burke County, North Carolina.

The Warp is of 2/20 cotton and the weft of a dark blue wool. A No. 30, or a No. 15, reed is used. The threading, tie-up and treadling are all found in the draft.

Figure 186 is an illustration of the finished pattern.

Tie-Up

1 and 2 to the first treadle.

2 and 3 to the second.

3 and 4 to the third

1 and 4 to the fourth

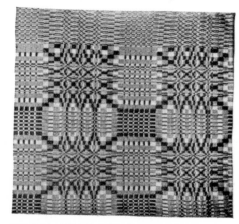

Fig. 184—Finished Cloth.　Pine Cone Bloom

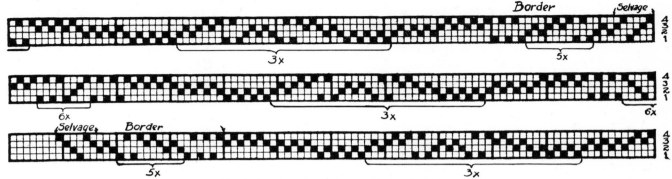

Fig. 183—Pine Cone Bloom. Draft of Pattern

Plain Weave

1 and 3 to right middle treadle
2 and 4 to left middle treadle.

Martha Washington Bag, Fig. 191

The draft shown in Figure 192 was taken from a bag like the one shown in Figure 191.

The bag was woven at Berea and is known as Martha Washington.

Those interested in weaving will find it a great assistance in their work to know enough of cloth analysis to analyze four harness drafts.

The writer well remembers the time when he knew nothing of cloth analysis. At that time he wrote to a well established center for foot power loom weaving and asked if he might buy a few drafts. The reply came stating very emphatically that nothing could be done for him. He lost

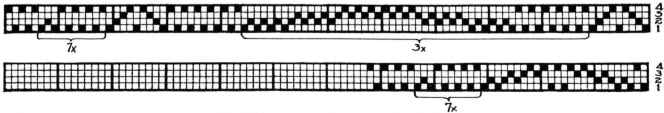

Fig. 185—Lily of the Valley. Draft of Pattern

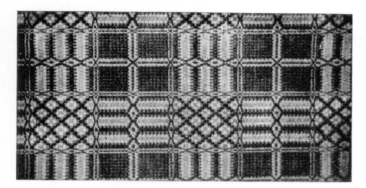

Fig. 186—Lily of the Valley

no time in learning a little about cloth analysis, and then purchased of the above mentioned center, finished squares of their various patterns and analyzed them.   In this way every piece of weaving produced by the center was analyzed and the pattern reproduced.

The Martha Washington draft adapts itself very beautifully to an all over pattern and may be used in pillow tops, table runners and even counterpanes.

Fig. 187—The Honey Suckle.   Draft of Pattern

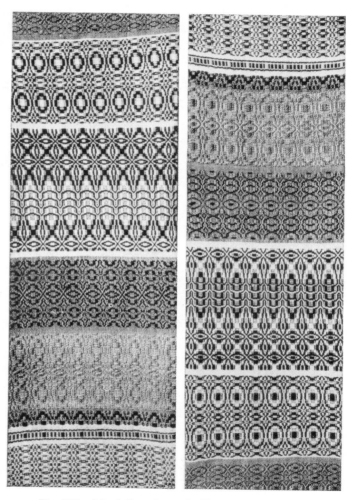

Fig. 188—Adaptations from the Honey Suckle Pattern

Fig. 189—Bag

Fig. 190—Hand Bag

Fig. 191—Martha Washington Bag

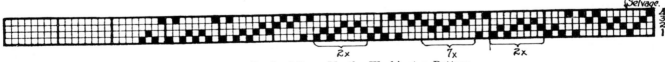

Fig. 192—Draft of Bag—Martha Washington Pattern

CHAPTER IV

The Analysis of Woven Patterns

How to Make a Draft From a Woven Pattern

To analyze a woven piece of fabric and again reproduce it on a foot-power loom is one of the most interesting phases of elementary textile work. So often pieces of old coverlids and linen towels may be found in the most out-of-the-way places. The amateur weaver always has a strong desire to reproduce these most interesting old designs.

In order to do this it is necessary to secure a piece of checked paper consisting of four lines representing the four heddles to be used in the weaving. All four-heddle drafts are written in this way.

Before making a draft it is necessary to know the following principles which underlie all four-heddle weaving.

First—There are six possible combinations of the heddles: 1-2, 1-3, 1-4, 2-3, 2-4, 3-4.

Second—Of these combinations, 1-3 and 2-4 are usually reserved for plain weaving.

Third—The combinations 1-2, 1-4, 2-3, 3-4, make the pattern.

Fourth—The last thread under one block of color is usually the first thread under the next block of color.

Fifth—All blocks in vertical and horizontal lines are made by the same combinations of heddles.

Sixth—There is a row of plain weaving after each row of pattern.

It is well in the beginning to select a small pattern such as is shown in Fig. 193. From this pattern pick out the unit of design which is repeated over again from the first. This consists of a square which extends from A to B.

When this is decided, we are ready to represent our blocks of color, beginning at the upper-right-hand corner of the unit and working diagonally to the lower-left-hand end. Fig. 194.

Any one of the four heddle combinations may be chosen for the first block of color. Count the number of warp threads under the block. In this case there are eight. Suppose the first combination is 4-1; we then mark alternately on the lines representing the fourth and first heddles, using as many as will correspond to the number of warp threads needed.

According to principle 4, the next combination may be one that has in it the last number just used. In the diagram, the last number was 1, so the combination 1-2 must be used next. This is represented as before on the

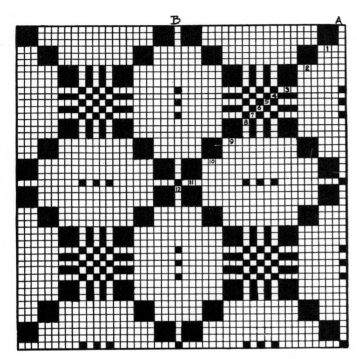

Fig. 193—Complete Pattern Repeated

lines representing those heddles, counting the 1 already there as the first number and using as many alternately, as there are to be warp threads under the second block of color—in this case 8.

Again according to principle four, the next combination (block 3) may be one that has in it the last num-

ber just used. In the diagram the last number was 2, so the combination 2-3 must be used next. This is represented as before on the lines representing those heddles, counting the 2 already there as the first number and using as many alternately, as there are to be warp threads under the third block of color—in this case 8.

Block 4 is the next to be considered.

This block may be one that has in it the last number just used. The last number was 3, so the combination 3-4 must be used next. This is represented as before on the lines representing those heddles, counting the 3 already there as the first number and using as many alternately as there are to be warp threads under the fourth block of color—in this case 4.

Block 5 is the next to be considered.

According to principle five, it is easily seen that block 5 is simply a repetition of block 3 and is represented by the combination 2-3. Here is the first difficulty. The last heddle used was 4, and our next block in order to be like the third, must be made with the combination 2-3. In order to have the last thread be the first in the next, 3 must be the last heddle used. This can be made right by adding another thread to the warp threads under the fourth block and putting it through the third heddle. We are then ready to use 3-2 two times, using the third heddle first.

Block 6 is to be next considered.

According to principle five, block 6 is on a line vertically and horizontally with block 4 and should be represented by the combination 3-4. In order to have the last thread the first in the next, 3 must be the last heddle used. This can be made right by adding another thread to the warp threads under the fifth block and putting it through the third heddle. We are then ready to use 3-4 two times.

Block 7 is to be next considered.

According to principle five, block **7** is on a line vertically and horizontally with block 5 and should be represented by the combination 3-2. The last thread used was 4. This can be made right by adding another thread to the warp threads under the sixth block and putting it through the third heddle. We are then ready to use 3-2 two times, using the third heddle first.

Block 8 is the same as blocks 6 and 4 and is represented by the combination 3-4. The last thread used in block 7 was 2. Another thread must now be added to the warp threads of block 7 and threaded through the third heddle. We are then ready to use 3-4 two times.

Block 9 is the same as block 3 and should be represented by the combination 2-3. Since the last thread of block 8 was four, it becomes necessary to add another warp thread to block 4 and thread it through the third heddle. We are then ready to use 3-2 eight times.

Block 10 is the same as block 2 and is represented by the combination 1-2. Since the last thread of block 9 was **2**, we are ready to use 2-1 four times.

Block 11 is the same as block 1 and is represented by the combination 4-1. Since the last thread of block 10 was **1**, we are ready to use 4-1 four times.

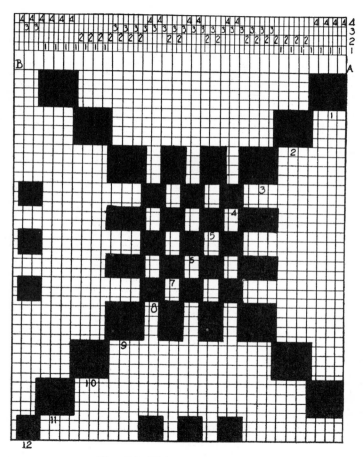

Fig. 194—Unit to be Analyzed

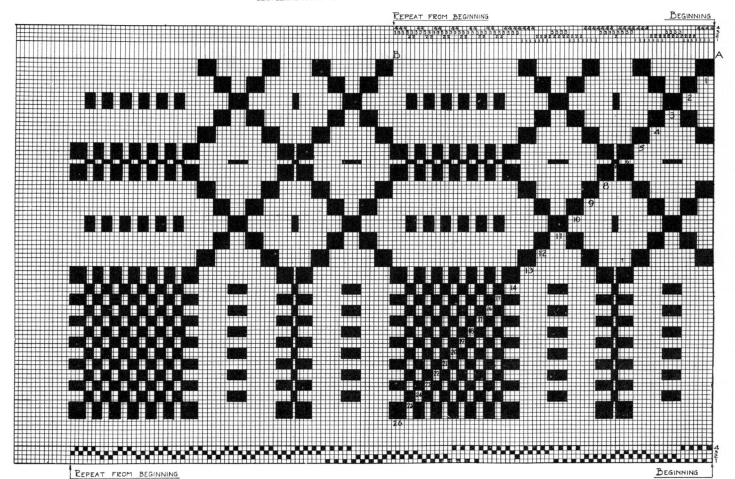

Fig. 195—A Pattern Analysis

Block 12 is the same as blocks 4, 6, and 8, and is represented by the combination 3-4. The last thread in block 11 was 4. We are ready to use the combination 4-3 two times.

The draft as written at the top of Fig. 194 when repeated several times makes a very interesting all-over pattern.

It will be observed that the draft ends with a "4". In repeating it the first "4" at the beginning must be omitted.

If both the last and first "4" are used it will bring two threads on the same heddle stick, thus causing two threads to go down or up, as the case may be.

Another Analysis

Always, before beginning any analysis, pick out of the pattern the unit of design which is repeated backward or over again to produce the all-over pattern.

Fig. 195 shows a more complicated pattern, consisting of two parts—a diamond and a square extending from A to B.

Number the blocks of color, beginning at the upper right-hand corner of the unit, diagonally to the lower left-hand end, as shown in Fig. 195.

Any one of the four heddle combinations may be chosen for the first block of color and for counting the number of warp threads under the block. In this case there are eight.

Suppose 4-1 is chosen for the first combination. This combination is then written as many times as will correspond to the number of warp threads needed, as shown above, block 1. (Fig. 195.)

Block No. 2 is represented by the combination 2-1.
Block No. 3 is represented by the combination 2-3.
Block No. 4 is the same as number 2.
Block No. 5 is the same as number 1.
Block No. 6 is represented by the combination 3-4.
Block No. 7 is the same as block 3.
Block No. 8 is the same as block 6.
Block No. 9 is the same as block 1.
Block No. 10 is the same as block 2.
Block No. 11 is the same as block 3.
Block No. 12 is the same as block 4.
Block No. 13 is the same as block 1.
Block No. 14 is the same as block 6.
Block No. 15 is the same as block 3.

From here the blocks are the same as 6 and 3, alternately. It must always be remembered that all blocks in the same lines vertically and horizontally are represented by the same combination.

The draft at the top of Fig. 195 shows the combinations in figures. The draft below shows the same threading.

How to Block Out a Pattern From a Draft

Blocking a pattern from a given draft is no less interesting than making a draft from a woven piece of fabric.

Drafts may be had from various sources without the woven fabric.

It is a great satisfaction to the amateur weaver to be able to block out the draft at hand and thus know before the loom is threaded what sort of pattern a certain draft will look like when woven.

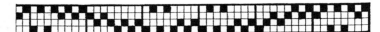

Fig. 196—Draft of Solomon's Delight

The draft shown in Fig. 196 is known as Solomon's Delight. To block out this draft, first secure a piece of paper ruled in one-eighth inch squares. Along the left edge write the draft as shown in Fig. 197. The first combination is 1-4. There are four threads in this combination, but as a matter of convenience only two threads are shown in Fig. 197. The 1-4 is written; the sign (") below indicates another 1-4. Each square represents a thread. The entire draft is written in this way. There is no objection to using the number of threads shown in the draft. This simply doubles the size of the blocks.

The draft is again written at the top of the checked paper. In Fig. 197 each vertical row of squares represents a warp thread.

To fill in the blocks as shown in Fig. 197 begin at the upper left-hand corner. The first combination at the left is 1-4, and the first combination at the top is 1-4. The four small squares are filled in with a colored pencil. Fol-

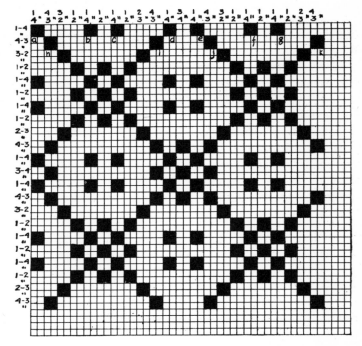

Fig. 197—Preliminary Blockout of Draft, Solomon's Delight

lowing across the paper each time that the combination 1-4 is reached a square is filled in as shown at a, b, c, d, e, f, and g.

The next combination at the left is 4-3 and the second combination at the top is 4-3. This means that where the vertical and horizontal threads cross, the block is colored as shown at h, i, j, and k. In this way the entire pattern is blocked out on the squared paper and provides a means by which the weaver may get a good idea of the pattern without threading the entire loom.

It will be observed that the draft in Fig. 196 has been repeated along the left side and also across the top of the checked paper, in Fig. 197. This is done to give the weaver a better idea of the pattern.

Any four-harness draft may be worked out in this way and is a means of detecting mistakes so often made in copying drafts. Any mistake in a draft is easily found and may be made right by the one who is checking it over.

Another Method of Blocking Out Pattern

The method of Blocking out a pattern from a given draft, as described in the preceding paragraphs, gives a very good idea of what the pattern will look like when woven, but it is not the most exact method.

Figure 198 shows the result of the more exact method of blocking out the pattern, of Solomon's Delight, the draft of which is given in Figure 196.

Using squared paper and with the draft at hand. mark each vertical row of squares as representing one thread in the warp. Starting then with the first thread at the right hand end of the draft, mark the first vertical row of squares (starting from the right hand side of the squared paper) number "4" which represents a thread threaded through a heddle on the fourth heddle sticks. The second

Fig. 198—Exact Method, Blockout of Draft.   Solomon's Delight

thread in the draft is threaded through the third heddle sticks, so mark the second vertical row of square Number "3." Continue in this way until all the threads in the draft have been marked on the top edging of the squared paper, then repeat the pattern once more.

This completes the marking of the upper edge.

Going back to the beginning of the draft, we find the first combination to be three and four. There being three threads in this combination, mark off four horizontal rows of squares (on the right hand side of the squared paper beginning at the top) with a bracket and the Numbers "3-4." Now wherever two or more vertical rows of 3 and 4 are crossed by the combination "3-4," we will get a square or rectangle depending on the number of vertical rows of "3" and "4" that come together.

Referring back to the draft, the next combination is "1 and 4;" mark the combination underneath combination "3-4," enclosing four horizontal rows of squares in the bracket. Continue until pattern is complete as shown in Figure 198.

The foregoing directions apply only to patterns where the threading drafts are followed in the treadling, but often patterns are encountered, in the weaving of which, the threading drafts were not followed in the treadling. In the blocking out of such patterns, the threading draft is followed in marking the vertical rows of squares on the top edge of the squared paper, and it is not used further.

For marking the horizontal rows of squares on the right hand side of the squared paper, the treadling draft is used. The method of blocking out the squares and rectangles is the same as heretofore described.

CHAPTER V

Linen Weaves

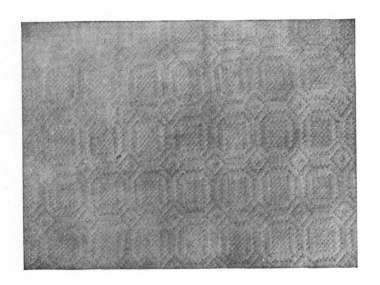

Fig. 200—Finished Pattern. Martha Washington Towel

Linen Weaves

So new is the return of weaving that few amateurs have ventured to do much in the way of reproducing the old linen weaves so generally used in the early days.

Under ordinary conditions linen threads are not in the least difficult to secure from various dealers in textile materials.

It is a very simple matter to raise one's own linen, thus making the linen products of the loom doubly interesting. The apparatus necessary to the heckling, scutching, and spinning of the flax may be purchased of the Community Shop, Lockport, Illinois.

The following drafts are not only suitable to the weaving of linens, but any material used in other weavings may be here used with great success.

Martha Washington Towel

The draft shown in Fig. 199 is that for the Martha Washington Towel.

Fig. 199—Martha Washington Towel. Draft of Pattern

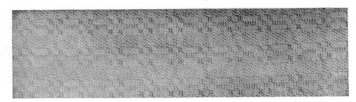

Fig. 201—Finished Pattern of Draft

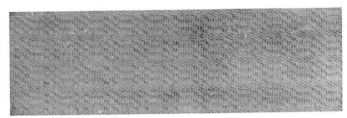

Fig. 202—Modified Treadling

The Warp

Owing to the scarcity of linen, the warp may be of cotton. Jap Silk, No. 70, makes a fine warp.

The Reed

There should be at least 48 threads to the inch and one thread through each dent, excepting at the edges where two threads are drawn through each of the first and last three dents. The filler is of a fine one-ply linen. A number 5, mercerized cotton makes a very interesting filler.

Fig. 200 shows the finished woven pattern.

Tie-Up

Attention is called to the numbering of the harnesses, counting the back harness No. 1, the next No. 2, etc.

The harnesses are tied as follows:
Numbers 1, 2, and 3 to the first treadle.
Numbers 1, 2, and 4 to the second treadle.
Number 5 to the third treadle.
Numbers 1, 3, and 4 to the fourth treadle.
Numbers 2, 3, and 4 to the fifth treadle.

Treadling Draft

Tramp treadle 5 and then treadle 3.
Tramp treadle 5 and then treadle 3.
Tramp treadle 4 and then treadle 3.
Tramp treadle 4 and then treadle 3.
Tramp treadle 2 and then treadle 3.
Tramp treadle 2 and then treadle 3.
Tramp treadle 1 and then treadle 3.
Tramp treadle 1 and then treadle 3.
Tramp treadle 5 and then treadle 3.
Tramp treadle 5 and then treadle 3.
Tramp treadle 4 and then treadle 3.
Tramp treadle 4 and then treadle 3.
Tramp treadle 5 and then treadle 3.
Tramp treadle 5 and then treadle 3.
Tramp treadle 1 and then treadle 3.
Tramp treadle 1 and then treadle 3.
Tramp treadle 2 and then treadle 3.
Tramp treadle 2 and then treadle 3.
Tramp treadle 4 and then treadle 3.
Tramp treadle 4 and then treadle 3.
Tramp treadle 5 and then treadle 3.
Tramp treadle 5 and then treadle 3.

Tramp treadle 1 and then treadle 3.
Tramp treadle 1 and then treadle 3.
Tramp treadle 2 and then treadle 3. } 11 times
Tramp treadle 2 and then treadle 3.

Only one shuttle is used.

Use the double tie-up as described on page 129.

Betsy Ross Towel

Fig. 203 shows the threading draft of the Betsy Ross Towel. This is a most interesting four-harness pattern.

Fig. 201 illustrates the finished pattern.

Fig. 202 shows another pattern made by a slight change in the order of treadling.

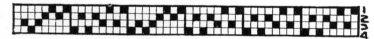

Fig. 203—Betsy Ross Towel. Draft of Pattern

Use a No. 48 reed, one thread to the dent, excepting the first and last two through which two threads are drawn. For warp use the No. 70 Jap Silk. Attention is called to the numbering of the harnesses:

Tie-Up

The treadles are tied as follows:

1-3 tie to the first treadle.

1-4 tie to the second treadle.

2-4 tie to the third treadle.

2-3 tie to the fourth treadle.

1-2 tie to the fifth treadle.

3-4 tie to the sixth treadle.

Treadling Draft

Tramp 1 then 3
Tramp 1 then 4
Tramp 2 then 4 } Repeat this group six times
Tramp 2 then 3

Tramp 1 then 2
Tramp 3 then 4 } Repeat this group eight times

Tramp 1 then 3
Tramp 2 then 4 } Repeat this group eight times

Tramp 1 then 2
Tramp 3 then 4 } Repeat this group eight times

Any number of modified weavings may be had by changing the order of the treadling groups.

Mollie Pitcher Towel

Fig. 205 illustrates the threading draft for the Mollie Pitcher Towel. The weave is most interesting and involves the use of only one shuttle as do all the other linen weaves.

Fig. 204 is the finished pattern obtained by following the treadling as given above, while Fig. 206 shows another pattern produced by making a slight change in the order of treadling.

Use a No. 48 reed; one thread to each dent, excepting the first and last three into which two threads are drawn.

For warp, use a No. 70 Jap Silk.

Tie-Up

Use the double tie-up, as shown by Fig. 262.
Harnesses 1, 2, and 4 tie to the first treadle.
Harnesses 1, 2, and 3 tie to the second treadle.
Harness 5 tie to the third treadle.
Harnesses 2, 3, and 4 tie to the fourth treadle.
Harnesses 1, 3, and 4 tie to the fifth treadle.

Treadling Draft for Fig. 204

Tramp 1 then 3 ⎫
Tramp 2 then 3 ⎬ 8 times

Tramp 1 then 3 ⎫
Tramp 4 then 3 ⎬ 4 times
Tramp 5 then 3 ⎭

Tramp 4 then 3

Tramp 2 then 3 ⎫
Tramp 2 then 3 ⎪
Tramp 1 then 3 ⎪
Tramp 1 then 3 ⎪
Tramp 2 then 3 ⎪
Tramp 2 then 3 ⎬ 3 times
Tramp 5 then 3 ⎪
Tramp 5 then 3 ⎪
Tramp 4 then 3 ⎪
Tramp 4 then 3 ⎪
Tramp 5 then 3 ⎪
Tramp 5 then 3 ⎭

Tramp 2 then 3
Tramp 2 then 3
Tramp 1 then 3
Tramp 1 then 3
Tramp 2 then 3
Tramp 2 then 3

Tramp 4 then 3 ⎫
Tramp 5 then 3 ⎬ 4 times

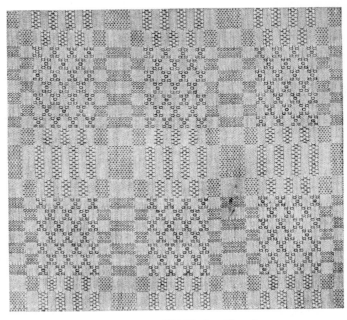

Fig. 204—Mollie Pitcher Towel

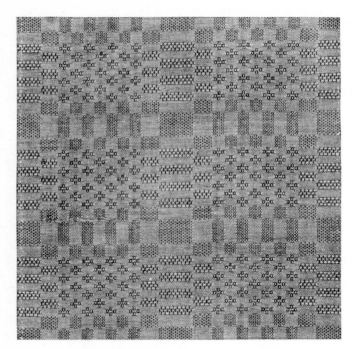

Fig. 206—Adaptation of Mollie Pitcher Towel

Tramp 4 then 3
Repeat from beginning.

Treadling Draft for Fig. 206

Tramp 1 then 3 ⎫
Tramp 2 then 3 ⎬ 8 times
Tramp 1 then 3

Tramp 4 then 3 ⎫
Tramp 5 then 3 ⎬ 4 times
Tramp 4 then 3
Tramp 1 then 3
Tramp 1 then 3
Tramp 2 then 3
Tramp 2 then 3
Tramp 1 then 3
Tramp 1 then 3
Tramp 4 then 3
Tramp 4 then 3
Tramp 5 then 3
Tramp 5 then 3
Tramp 4 then 3
Tramp 4 then 3

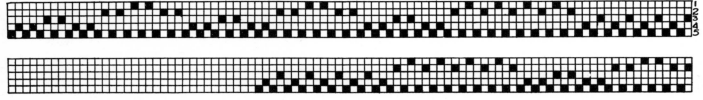

Fig. 205—Draft for Mollie Pitcher Towel

Fig. 207—Draft for Three Harness Weave

Tramp 1 then 3 ⎤
Tramp 1 then 3 ⎟
Tramp 2 then 3 ⎟
Tramp 2 then 3 ⎬ 4 times
Tramp 1 then 3 ⎟
Tramp 1 then 3 ⎟
Tramp 4 then 3 ⎟
Tramp 5 then 3 ⎦

Tramp 4 then 3
Repeat from beginning.

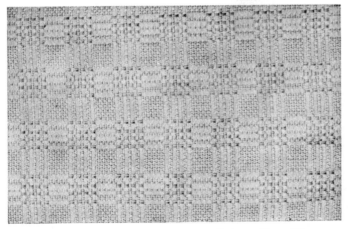

Fig. 208—Finished Pattern of Three Harness Linen Weave

Three Harness Linen Weave

Fig. 207 gives the draft for the weaving of very practical towels.

Use the same materials as described in previous towel drafts.

There are only three harnesses, six treadles, thus giving a variety in weave. Fig. 208 shows the finished pattern.

Harnesses 1 and 3 tie to the first treadle.

Harnesses 1 and 2 tie to the second treadle.

Harness 3 tie to the third treadle.

Harness 2 tie to the fourth treadle.

Harnesses 2 and 3 tie to the fifth treadle.

Harness 3 tie to the sixth treadle.

The double tie-up shown by Fig. 260 is best for all linen weaves, especially when an odd number of harnesses is involved.

Treadling Draft

Tramp 4 then 1 ⎤
Tramp 4 then 3 ⎬ 4 times
Tramp 1 then 2 ⎟
Tramp 3 then 4 ⎦

Tramp 2 then 1 ⎤
Tramp 4 then 1 ⎬ 3 times
Tramp 5 then 6 ⎦

Tramp 3 then 2 ⎫
Tramp 3 then 4 ⎪
Tramp 2 then 1 ⎬ 3 times
Tramp 4 then 1 ⎪
Tramp 5 then 6 ⎭
Tramp 3 then 2 ⎫
Tramp 3 then 2 ⎬ 3 times
Tramp 5 then 6 ⎭
Tramp 1 then 4
Tramp 1 then 2 ⎫
Tramp 4 then 3 ⎪
Tramp 2 then 1 ⎬ 4 times
Tramp 3 then 4 ⎭
Tramp 1 then 4
Repeat from beginning.

Fig. 209—M's and O's. Draft of Pattern

M's and O's

The short threading draft shown in Fig. 209 is known in Kentucky as M's and O's.

Use cotton for the warp, and a number 20 linen for

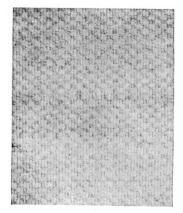
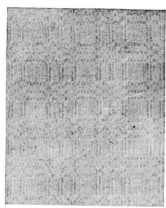

Fig. 210—Preliminary Pattern,   Fig. 212—Complete Pattern
M's and O's   of Fig. 211

the filler. The 2/20 cotton unbleached used in the counterpanes is suitable for this pattern. Fig. 210 shows the finished pattern.

The Tie-Up

Harnesses 3 and 4 are tied to the first treadle.
Harnesses 1 and 2 are tied to the second treadle.
Harnesses 1 and 3 are tied to the third treadle.
Harnesses 2 and 4 are tied to the fourth treadle.

Fig. 211—Modified Draft in M's and O's

Treadling Draft

Tramp first two treadles eight times alternately, then 3 and 4 treadles eight times alternately, always beginning at the right.

Fig. 211 shows a modified draft of the M's and O's. Fig. 212 shows the finished piece of work.

The weaver must remember that the horizontal dimensions in weaving depend upon the number of times certain threads are repeated in the draft. The vertical dimensions depend upon the number of times certain treadles are pressed down. This is very clearly demonstrated in the modified draft.

Only one shuttle is used, as no binder is necessary in any of the linen weaves.

CHAPTER VI

Danish and Norwegian Weaving

Ways of Expressing Danish Patterns

It has been stated already that no attempt has been made to make this manual technical. The plan is to keep every pattern simple and to tell of its execution in as simple a way as possible.

The Danes, Swedes, and Norwegians have carried weaving on the foot-power loom to a high degree of *efficiency*. The work is carried on to a very great extent in the homes. This is largely due to the fact that the governments of these countries encourage weaving as a home industry. Each of these countries has its own way of writing and reading drafts. It is the purpose of this manual to give to amateur weavers an explanation of the way each of the three nationalities writes and interprets its drafts.

Reading a Draft

Fig. 213 shows a four-harness pattern woven by using three treadles. The lower heddle sticks are tied one to each lam.

The treadles are tied as indicated by the stars placed on the horizontal lines just to the right of the threading. The tie-up is interpreted as follows:

Lams 2 and 4 tie to the first treadle.

Lams 1 and 3 tie to the second treadle.

Lams 1 and 2 tie to the third treadle.

The order in which the treadles are pressed down is indicated by the stars on the vertical lines just to the right of the woven pattern. Treadle No. 3 is pressed down first, then treadle No. 2, then back to No. 3, next No. 1, and then back to No. 3, etc.

Fig. 214 shows the draft and a woven sample for a two-treadle loom. Each horizontal line above the woven pattern stands for a pair of heddle sticks (harness). Each vertical line stands for a treadle. This draft is threaded in the following way:

The first thread passes through the eye of the heddle on the first pair of heddle sticks. The second thread passes through the eye of the heddle on the second pair of heddle sticks. Each time a heddle is threaded, it is pushed along. The third thread passes through the eye of the heddle on the third heddle stick and is pushed along. The fourth thread passes through the eye of the first heddle on the fourth heddle stick and is pushed along. The fifth thread goes back to the first heddle stick and is threaded through the eye of the second heddle and is pushed along. The threading continues the same as the first four threads, the

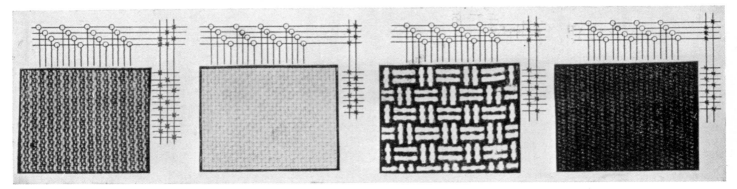

Fig. 213   Fig. 214   Fig. 215   Fig. 216

order being 1, 2, 3, 4. This is continued until the desired number of threads have been threaded.

It will be observed that only two treadles are used while there are four harnesses for plain weaving. The beginner might ask why use four harnesses when two might answer the purpose. If any great number of threads is to be used in plain weaving, it is better to use four harnesses instead of two, threading as above described.

Tying the Treadle

It will be observed that the lower heddle sticks 2 and 4 are tied to the right treadle, and 1 and 3 to the left treadle. This is indicated by the stars placed on the vertical lines to the right of the threading draft. With this tie-up, each time a treadle is pressed down, one-half the threads are drawn down. This practically does what two

harnesses would do. By using four sets the threads are not crowded so closely together. The stars placed on the vertical lines to the right of the woven sample indicate the order in which the treadles are to be pressed down.

Fig. 215 shows a somewhat checked material. To produce this pattern the warp is made up of blue and white threads. The threading is done the same as in Fig. 214, but first two blue and then two white threads are threaded until the entire number of threads have been used. When weaving, two blue threads are used and then two white. This necessitates the use of two shuttles. It is also understood that when preparing the warp chain, the spools of warp are so placed on the spool rack that two blue and two white threads are reeled or warped at one time. The stars marked on the vertical lines indicate that first one treadle and then the other is to be pressed down.

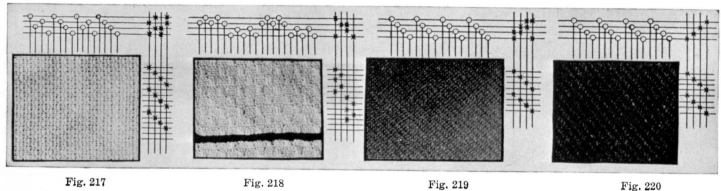

Fig. 217   Fig. 218   Fig. 219   Fig. 220

Fig. 216 shows another four-harness, but practically only two-harness pattern. The threading is done the same as in the two already described. Harnesses 1, 2 and 3 are tied to the left treadle, and harness 4 to the right treadle. This is indicated by the stars placed on the vertical lines to the right of the threading draft.

The stars on the vertical lines to the right of the woven pattern indicate the order in which the treadles are pressed down.

Figure 217 shows a four-harness pattern, a little more irregular in its threading. The greatest care must be exercised when threading.

In tying up this pattern, the lams are tied one to each lower heddle stick. The stars on the vertical lines to the right of the threading indicate the order in which the treadles are tied to the lams. Treadle No. 1 is tied to the 3rd and 4th lams. Treadle No. 2 is tied to the 1st and 2nd lams. Treadle No. 3 is tied to the 2nd and 4th lams. Treadle No. 4 is tied to the 1st and 3rd lams.

The stars on the vertical lines, to the right of the woven pattern, indicate the order in which the treadles are to be pressed down. The order is first treadle 4, then 3, 2 and 1. Then back again to 4, 3, 2, 1. This order is continued throughout the entire weaving.

Fig. 218 shows a most interesting weave for towels. The warp and woof should be of linen. The threading is done as shown in the draft. Lams and treadles are tied as shown by stars to the right of the threading draft. The order of treadling is shown by stars on vertical lines to the right of woven sample.

Figure 219 shows a serge. The warp and woof should

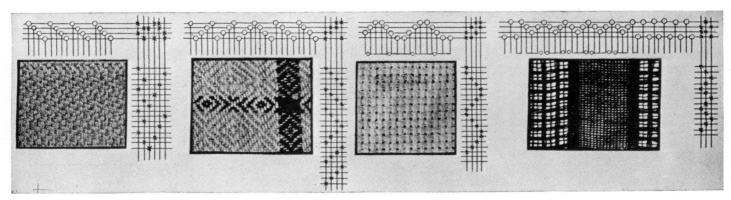

Fig. 221   Fig. 222   Fig. 223   Fig. 224

be of wool. Threading and tie-up are as indicated in the draft.

Fig. 220 shows another serge weave.

Fig. 221 shows a pattern woven on a six treadle loom. The method of handling more than four harnesses will be treated a little later. It is a very interesting weave which may be used for winter coats. The warp and woof are of wool. Two threads are drawn through each dent of the reed. Note the irregular way in which the treadles are pressed down.

Figure 222 shows an interesting weave to be used in towels. The dark, vertical stripe shows a number of colored threads reeled in the warp, while the horizontal dark stripe indicates that the same color is used as woof.

This pattern is commonly known as the "Goose Eye."

The threading and treadling are done as indicated. Two threads are drawn through each dent.

Figure 223 shows a canvas weave. The threading is done the same as in previous patterns. The little circle placed below and between the groups of threads only indicates that a dent in the reed is to be omitted and has no reference to the threading of the pattern.

It will be observed that the threads are in groups, four in each. Each group of four threads is drawn through every other dent of the reed. In other words, every other dent of the reed is left vacant. The threads on heddle sticks 1 and 2 make one group and the threads on heddle sticks 3 and 4 make another group. This is clearly shown in the draft. When weaving, the first and fourth woof threads are to be double.

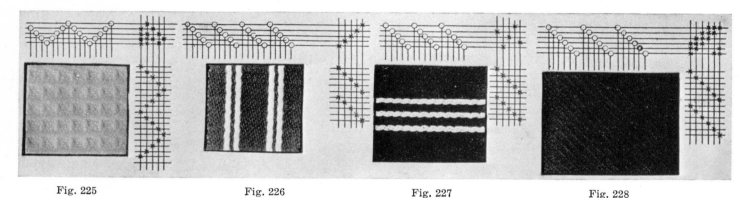

Fig. 225   Fig. 226   Fig. 227   Fig. 228

Figure 224 shows a very interesting curtain material woven by using four harnesses and three treadles.

The plain stripe is shown in the first part of the threading draft. This number of threads may be increased so as to make any width desired. The closely woven bands at the edges of the plain stripe are obtained by drawing two threads through each dent.

The open work is produced by drawing the three threads, held together at the base, through a single dent. The small circles between the groups indicate a dent to be omitted. The tie-up and treadling are done as indicated in the draft.

In Figs. 225, 226, 227 and 228 are given examples of five and six harness patterns. While these drafts are threaded and tied up the same as other patterns, the method of hanging the harnesses is somewhat different and will be taken up in detail a little later.

Norwegian Patterns

The three patterns which follow show that the Danish and Norwegian ways of writing patterns are very much the same.

Figure 229 shows a very interesting pattern and draft which may be produced on a four-harness loom, using eight treadles. In reeling the warp, eight threads of one color are used (say blue) and then eight threads of white. Two threads are drawn through the eye of each heddle and also through each dent of the reed. The woof thread is also wound double on the bobbins so that each time the shuttle passes through the shed two threads are carried at the same time.

The horizontal parallel lines represent the harnesses, which are the same as heddle sticks. The vertical parallel lines represent the treadles. The stars indicate the way the treadles are tied to the lams. The little dashes on the vertical lines indicate the order in which the treadles are pressed down. This order of treadling is continued until the desired amount of fabric is woven.

Figure 230 shows a pattern in which the reeling is done by running three blue threads and one white thread on the beam. The entire warp is made up in this way.

three blue and one white. Each thread passes through the eye of a heddle, and only one thread to each dent of the reed. When weaving, three blue woof threads are woven and then one white.

In warping for the pattern shown in Fig. 231, two blue and two white threads are warped at the same time. The threading is done by threading singly two blue and then two white, as indicated in the draft. Two threads are drawn through each dent of the reed.

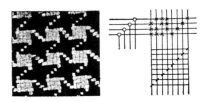

Fig. 229

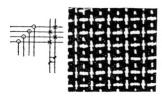

Fig. 230

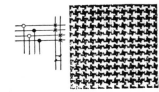

Fig. 231

CHAPTER VII

Swedish Weaving

Swedish Way of Writing a Draft

In many respects the Swedish way of writing a draft is more simple than any of the other ways described.

The patterns which follow are all written in the Swedish manner and are interpreted in the following way: Fig. 232 shows a plain two-harness weave. Each vertical line indicates a thread.

In Figure 233 is shown a two-harness pattern. The threading indicates that two threads are drawn through each eye of the heddles; two through the eye of the first heddle on the back heddle sticks, and then two through the eye of the first heddle on the first or front heddle sticks.

It may also be done by threading only one thread through each eye but using two heddles on the same sticks. Two threads may be drawn through each dent of the reed.

Figure 235 shows what may be called either a two-treadle or four-treadle draft. If two treadles are used, two lams tie to each treadle. It must always be remembered that each lam is tied to a lower heddle stick. Tying to the lams is the same as tying to the lower heddle sticks.

When the foot presses a treadle it draws down two harnesses.

If four treadles are used, one to each lam, it is necessary to use both feet in pressing down two treadles at the same time. The treadles marked 1 and 1 indicate that these are the first to be pressed down and mean treadles 1 and 3. Two and 2 indicate the second change and indicate that the second and fourth treadles are pressed down.

Figure 234 shows the draft for a four-harness loom. The space between each pair of horizontal parallel lines stands for a pair of heddle sticks.

Each space between the vertical parallel lines represents a treadle. The little dots within the small squares indicate the order in which the treadles are to be tied to the lams.

The figures just below the dots indicate the order in which the treadles are pressed down.

Figure 234 is threaded by passing a thread through the eye of the heddle on the back or fourth heddle sticks. The second thread passes through the eye of the heddle on the third heddle sticks, the third thread passes through the eye of the heddle on the second, and the fourth thread passes through the eye of the first heddle on the first or front heddle sticks.

The entire draft is threaded by following this order:

The **lams** are tied one to each lower heddle stick. The pattern indicates according to the little dots that the fourth lam is tied to the first treadle, the second lam is tied to the second treadle, the third lam is tied to the third treadle, and the first lam is tied to the fourth treadle.

The figures just below the dots indicate that the treadles are pressed down in the order of first 1, then 2, 3, and 4. This order of treadling is kept up until the desired amount of material is woven.

In Fig. 236 is shown the same threading, but a different order of tying.

Lams 1 and 2 are tied to the first treadle. Lams 1 and 3 are tied to the second treadle. Lams 1 and 2 are tied to the third treadle. Lams 2 and 4 are tied to the fourth treadle.

The order of pressing the treadles is shown by the figures.

In Fig. 237 the threading is the same as in the two previous patterns. The lams are tied as follows:

1, 3 and 4 to the first treadle.
2 and 3 to the second treadle.
1, 2 and 3 to the third treadle.
2 and 4 to the fourth treadle.
1 to the fifth treadle.
2 to the sixth treadle.

While this pattern requires six treadles, there will be no difficulty in understanding the tie-up.

Figure 238 shows the same threading and two ways

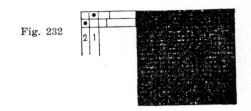

Fig. 232

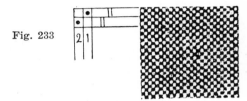

Fig. 233

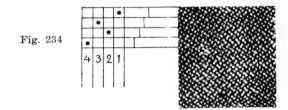

Fig. 234

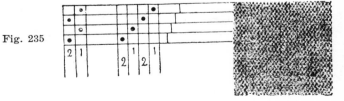

Fig. 235

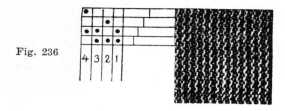

Fig. 236

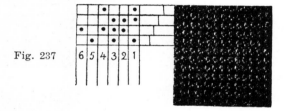

Fig. 237

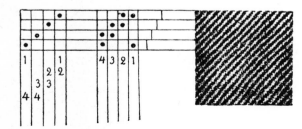

Fig. 238

of "tie-up." The first shows each lower heddle stick tied to a treadle. In such cases treadles 1 and 4 are pressed down the first time, indicated by the two ones. The next time treadles 1 and 2 are pressed down at the same time, indicated by the two twos. The third time treadles 2 and 3 are pressed down, indicated by the two threes. The fourth time treadles 3 and 4 are pressed down, indicated by the two fours. After following this order once it is gone right over again and continued until the desired amount of material is woven.

The other tying gives exactly the same result because of the fact that two lams are tied to one treadle. This latter plan is better and makes it possible to accomplish much greater results in the amount of fabrics woven.

In the next four patterns, 239 to 242 inclusive, the threading is the same as in previous patterns. The treadling is done by following the order of numbering.

In Fig. 241 the number 5 means that the third treadle is to be pressed down, and number 6 indicates the second treadle pressed down.

In Fig. 243 the threading is done the same as in tne two-harness loom draft shown in Fig. 233.

Irregular Threading

In Fig. 244 is shown the first irregular threading. The first thread passes through the first heddle on the fourth heddle stick, the second thread passes through the first heddle on the third heddle stick, the third thread goes back to the second heddle on the fourth heddle stick, the fourth thread to the second heddle on the third heddle stick, the fifth thread through the first heddle on the second heddle stick, the sixth thread through the first heddle on the first heddle stick, the seventh thread through the second heddle on the second heddle stick, and the eighth thread through the second heddle on the first heddle stick

In Fig. 245 is shown another irregular threading; first between the 3rd and 4th heddles and then between the 1st and 2nd. Observe the grouping of the treadling.

The lams are tied as indicated by the dots. The treadles are pressed down as indicated by the figures. The first time treadle 1 is pressed down. The next No. 2, the third time No. 1 again, the fourth time No. 2 again. The fifth time No. 1. The next five times are between treadles 3 and 4. The next goes back to the first and second treadles. This order is kept up until the desired amount of material is woven.

Figure 246 shows what is known as the "Honey Comb Weave." There will be no difficulty in understanding the threading. The first fourteen threads are on the third and fourth harnesses. The second fourteen threads are on the first and second harnesses. To produce the effect shown in the finished pattern the entire warp is threaded just as shown in the draft. If a variation is desired the loom may be threaded so six inches will be the same as shown in the finished pattern. A four-inch stripe may be threaded by drawing 28 threads through the heddles on the third and

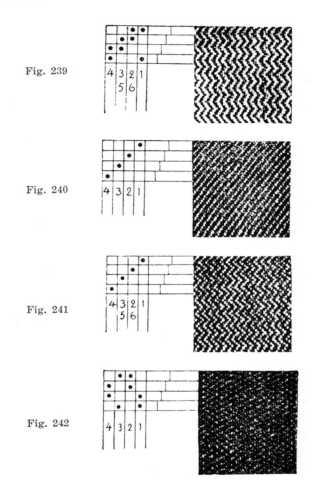

Fig. 239

Fig. 240

Fig. 241

Fig. 242

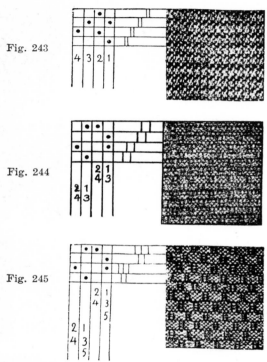

Fig. 243

Fig. 244

Fig. 245

The next is to press down treadles one and three at the same time. This is indicated by 1 and 1, a heavy thread passed through the shed. The next is to press down treadles two and four at the same time, and is indicated by the figures 2 and 2 and a heavy thread passes through the shed. The next fourteen threads are woven in by pressing down treadles three and four as indicated by the figures placed in the vertical spaces. This order of treadling is kept up until the material is woven.

Figure 248 shows a threading which is the same as that of the Rose Path. By following the order of treadling as indicated by the figures used, a most pleasing all-over pattern results.

Figure 249 shows two threads passing through the eye of the heddle on the fourth heddle sticks, then one thread each through the third and second, and then two through the eye of the first heddle on the first heddle sticks.

The draft indicates two single threads and then one double. In threading, two threads may be drawn through each dent of the reed, or a double thread may be drawn through the first and then two single, as indicated in the draft.

Observe the order of treadling, first the first treadle, then the second, and then the third. The fourth step indicates that the first, "marked four," is pressed down and then the second, "marked five." The sixth time the foot presses down a treadle, it is the fourth one.

The figures indicate the number of times the foot is

fourth harnesses and then 28 on the first and second. This is continued until the desired width is obtained. The next step is to go back to the fourteen threads. The treadles are tied one to each lam. In weaving, the first fourteen threads of the woof are woven by pressing down the first and then the second treadles.

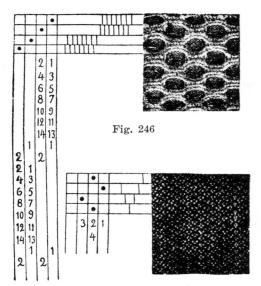

Fig. 246

Fig. 247

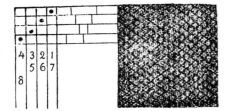

Fig. 248

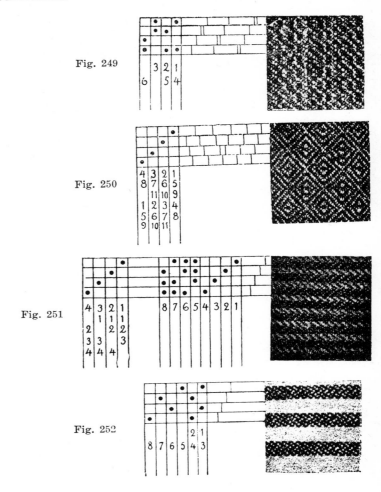

Fig. 249

Fig. 250

Fig. 251

Fig. 252

changed from one treadle to another.   The space in which the figure is placed is the treadle to be pressed down.

Figure 250 shows the Swedish way of expressing the pattern known as the "Goose Eye."   Observe the order of treadling.   The treadles are pressed down in their order from 1 to 4, then back to 1, indicated by the number 5; back to the fourth indicated by the number 8; back to number 1 for the third time, indicated by the number 9.

The second change consists of the reverse order of treadling.

Figure 251 shows a four-harness pattern which may be accomplished by using four treadles or eight treadles. Observe the difference in the tie-up. If four treadles are used they are pressed down in their regular order, 1 to 4.

The next time treadles 1, 2, and 3 are all pressed down at the same time.   This is indicated by the three ones.

Treadles 1, 2, and 4 are next pressed down, indicated by three twos.

The next time treadles 1, 3 and 4 and the next 2, 3 and 4.

If eight treadles are used and tied as indicated the work is more rapidly carried on.

Figure 252 shows a four-harness loom. The pattern is accomplished by tying and treadling as indicated in the draft.

Three-Harness Draft

The amateur weaver by this time has no doubt gained sufficient knowledge of the two and four-harness drafts not

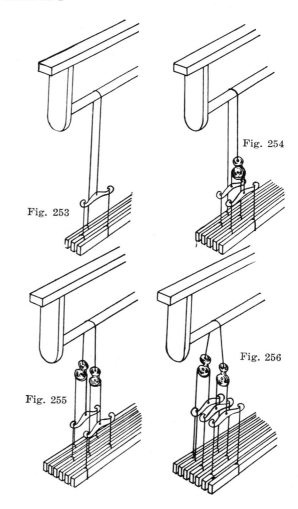

Fig. 253

Fig. 254

Fig. 255

Fig. 256

only to do the threading successfully but also to "tie-up" for any pattern desired. Occasionally a draft appears which is written in three harnesses, as shown in Fig. 224. When such is the case the upper heddle sticks are tied as shown in Fig. 253. The tying of the treadles is the same as for patterns already described.

Figure 254 shows the way five harnesses are tied.

Figure 255 shows the tie-up for a six-harness draft and Fig. 256 shows the tie-up for seven harnesses. Any of the above may be tied as shown in Fig. 262. The pulleys used may be purchased of any dealer in hardware or may be made of wood, being turned on a wood lathe.

Figure 257 shows a plain diagonal weave in three harnesses. The threading is simple and the tie-up consists in tying a treadle to each lower heddle stick.

The drawing shown in Fig. 253 shows the way the upper heddle sticks are tied.

Figure 258 shows a threading quite different from that shown in Fig. 257.

The first thread is drawn through the eye of the first heddle on the third heddle stick, the second thread through the eye of the first heddle on the second heddle stick, the third thread goes back to the eye of the second heddle on the third heddle stick.

The next three threads are on heddle sticks 1 and 2.

Figure 259 shows the draft and sample of an interesting curtain material.

The threading is done by following the draft. The

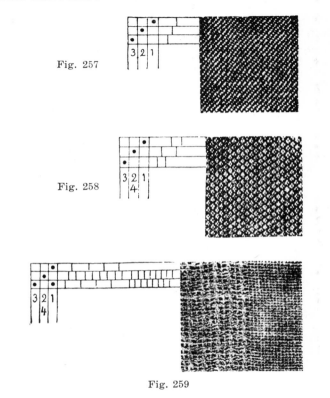

Fig. 257

Fig. 258

Fig. 259

threads on harnesses 1 and 2 make the plain weave. The somewhat irregular threading makes the stripe.

When threading the reed draw one thread through each dent for the plain stripe.

Skip one dent and then draw the three threads on heddle sticks 2 and 3 through the same dent.

Skip a dent and then draw the one thread on the first heddle sticks through a dent, skip a dent and draw three, skip, draw one, skip and draw three, etc.

Eight-Harness Pattern

Figure 260 shows the way the upper heddle sticks for an eight-harness loom are tied. There are always as many lams used as there are lower heddle sticks. Ordinarily

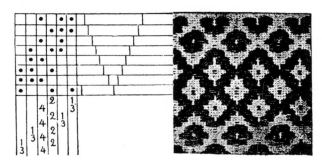

Fig. 261

the eight-harness loom works fairly well when tied up as shown in Fig. 260.

The difficulty, if there is any, grows out of the fact that the heddle sticks or harnesses after being drawn down refuse to return to their original position when the foot releases the treadle. Sometimes weights consisting of rectangular pieces of iron are hung at each end of the heddle sticks. These weights draw the harnesses back in place when raised.

Heddle Frames

Sometimes wire heddles are used instead of those made of cord. The wire heddles are placed in wooden frames. These frames may be suspended the same as when heddle sticks are used.

Figure 261 shows an eight-harness pattern, threading and treadling drafts.

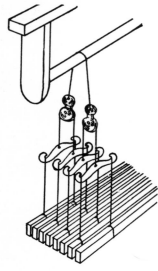

Fig. 260

Another Way of "Tie-Up"

Figure 262 shows a way of "tie-up" that requires two sets of lams. The second set of lams may be held in place by an iron rod pushed through the same brackets which hold the upper lams, only lower down. This is shown in the construction of the loom. The loom should be about four inches higher in order to give sufficient space for the two sets of lams. This may be brought about by adding a four-inch piece to each leg of the loom. For all ordinary purposes the original working drawing of the loom answers all conditions. By using this method the heddle horses are done away with, and each harness is tied so it must pull either up or down when pressure is applied to the treadle. The roller over which the heddle horses are hung is removed and replaced by the apparatus shown at A and B, Fig. 262. A detailed section is shown at Fig. 263. If an eight-harness loom is desired, sixteen pieces are constructed as shown in Fig. 263. Eight of these are placed to the right upper half of the loom and the other eight to the left upper half. The various sections are held in place by a half-inch dowel rod as shown at 1 and 2, Fig. 262. The rods are supported by two pieces of ⅞" maple constructed as shown in Fig. 264. This sort of frame work replaces the roller as shown in the finished loom in Fig. 265.

The "Tie-Up"

Returning to Fig. 262, loops of No. 12 blocking cord are tied and hung from each outer end of the levers as shown at C and D in Fig. 262. Two ends of the cord are

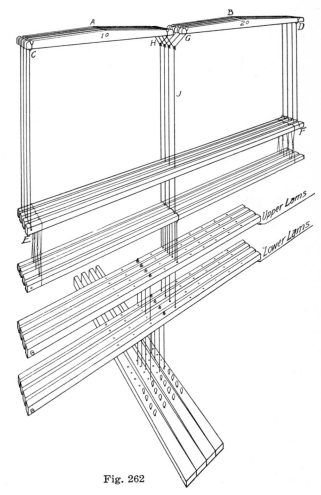

Fig. 262

fastened to each end of the upper heddle sticks, as shown at E and F. The loops and ends are tied just the same as the treadles are tied to the lams. From the inner ends of the levers H and G. a piece of blocking cord is tied, one end to one, and the other end to the other as shown. From each loop a piece of blocking cord extends to the lower set of lams by passing between the harness and ties the same

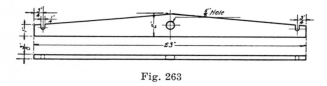

Fig. 263

as all other connections have been made. Each lower heddle stick ties to an upper lam the same as in the two and four-harness looms. Loops of blocking cord are now drawn through the holes of the treadles, one in each. The upper lams are tied to the treadles the same as in every other "tie-up," the cord passing between the lower lams. The lower lams are also tied to the treadles by using the loops not used in tying the upper lams.

By tying a loom in this way all harnesses making the pattern are drawn down while the other harnesses are drawn up. No part remains stationary. The weights previously mentioned for drawing the harnesses back in place are no longer necessary. Fig. 262 shows only a four-treadle loom. This is done to avoid complication in the explanation. Any number may be used. This method of tie-up is especially desirable when an odd number of heddle sticks (harnesses) are used. It does away with pulleys and heddle horses, as shown by Fig. 265. The fact that each part of the harness must either pull up or down makes a most perfect shed, thus avoiding the skipping of threads, so common in weaving when the shed is not perfect.

Figure 267 shows a very interesting pattern produced by either five or six harnesses. The tie-up for each is given in the draft, Fig. 266.

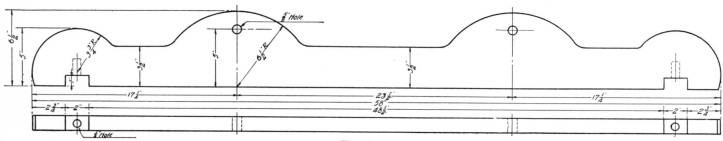

Fig. 264

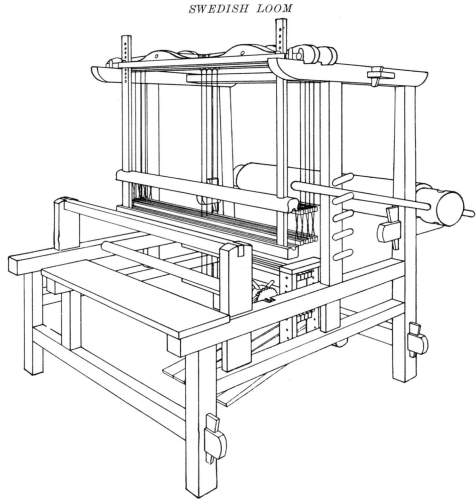

Fig. 265

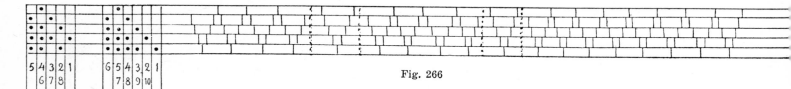

Fig. 266

The order of treadling is indicated by the figures just below the dots indicating the "tie-up."

The material produced may be used in a counterpane as well as in a bathrobe, if so desired.

The warp is run off in two colors in the following order:

112 white	18 red	62 white
18 red	814 white	18 red
62 white	18 red	112 white

The woof is of both red and white.

Six-Harness Draft

The secret of success in weaving is getting all parts "tied-up" so there is no irregular pulling in any way. Great care should be exercised in using the knots in "tie-up" as has been suggested. This will enable the weaver quickly to adjust any irregular pulling without untying the hard knots so often used by the amateur weaver. It takes some time to adjust each part before arriving at the stage where everything moves smoothly.

In the various drafts which follow no attempt has been made to give a minute description of each pattern. The thought is that each weaver will use the draft best suited to the needs at hand. Among the patterns given are drafts for towels, dress goods, coats, upholstering, table runners, curtains, couch covers, counterpanes, suiting, pillow tops, etc. The part of any draft to be repeated is placed between two arrows and marked "Pattern."

The threading, tie-up and the order of treadling have been so minutely described that further explanation is not necessary. If possible, the loom should be equipped with the parts shown in Figs. 263 and 264, and placed as shown in Fig. 265.

For the regulation four-harness loom the one shown in Fig. 20 is very satisfactory. It is well to start out with the loom just as shown in Fig. 20. As the work advances the various additions may be added as the necessity requires.

Six-Harness Loom

The Swedish loom, as described and illustrated in this manual, is constructed in such a way as to permit of additional parts, making possible the production of many complicated patterns. The drawing shown in Fig. 262 shows the construction of parts which make easy the weaving with six harnesses.

The various drafts in six harnesses which follow have been very carefully worked out and found practical in every respect. Among the drafts given are those suited to upholstering, dress goods, toweling, heavy suiting, coats, etc. The interested weaver will find no end of suggestions.

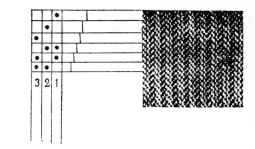

Fig. 268

Fig. 267

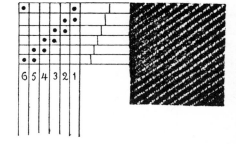

Fig. 269

Fig. 270

This, together with a little originality, will greatly simplify the working out of new and attractive patterns.

It is not necessary to confine the work only to certain materials. Many times a pattern worked out in the finest of threads may be worked out in a very coarse thread and made to serve an entirely different purpose from what it was originally intended.

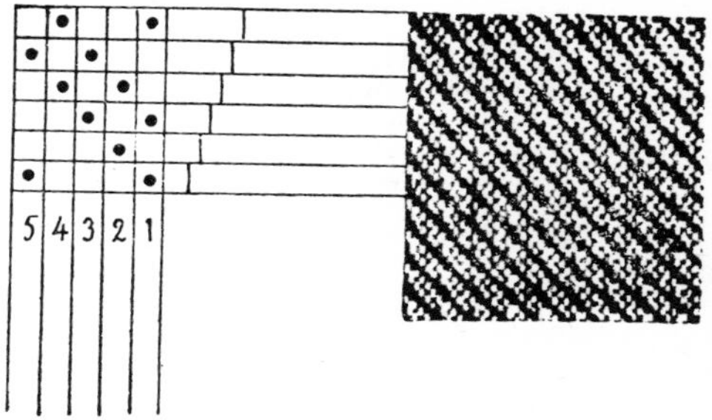

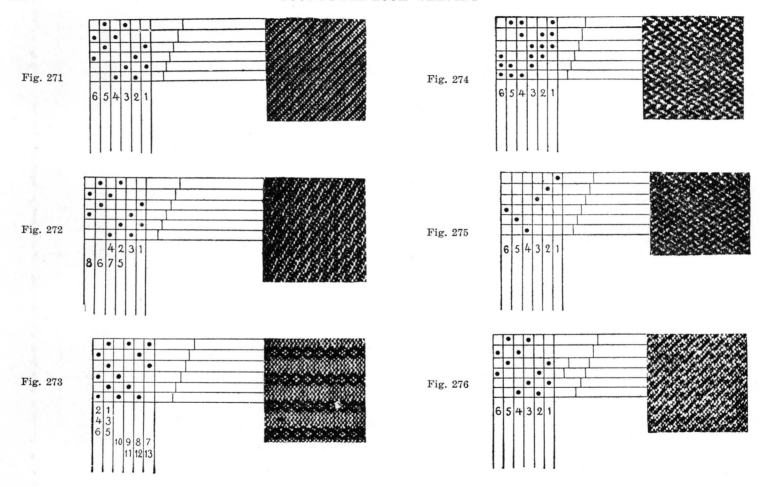

Fig. 271

Fig. 272

Fig. 273

Fig. 274

Fig. 275

Fig. 276

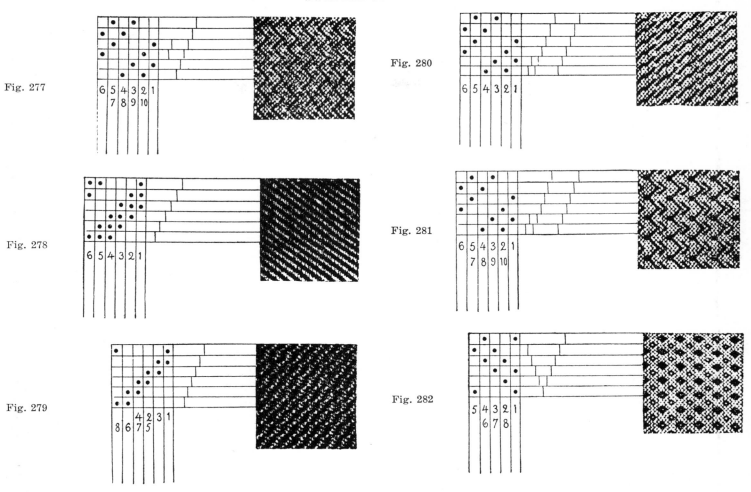

Fig. 277

Fig. 278

Fig. 279

Fig. 280

Fig. 281

Fig. 282

To enjoy weaving great care must be exercised in the "tie-up." All parts must be made to pull evenly. To do this the blocking cord must be used and the method of tying must be observed in order to adjust readily.

Eight-Harness Loom

The loom as described for six harnesses will answer the description for the eight harness loom. The parts necessary are described in Figs. 262, 263 and 264. These parts are shown properly placed in the complete loom as illustrated by Fig. 265.

The next group of patterns from Fig. 286 to Fig. 433 inclusive, concerns the eight-harness loom. The threading and tie-up have been so carefully described in previous patterns that there can be no difficulty in understanding the drafts for the eight-harness patterns as here given. It will be found that the threading for many of the eight-harness patterns is the same, the change in pattern being brought about by a change in the tie-up. One threading therefore makes it possible to produce a variety of patterns by changing only the order of treadling.

In this way numerous interesting weaves which may be used for upholstering, suiting material, towels, etc., can be produced.

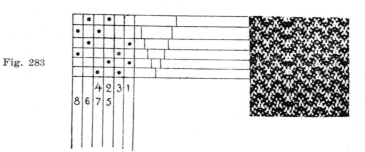

Fig. 283

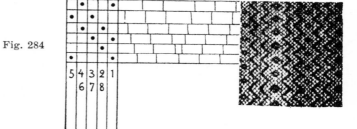

Fig. 284

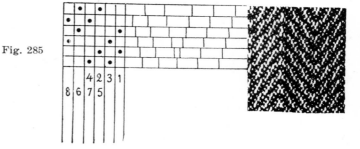

Fig. 285

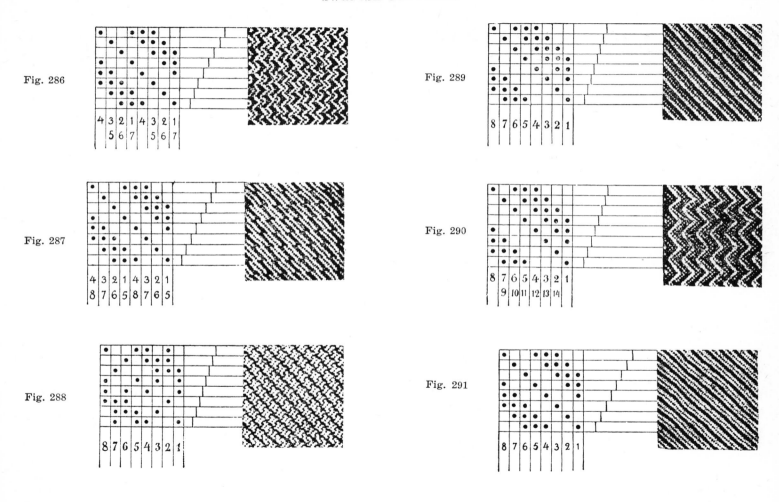

Fig. 286

Fig. 287

Fig. 288

Fig. 289

Fig. 290

Fig. 291

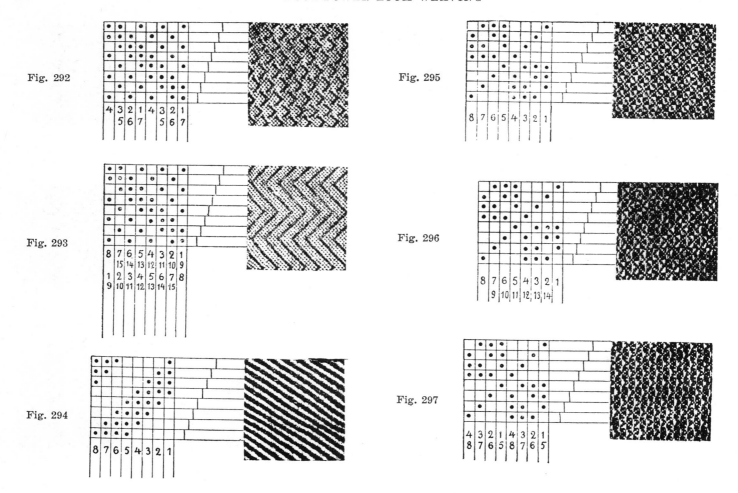

Fig. 292

Fig. 293

Fig. 294

Fig. 295

Fig. 296

Fig. 297

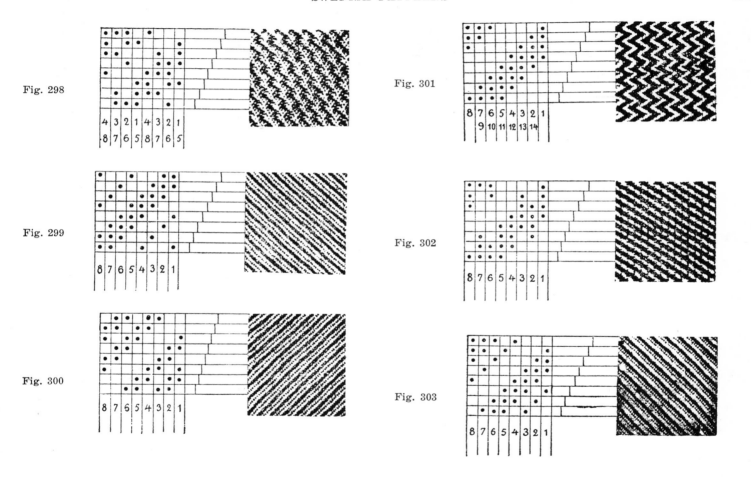

Fig. 298

Fig. 299

Fig. 300

Fig. 301

Fig. 302

Fig. 303

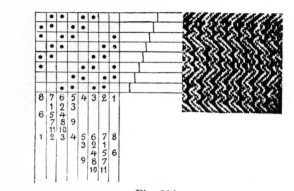

Fig. 304

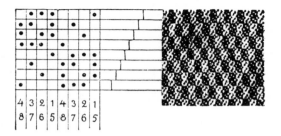

Fig. 306

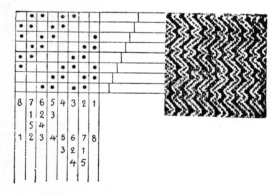

Fig. 305

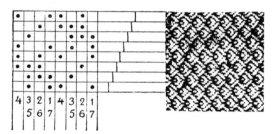

Fig. 307

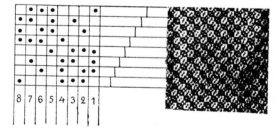

Fig. 308

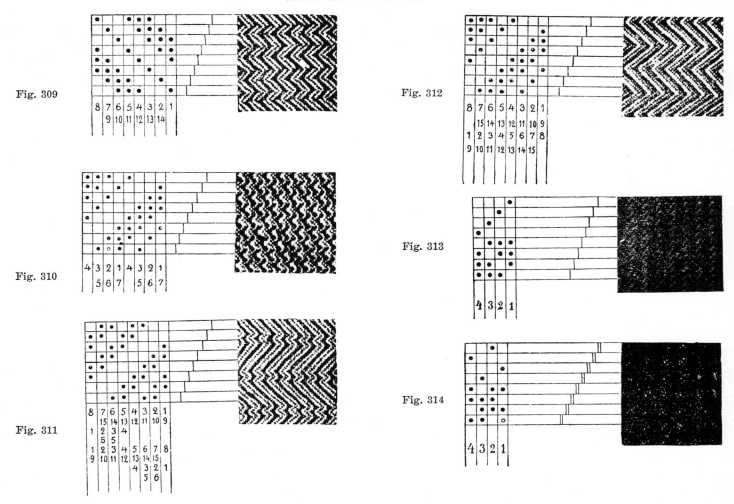

Fig. 309

Fig. 310

Fig. 311

Fig. 312

Fig. 313

Fig. 314

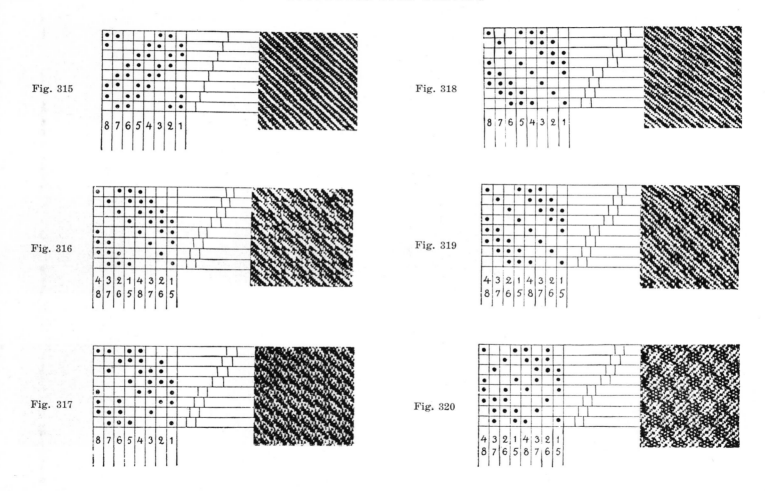

Fig. 315

Fig. 316

Fig. 317

Fig. 318

Fig. 319

Fig. 320

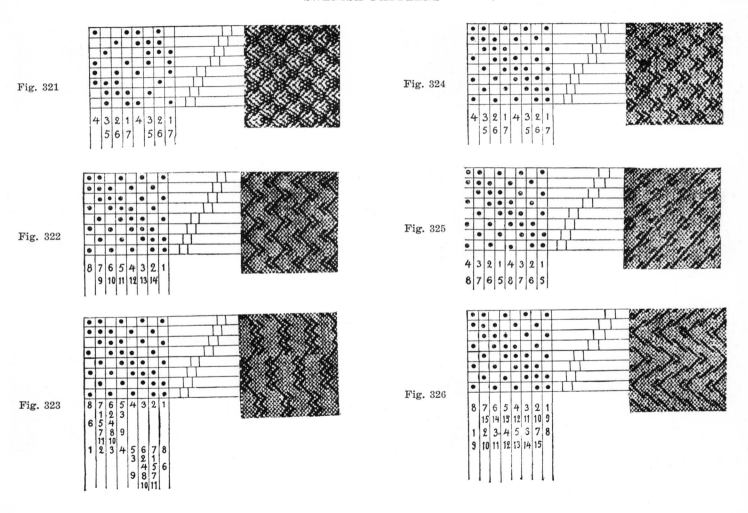

Fig. 321

Fig. 322

Fig. 323

Fig. 324

Fig. 325

Fig. 326

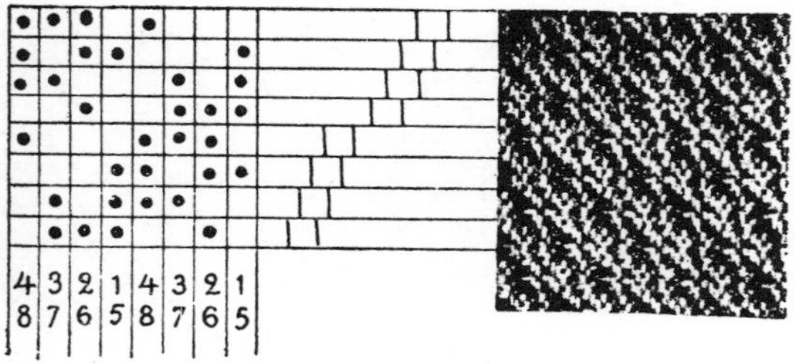

Fig. 327

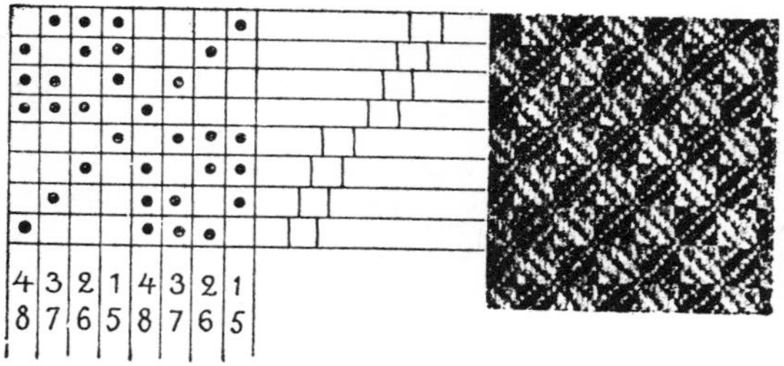

4	3	2	1	4	3	2	1
8	7	6	5	8	7	6	5

Fig. 330

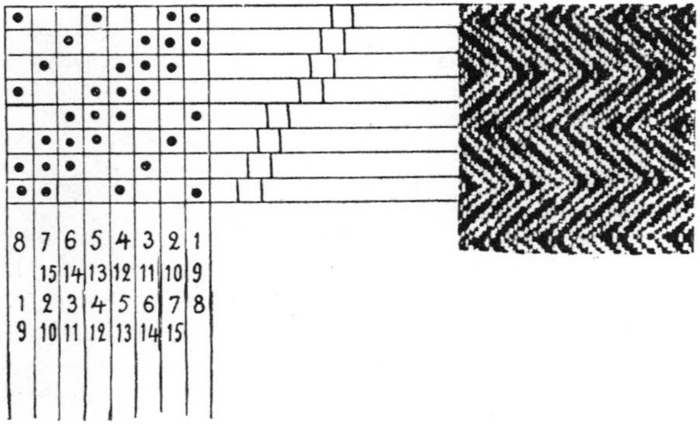

4	3	2	1	4	3	2	1
8	7	6	5	8	7	6	5

Fig. 328

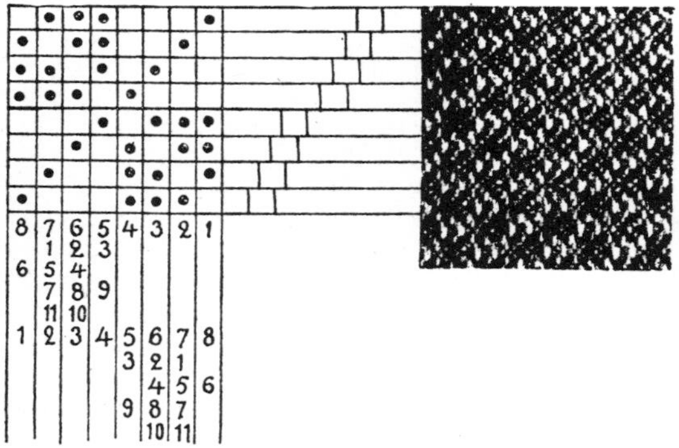

8	7	6	5	4	3	2	1
	15	14	13	12	11	10	9
1	2	3	4	5	6	7	8
9	10	11	12	13	14	15	

Fig. 331

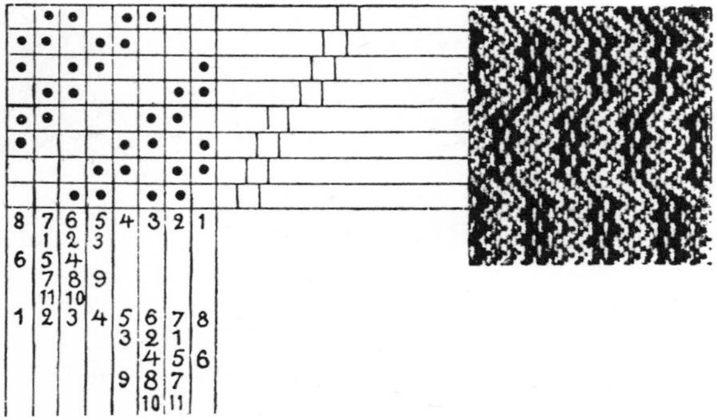

8	7	6	5	4	3	2	1
6	1	2	3				
	5	4					
	7	8					
	11	10					
	2	3					
1			4	5	6	7	8
				3	2	1	6
				4	5	7	
					8		
					9		
					10	11	

Fig. 329

8	7	6	5	4	3	2	1
6	1	2	3				
	5	4					
	7	8					
	11	10					
	2	3					
1			4	5	6	7	8
				3	2	1	6
				4	5	7	
					8		
					9		
					10	11	

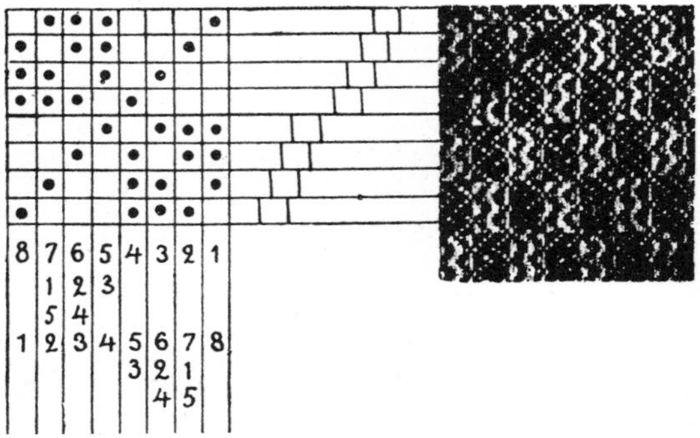

Fig. 332

8	7	6	5	4	3	2	1
	1	2	3				
	5	6					
1	2	3	4	5	6	7	8
				3	2	1	
					4		

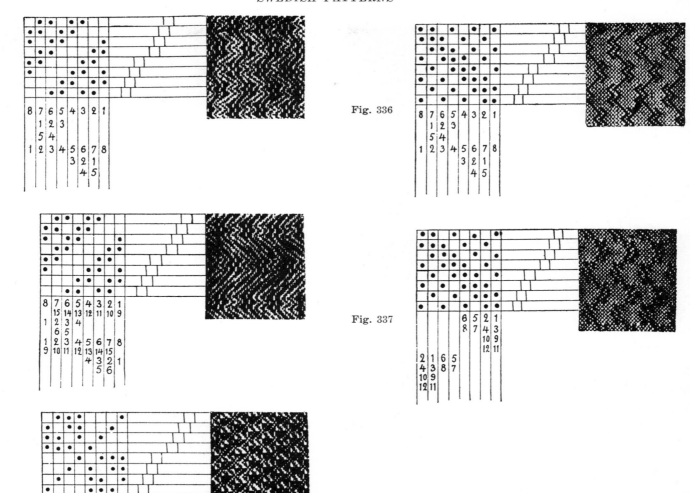

Fig. 333

Fig. 334

Fig. 335

Fig. 336

Fig. 337

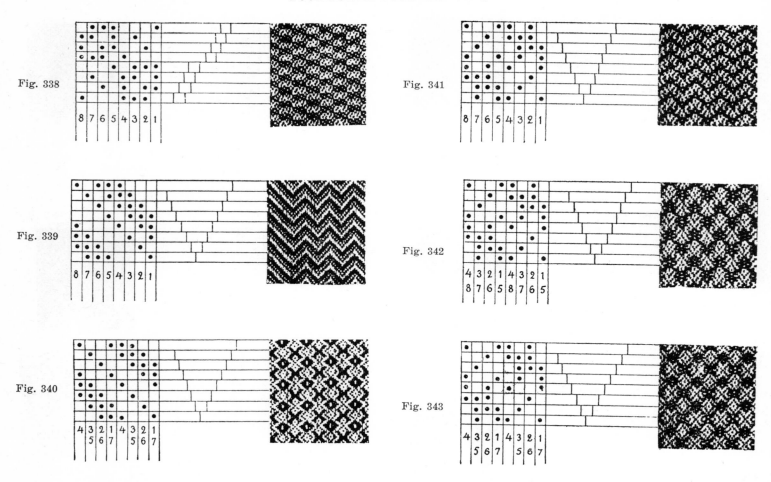

Fig. 338

Fig. 339

Fig. 340

Fig. 341

Fig. 342

Fig. 343

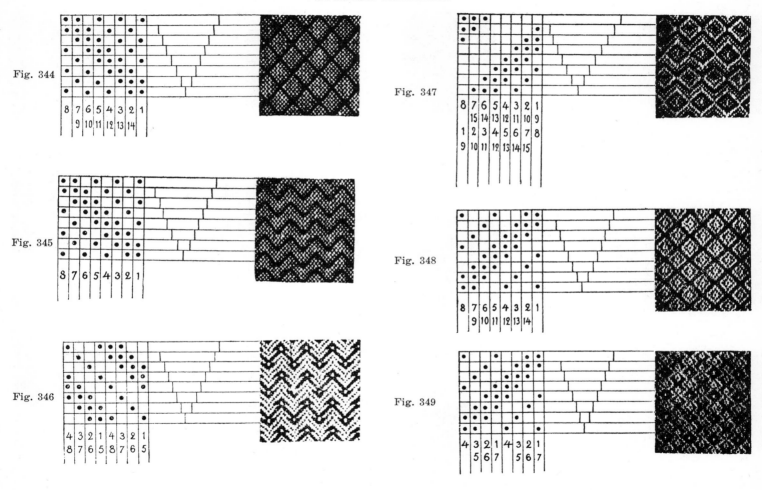

Fig. 344

8 7 6 5 4 3 2 1
9 10 11 12 13 14

Fig. 347

8 7 6 5 4 3 2 1
15 14 13 12 11 10 9
1 2 3 4 5 6 7 8
9 10 11 12 13 14 15

Fig. 345

8 7 6 5 4 3 2 1

Fig. 348

8 7 6 5 4 3 2 1
9 10 11 12 13 14

Fig. 346

4 3 2 1 4 3 2 1
8 7 6 5 8 7 6 5

Fig. 349

4 3 2 1 4 3 2 1
5 6 7 5 6 7

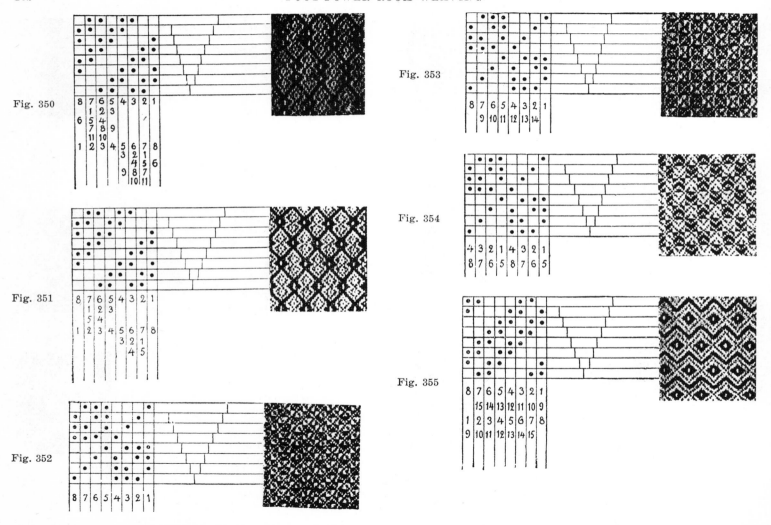

Fig. 350

Fig. 351

Fig. 352

Fig. 353

Fig. 354

Fig. 355

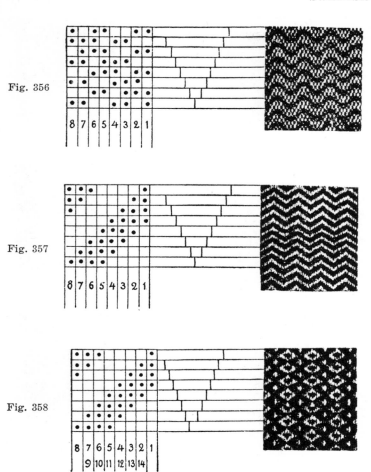

Fig. 356

Fig. 357

Fig. 358

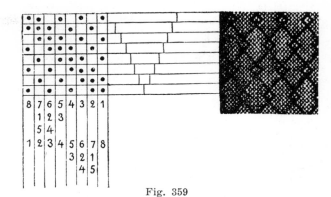

Fig. 359

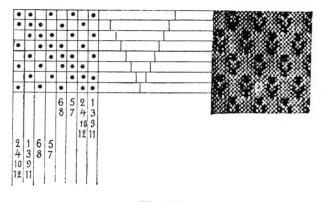

Fig. 360

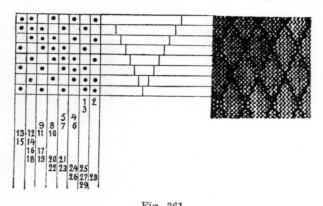

Fig. 361

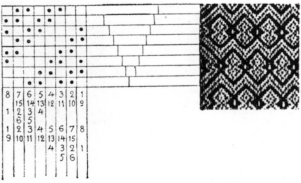

Fig. 362

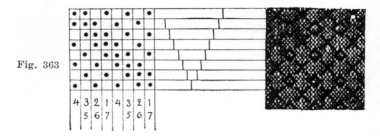

Fig. 363

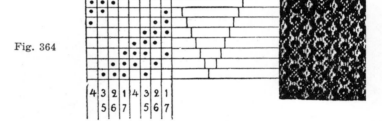

Fig. 364

Fig. 365

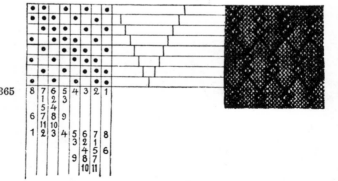

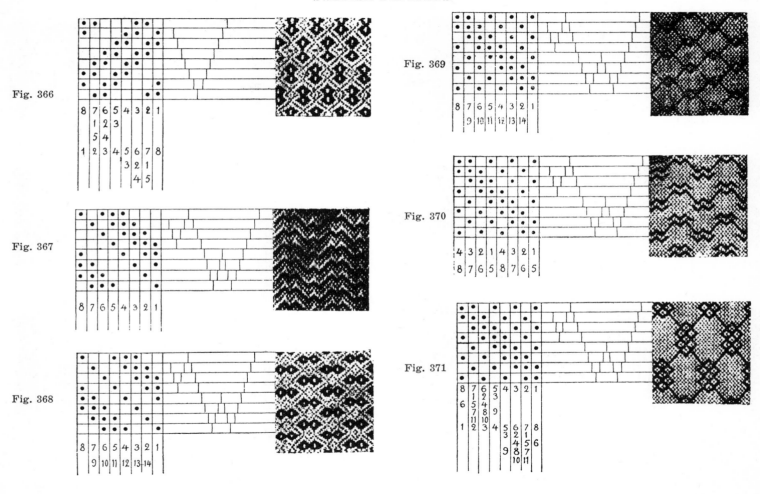

Fig. 366

Fig. 367

Fig. 368

Fig. 369

Fig. 370

Fig. 371

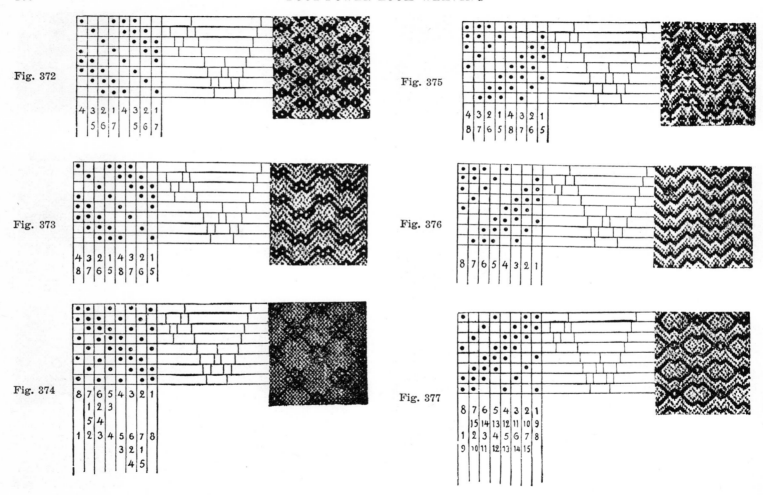

Fig. 372

Fig. 373

Fig. 374

Fig. 375

Fig. 376

Fig. 377

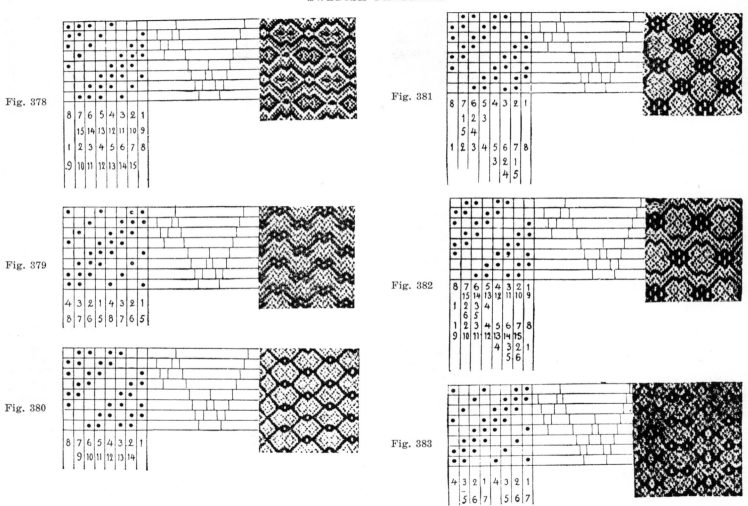

Fig. 378

8	7	6	5	4	3	2	1
15	14	13	12	11	10	9	
1	2	3	4	5	6	7	8
9	10	11	12	13	14	15	

Fig. 379

4	3	2	1	4	3	2	1
8	7	6	5	8	7	6	5

Fig. 380

8	7	6	5	4	3	2	1
	9	10	11	12	13	14	

Fig. 381

8	7	6	5	4	3	2	1
	1	2	3				
	5	4					
1	2	3	4	5	6	7	8
				3	2	1	
				4	5		

Fig. 382

8	7	6	5	4	3	2	1
15	14	13	12	11	10	9	
1	2	3	4				
	6	5					
1	2	3	4	5	6	7	8
9	10	11	12	13	14	15	
				4	3	2	1
					5	6	

Fig. 383

4	3	2	1	4	3	2	1
5	6	7		5	6	7	

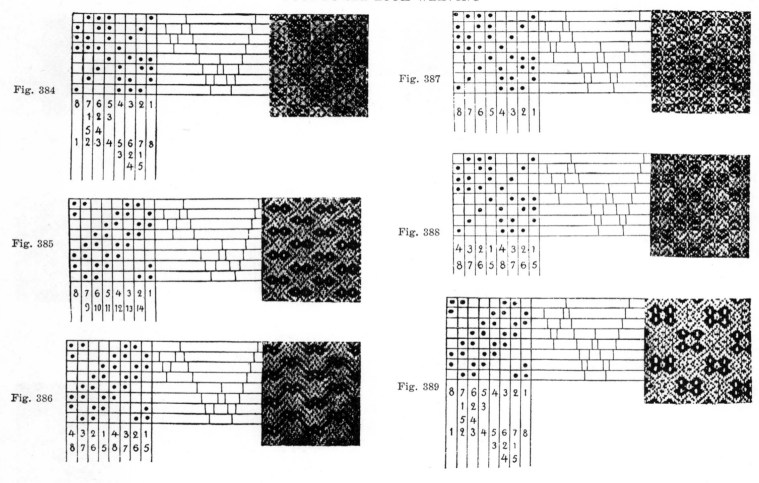

Fig. 384

Fig. 385

Fig. 386

Fig. 387

Fig. 388

Fig. 389

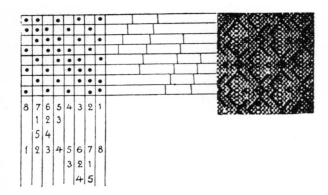

Fig. 390

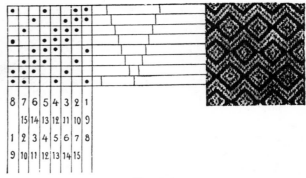

Fig. 392

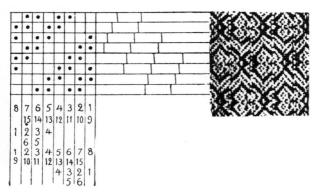

Fig. 391

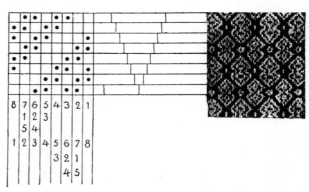

Fig. 393

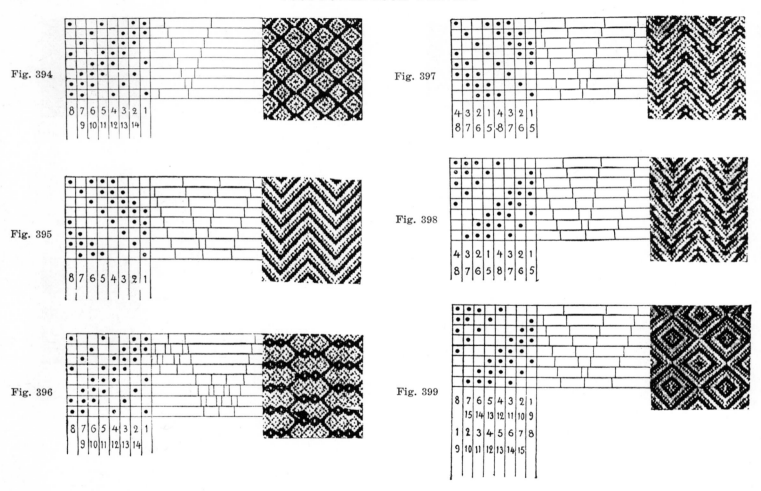

Fig. 394

Fig. 395

Fig. 396

Fig. 397

Fig. 398

Fig. 399

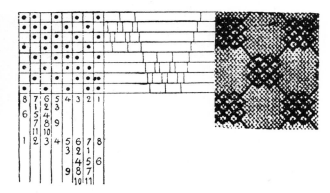

Fig. 400

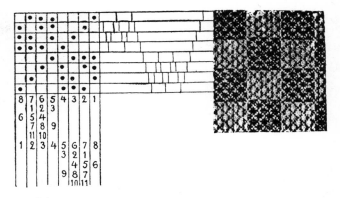

Fig. 402

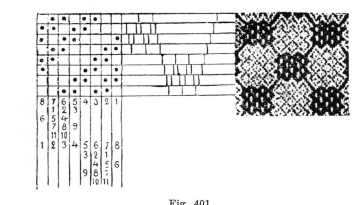

Fig. 401

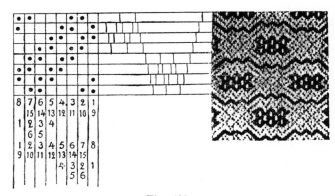

Fig. 403

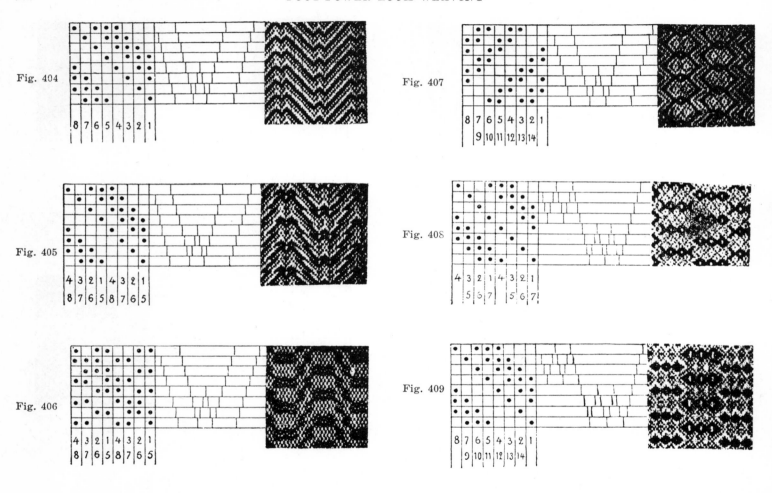

Fig. 404

8 7 6 5 4 3 2 1

Fig. 407

8 7 6 5 4 3 2 1
9 10 11 12 13 14

Fig. 405

4 3 2 1 4 3 2 1
8 7 6 5 8 7 6 5

Fig. 408

4 3 2 1 4 3 2 1
5 6 7 5 6 7

Fig. 406

4 3 2 1 4 3 2 1
8 7 6 5 8 7 6 5

Fig. 409

8 7 6 5 4 3 2 1
9 10 11 12 13 14

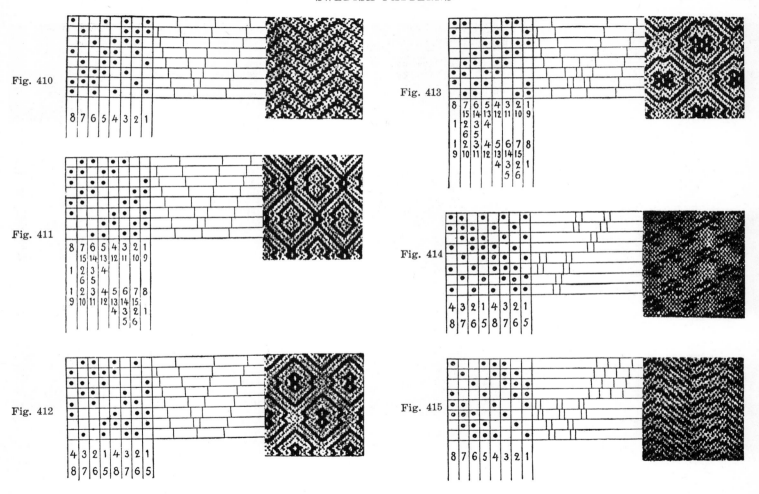

Fig. 410

Fig. 411

Fig. 412

Fig. 413

Fig. 414

Fig. 415

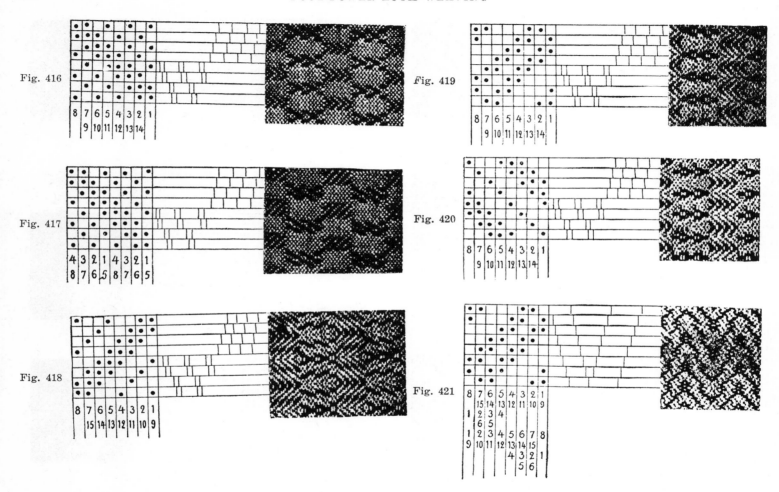

Fig. 416

8 7 6 5 4 3 2 1
 9 10 11 12 13 14

Fig. 417

4 3 2 1 4 3 2 1
8 7 6 5 8 7 6 5

Fig. 418

8 7 6 5 4 3 2 1
 15 14 13 12 11 10 9

Fig. 419

8 7 6 5 4 3 2 1
 9 10 11 12 13 14

Fig. 420

8 7 6 5 4 3 2 1
 9 10 11 12 13 14

Fig. 421

8 7 6 5 4 3 2 1
 15 14 13 12 11 10 9
1   2 3 4
    6 5
    3
1   2 3 4 5 6 7 8
9 10 11 12 13 14 15
          4 3 2 1
          3 5 6

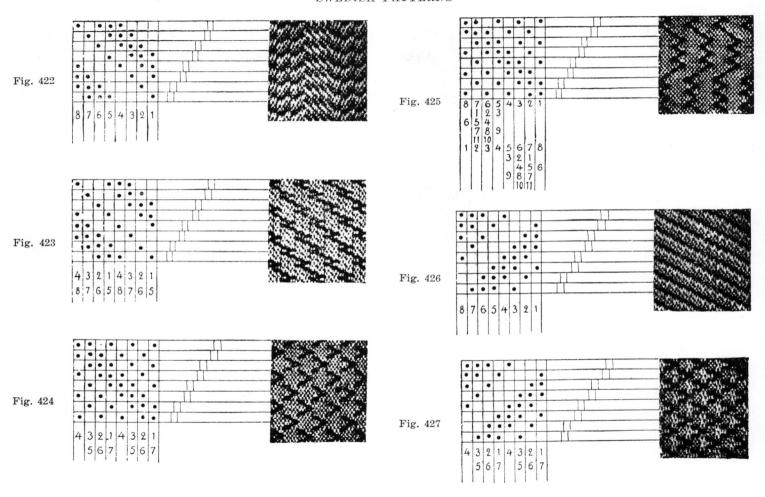

Fig. 422

8 7 6 5 4 3 2 1

Fig. 423

4 3 2 1 4 3 2 1
8 7 6 5 8 7 6 5

Fig. 424

4 3 2 1 4 3 2 1
5 6 7 5 6 7

Fig. 425

8 7 6 5 4 3 2 1
6 1 5 2 3
  5 4
  7 9
  11 10
1 2 3 4 5 6 7 8
    3 2 1
      4 5 6
      8 7
      9 10 11

Fig. 426

8 7 6 5 4 3 2 1

Fig. 427

4 3 2 1 4 3 2 1
5 6 7 5 6 7

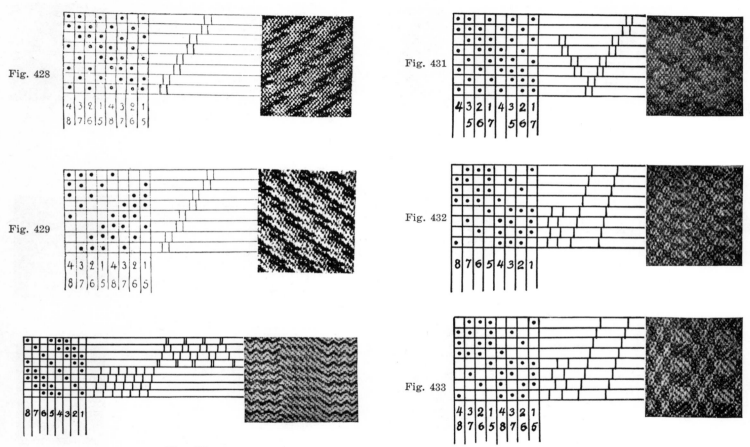

Fig. 428

Fig. 429

Fig. 430

Fig. 431

Fig. 432

Fig. 433

CHAPTER VIII

Damask Weave

Damask Weave

Figure 434 shows a most interesting ten-harness damask weave which may be used in weaving napkins and tablecloths. The draft is written just as the Norwegians write it. There will be little or no difficulty in accomplishing the weave after the threading and treadling are understood.

It has already been stated that each horizontal line means a pair of heddle sticks. The draft shows that there are ten, divided into two sections or groups, marked I and II. The first group consists of the first five harnesses and the second group of the second five.

The threading is indicated by the slanting lines which cross the horizontal parallel lines. Each horizontal line crossed by a slanting line means a thread in each heddle.

The first thread passes through the eye of the first heddle on the first heddle sticks. Each thread is taken in its regular order, passing through the eye of the first heddle on each pair of heddle sticks from the first through the tenth.

The draft indicates that this order is again repeated. The threading now changes and the heddles on the first five harnesses only are used. This is continued for nine

repeats as shown by the nine slanting lines. The third change is the same as the first, which threads from the first through the tenth.

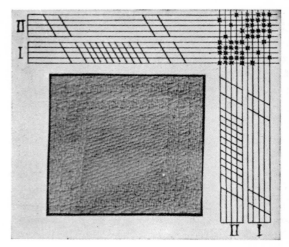

Fig. 434

The entire pattern is made up by repeating the draft shown in Fig. 434.

Threading the Reed

Each thread passes through the eye of a heddle.

In threading the reed, three threads may be drawn through each dent. Sometimes when a large number of threads is used to the inch, four threads are drawn through a dent. This makes it possible to use a coarser reed, thus simplifying the threading.

"Tie-Up"

It will be observed that each vertical line indicates a treadle. These treadles are divided into two groups, I and II.

Group I operates the first five, and Group II operates the second five.

The treadles are tied as indicated by the stars. The double set of lams should be used. See Fig. 262.

The treadling is done by pressing down the tenth treadle, then the ninth, and so on through the ten. This order is again repeated. From here only the second group treadles are pressed down in their regular order nine times. After that the treadling goes back to the tenth through the ten twice. This order of treadling is continued throughout the entire weaving. The weaver soon learns to repeat any order of treadling as many times as is necessary to produce the desired effect.

Ten-Harness "Tie-Up"

If the plan for "tie-up" suggested in Fig. 262 is not used, the device shown in Fig. 435 is easily constructed and used to work ten harnesses.

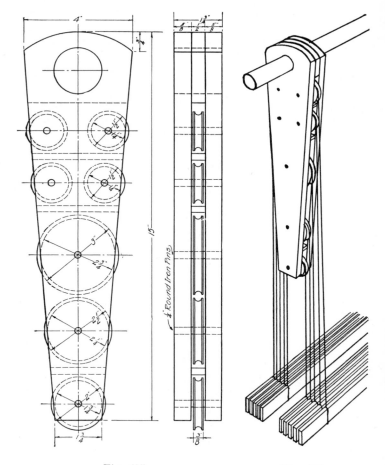

Fig. 435   Fig. 436

Border.

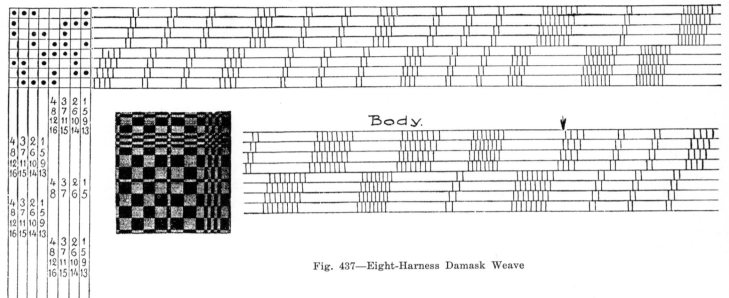

Body.

Fig. 437—Eight-Harness Damask Weave

The lowest pulley controls the two middle harnesses, the one above controls the two harnesses, one at each side of the two center ones. The third pulley controls two other harnesses in a similar way as just mentioned. In the case of two small pulleys, the rope passes over the two, one end tied to one harness and the other to another. The two top pulleys control the first and last harnesses.

No heddle horses are required.

The drawing shown in Fig. 436 shows the ropes tied to one end of the heddle sticks.

Figure 437 shows the draft for an eight-harness damask weave written in the Swedish way. In this draft the space between two lines represents a pair of heddle sticks.

The threading begins at the right and is read toward the left. When the first part is threaded, begin at the left of the second.

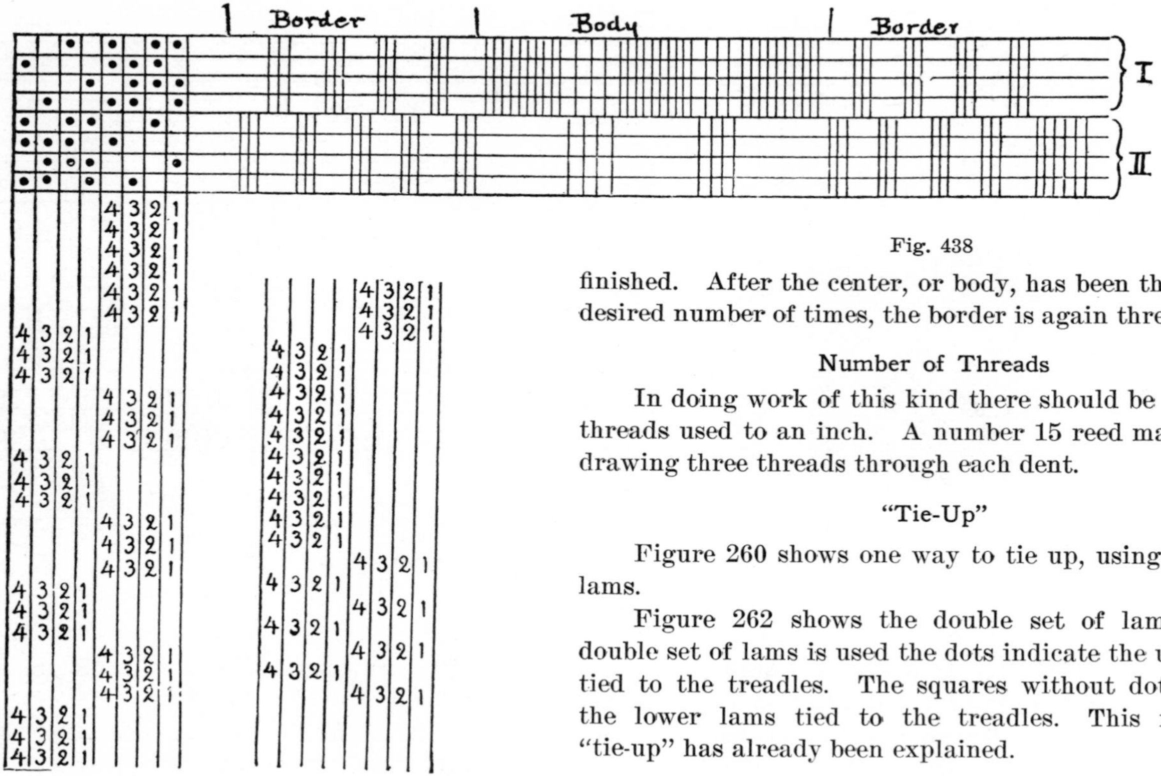

Border   Body   Border

I

II

Fig. 438

finished. After the center, or body, has been threaded the desired number of times, the border is again threaded.

Number of Threads

In doing work of this kind there should be at least 45 threads used to an inch. A number 15 reed may be used, drawing three threads through each dent.

"Tie-Up"

Figure 260 shows one way to tie up, using one set of lams.

Figure 262 shows the double set of lams. If the double set of lams is used the dots indicate the upper lams tied to the treadles. The squares without dots indicate the lower lams tied to the treadles. This method of "tie-up" has already been explained.

Order of Treadling

The figures just below the dots indicating the "tie-up" show the order in which the treadles are pressed down. This has already been explained in detail.

The arrow indicates the end of the border.

The center begins with the arrow and includes all threads to the left. The number of times the center is repeated depends upon the width the material is to be when

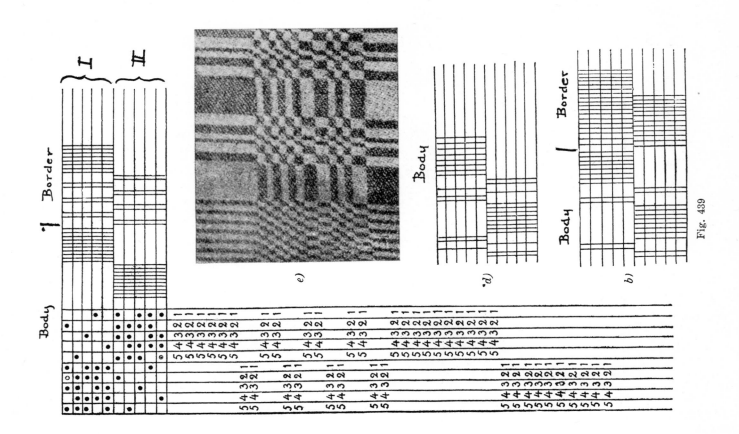

Fig. 439

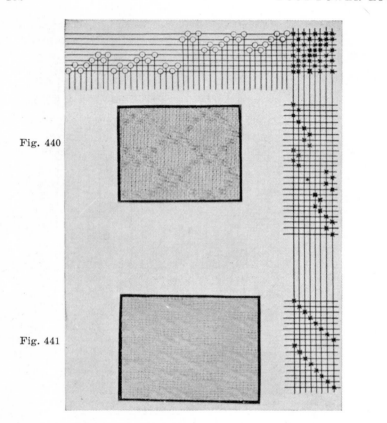

Fig. 440

Fig. 441

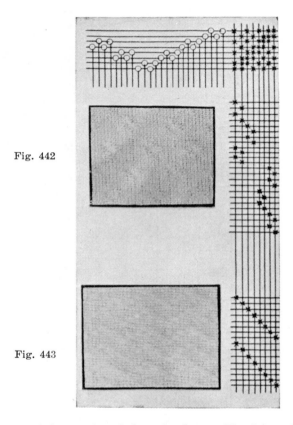

Fig. 442

Fig. 443

Figure 438 shows another interesting damask weave done with eight harnesses and eight treadles.

The tie-up is indicated by the dots and the order of treadling by figures just below the dots. The "tie-up" may be with the one set of lams or with the double set.

The body part of the threading is repeated as many

times as is necessary to give the desired width. The border also may be repeated several times.

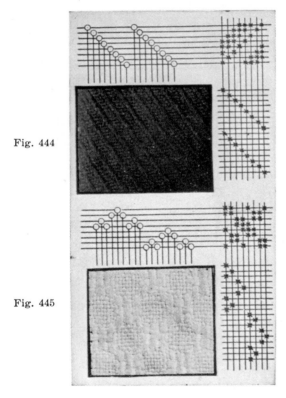

Fig. 444

Fig. 445

Fig. 439 shows the threading for a ten-harness damask weave. There are three arrangements shown. The tie-up

and order of treadling are given for the first one only. The weaver has, no doubt, learned by this time that the threading indicates the treadling.

While Figs. 440, 441, 442, and 443 do not show the regular damask weave, they do show good examples of linen toweling and even good examples of materials that might be used in upholstering. The threading and "tie-up" for Fig. 440 and Fig. 441 are the same. The difference in pattern is brought out by a difference in the order of treadling.

The stars on the vertical lines indicate the order of treadling.

The threading and "tie-up" for Fig. 442 and Fig. 443 are also the same, and the difference in pattern is also brought out by the difference in treadling.

Figure 444 shows a very good diagonal weave in eight harnesses. While this draft is not good for toweling, etc., it is exceptionally good for coats, suiting, etc. The threading, "tie-up" and treadling are all read from Fig. 444.

Figure 445 is a most excellent draft for linens. It is not a damask weave but makes a very satisfactory weave for towels. Threading, tie-up, and treadling are all read from the draft.

Table Mat

Figure 447 shows a table mat woven of No. 3 mercerized cotton warped in two colors. The draft shown in Fig. 446 indicates only two changes in the grouping of the threads. The colors used are green and golden brown

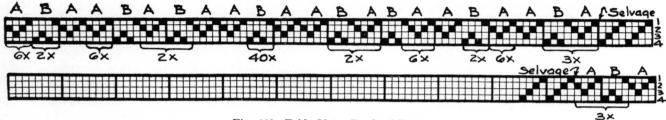

Fig. 446—Table Mat.　Draft of Pattern

The selvage is of green.　The first group of four threads, marked "A," is of golden brown.

The next four threads, marked "B," are green.

This is repeated three times, first A and then B.

It will be observed that the threads run in groups of four, A always being of golden brown and B of green.

Figure 447 requires 408 threads of two colors to be warped as above described, a number 20 reed, one pattern thread to a dent and two selvage threads to a dent of the first four and the last four dents of the draft.

The woof is the same material as the warp, a No. 3 mercerized cotton.　The binder must be a much finer thread and of a different color.　For the above colors, an orange binder works in very harmoniously.

The pattern lams are tied in the following order:
1 and 2 to the first treadle.
3 and 2 to the second treadle.
1 and 4 to the third treadle.
3 and 4 to the fourth treadle.

The plain weave is done by tying lams 1 and 3 to the right middle treadle, and 2 and 4 to the left middle treadle.

Figure 447, showing the finished mat, will give the weaver an idea of the way in which the treadles are operated to produce the design as given.　The vertical bands are unchangeable.　The horizontal bands may be made any width by repeating 1-2 and 3-2, always using the binder after each pattern thread.

The other combinations are 1-4 and 3-4.

The woof is all of the same color.

It is the way the warping is done and the treadling that makes the pattern.

The table mat has the effect of double weaving done with four harnesses.　It is really a six-harness pattern reduced to four.　A little experimenting will suggest a large variety of combinations of stripes and squares which the operator may work out.　The combination of threading may be varied so as to produce most interesting patterns.

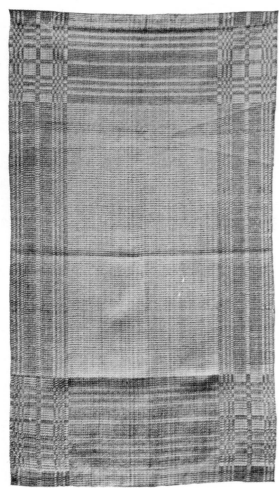

Fig. 447—Finished Mat

Fig. 448—Finished Rug

Rug Weaving in Wool

Figure 448 shows another kind of double weave. The weave in Fig. 447 requires a binder, while the finished rug shown in Fig. 448 does not require a binder of any kind.

Figure 449 shows the draft.

The draft requires 240 threads. This allows for six selvage threads at the beginning and the end. Three selvage threads are drawn through the eye of a heddle at one time. Only two heddles are used for the selvage. In threading the selvage through the reed, draw three threads through each of the two dents. The warp is of ordinary four-ply carpet warp.

The threading is done as shown in the draft, care being taken to repeat the number of times as indicated.

There are about seven threads to the inch.

Since the No. 15 reed is already in stock it may be used for the rug at hand, a thread being drawn through every other dent of the reed.

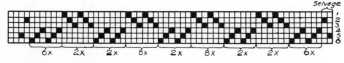

Fig. 449—Draft for Rug

The draft shows that there are six harnesses. It requires but four treadles to operate the six harnesses, which are tied in the following way:

Lams 2, 3 and 4 are tied to the first treadle.

Fig. 450—A Rug in Tan and Brown.

Lams 3, 4 and 5 are tied to the second treadle.

Lams 1, 3 and 5 are tied to the third treadle.

Lams 2, 4 and 6 are tied to the fourth treadle.

The double "tie-up" suggested in Fig. 262 may be used to advantage in weaving this particular pattern.

To produce the pattern shown in Fig. 448, two shuttles are used, one with a bobbin of white wool and one with a bobbin of blue wool. The wool used is similar to that used in kindergarten weaving. It is a kind of carpet yarn. It is almost as heavy as cotton roving.

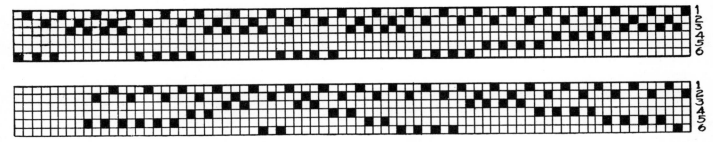

Fig. 451—Sea Shell. Draft of Pattern

Operating of Treadles

Treadle four is pressed down and the shuttle containing the blue is passed through the shed. Treadle one is next pressed down and the white thread is passed through the shed.

Treadle two is next pressed down and the blue used. Treadle three is pressed down and the white passed through the shed. This order of treadling is continued throughout the weaving of the entire rug shown in Fig. 448.

Figure 450 shows the same tie-up, but a different order of treadling. Instead of using blue and white for the woof, tan and brown are used. The weaving is started in the same way as in Fig. 448.

After the band of one color is as wide as is desired, the opposite color is made to reverse. This change is brought about by passing the same color through the shed twice. The order of treadling is exactly the same.

Sea Shell Pattern

The draft shown in Fig. 451 is that of a six-harness loom.

The draft shows that ten treadles are required to produce the pattern shown in Fig. 452.

It requires 148 threads for one repeat.

The warp is of a two-ply No. 30 Egyptian twine, and the woof is of a No. 5 mercerized cotton. There are thirty threads to the inch drawn through the dents of a No. 15 reed, two threads to the dent.

The lams are tied to the lower heddle sticks.

They are tied to the treadles in the following order:

Lams 1 and 3 are tied to the first treadle.

Lams 2 and 3 are tied to the second treadle.

Lams 1 and 4 are tied to the third treadle.

Lams 2 and 4 are tied to the fourth treadle.

Lams 1 and 5 are tied to the fifth treadle.

Lams 2 and 5 are tied to the sixth treadle.

Lams 1 and 6 are tied to the seventh treadle.

Lams 2 and 6 are tied to the eighth treadle.

The plain weave is done by tying:

Lams 1 and 2 to the right middle treadle.

Lams 3, 4, 5 and 6 to the left middle treadle.

Figure 452 shows the finished Sea Shell. It is a close weave and may be used for window side drapes, pillow tops, table runners, and because of the closeness of the weave it may very successfully be used in upholstering.

It is perhaps the most difficult to weave because of the six harnesses and ten treadles. If the double "tie-up" suggested in Fig. 262 is used, there will be no difficulty in securing a good shed.

Any shade of No. 5 mercerized cotton may be used.

The draft itself indicates the order of treadling. It will be remembered that each dark square indicates a woof thread. In the first combination of threads 1 and 3 are given. This means that the treadle controlling harnesses 1 and 3 is pressed down twice for the pattern threads with a binder after each pattern thread. Since the method of expressing the reading of this kind of draft has been carefully explained previously, it will not be necessary to again go into the detail of it at this time.

The six harness patterns do not require to be woven so finely as the four harness designs. A number 24 reed, one thread to the dent, makes a very fine fabric.

Figure 453 shows the draft for what is known as the

Fig. 452—Sea Shell

Fig. 453—Virginia Beauty. Four Harness

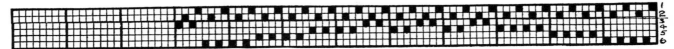

Fig. 454—Virginia Beauty. Six Harness

"Virginia Beauty," to be transposed into a six-harness draft.

To do this let the
Combination 1-4=Combination 1-6 and 2-6.
Combination 3-4=Combination 1-5 and 2-5.
Combination 2-3=Combination 1-4 and 2-4.
Combination 1-2=Combination 1-3 and 2-3.
right through the draft, with the draft shown by Fig. 454 as a result.

The Tie-Up

The tie-up for the pattern is found in the same way as for four heddle drafts.

1-6 is tied to the first treadle.
2-6 is tied to the second treadle.
1-5 is tied to the third treadle.
2-5 is tied to the fourth treadle.
1-4 is tied to the fifth treadle.
2-4 is tied to the sixth treadle.
1-3 is tied to the seventh treadle.

2-3 is tied to the eighth treadle.
Tie-up for the plain weave is as follows:
1-2 to the right middle treadle.
3-4-5-6 to the left middle treadle.

To Transpose a Four Heddle to a Six Heddle Draft

Designs best suited to transpose from four to six heddles are those written in two's, four's, and eight's, or even multiples.

The designs written in 3's, 5's, 7's, or 9's, or where those multiples appear in the design, are more complicated if transposed as written. The simplest way is to make such a draft over so that it reads in 2's, 4's, 8's, etc.

In re-arranging a draft an additional one or two may have to be added or the draft may be reduced to produce a smaller design.

The plain weave is found by checking through the draft, allowing the heddle stick that contains every other thread to be tied to one treadle, and the opposite half of the threads to be tied to the other middle treadle.

For example—the first thread appears on heddle No. 1. The next thread is on heddle No. 6. One and six cannot be used together in the plain weave because two threads would be brought down together.

The third thread is on the second heddle. The first and third threads may be used together because the second thread which is on heddle No. 6 comes between. Checking through the draft the plain weave is found to be as above stated.

CHAPTER IX

Double Weave

Double weaving is one of the most interesting phases of the art of weaving. It is a branch of the work that amateur weavers know the least about. It is difficult to understand just how the weavers of many years ago controlled the number of harnesses necessary to produce the seemingly complicated patterns found in old counterpanes possessed by many of the old settlers.

Plain double cloth of separate colors can be woven on a loom with a harness of four heddles, but the warp must be specially arranged for the purpose.

If it be decided to make one side of the cloth black and the other white, the warp must be so made that the threads on the warp beam are black and white. This is easily done while reeling the warp. The spools, black and white, may be so arranged on the spool rack that the black and white threads alternate. The placing of the warp on the beam is the same as for all other kinds of weaving.

Entering the Double Warp in Harness

There are four heddles hung in the usual way. The warp of black and white threads is entered the same as when threading any four heddle loom, as shown in Fig. 455.

The first thread is black and passes through the eye of the first heddle on the fourth heddle sticks. It will be found that all the threads on the fourth heddle sticks will be black.

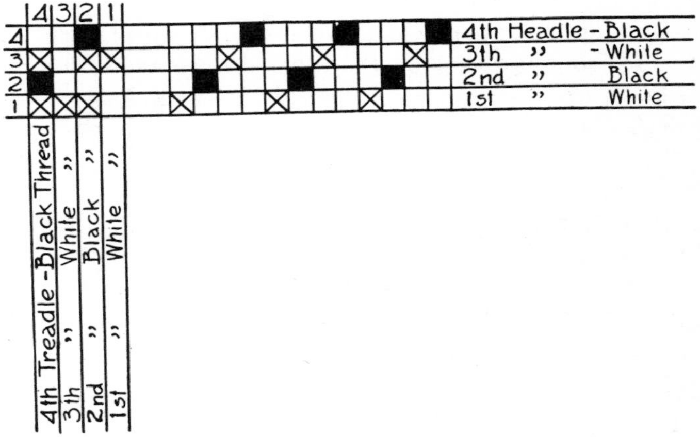

Fig. 455

The third heddle sticks will carry all white, the second all black and the first all white.

Weaving Double Cloth

It requires two shuttles to weave double cloth, one for the white thread and the other for the black.

When all is ready, weaving begins by drawing down all the white thread and half the black, as shown in Fig. 455, treadle 4. A black thread is now passed through the shed, thus formed. This begins the black cloth and is on the upper side of the weaving. The white cloth is to be formed on the underside. In order to bring this about one-half the white threads are drawn down, the other half of the white and all the black remaining up, as shown in Fig. 455, treadle 3.

A white thread is now passed through the shed.

The next thread in the plain cloth is to be a black one. To do this all the black threads left up in treadle 4 must be brought down together with all the white threads, as shown in treadle 2. A black thread is now passed through the shed.

The fourth thread must be another white one. The required shed is made by bringing down the white threads not brought down by treadle 3. By pressing down treadle 1, the right shed is made and a white thread is passed through. If this order of treadling is followed, a double cloth is woven which is black on the top and white below.

Double Pattern Weaving

To understand double pattern weaving it is best to first thread a loom, as described in the weaving of plain double cloth.

Through experimenting with the plain double tie-up one learns that only plain double cloth can be woven.

In other words, no change is possible. The cloth throughout is black on one side and white on the other. To produce a change it will be necessary to add four more heddles.

Figure 456 shows a double woven pattern which may be produced with eight heddles, four of which will give the black squares and four the white. The draft written below the pattern, Fig. 456, is written out in full, while the draft at the right is very much condensed, thus using less space.

The Warp

The warp may be of the regular four-ply carpet warp in two colors. It is reeled and handled throughout as described in the weaving of plain double cloth. There should be from 32 to 36 threads per inch, one-half being white and the other half black. Two threads, one black and one white, are drawn through each dent of a number 16 or 18 reed.

The Threading

The draft below Fig. 456 is so written as to show the number of threads that produce each part of the finished pattern. The little black square in the lower left hand corner of the finished pattern is taken care of by the first four threads in the draft. The little white square above it is taken care of by the second four threads. This is repeated four times. In the condensed form at the right this part of the draft is expressed by using a brace with

Fig. 456—Double Woven Pattern

the figures telling the number of times this order of threads is to be repeated.

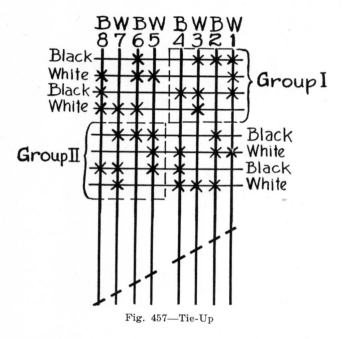

Fig. 457—Tie-Up

Observe the threading for the long narrow strip of black. Only heddles 8, 7, 6, and 5 are used. The white strip above is cared for by using only heddles 4, 3, 2, and 1. Note the way the changes and the repeats are expressed in the condensed way of writing the draft.

The weaver must remember that the horizontal spacing in any design is controlled by the number of times a certain portion of the draft is repeated. The vertical spacing depends upon the number of woof threads.

The draft at the right tells in a very simple way the whole story of the pattern at hand. The heddle sticks are numbered at the left of the threading draft. The treadles are numbered at the top. Just below is the treadling for the front border. The first treadle is pressed down and a white thread is passed through the shed. The second treadle is pressed down and a black thread is passed through the shed. The 3rd, 4th, 5th, 6th, 7th and 8th are taken in their regular order. This order of treadling is repeated four times. The remainder of the treadling draft is shown to the left.

Tie-Up

The tie-up part of the draft shows that heddles 8, 7, 6 and 3 are tied to the first treadle, heddles 8, 4, 3 and 1 to the second treadle, etc.

The black squares simply tell the black heddles and the cross the white heddles tied to a certain treadle. Attention is called to the fact that all the white threads are on heddle sticks 1, 3, 5 and 7, while all the black threads are found on heddle sticks 2, 4, 6 and 8.

Explanation of Tie-Up

In order to work intelligently the one operating the loom should understand the reasons for tying certain

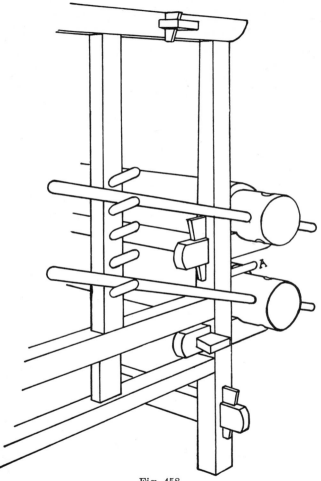

Fig. 458

heddles to certain treadles. For convenience the treadles may be grouped as shown in Fig. 457 and marked I and II. The harnesses may also be grouped and marked I and II. The black and white squares at the right mark the color of the threads carried by the various harnesses. The letters at the top, Fig. 457, indicate the color of the threads to be used as the filler. For example, a white thread is passed through the shed formed by pressing down the first treadle to the right. A black thread is used with the second treadle to the right, etc.

Since there are but two changes in the pattern, the treadling draft is made out in the following manner. Do not become confused by considering the whole pattern but take only the large square of black in the lower right hand corner and the white rectangle above it.

These two represent the two changes.

Four harnesses and four treadles are necessary for each change.

To weave in the first white thread of the white square beneath the large black one, it will be necessary to draw up all the black threads in this particular square and half the white throughout the pattern.

In group I, Fig. 457, to the right, both black threads are drawn up as indicated by the crosses opposite the black squares. The first white is drawn up, the second white is left down, the next white is brought up, the last white left down.

The second filler thread is to be black.

To produce this, all the white threads in groups I, treadle 2, must be left down, which is so indicated by the crosses on treadle 2, Group I; half of the black are up throughout the pattern. It is always true that when a black thread passes through the shed, half of the black threads are up and other half down. When a white thread passes through the shed, half of the white threads throughout the pattern are up and the other half down. Care must be exercised in not drawing up the same threads for either two successive white or black woof threads.

The third filler thread is a white and is woven in below the black square. All the black must be drawn up out of the way, as is indicated in Group I, third treadle. Half of the white must be drawn up. It is here that care must be taken not to take the same white as was taken when weaving in the last white thread. The second white thread is therefore drawn up and every other white thread throughout the pattern. The remaining black threads are left down as indicated on the third treadle. The fourth thread is black; therefore all the white threads in Group I are left down. All the other white threads are brought up. Half of the black are up. The first black at top, treadle 4, is left down because it was brought up on treadle 2. The second black thread, Group I, is brought up and every other black thread throughout is brought up as is indicated on treadle 4, Group I. The treadles in Group I, when used in their regular order, produce the large square. The order must be repeated until the desired square is woven.

Group II

Group II, Fig. 457, which is indicated by the dotted lines, takes care of the smaller black square. The first thread of the white square beneath the black, is white, and is woven in by raising all the black threads, and half the white in the group, using treadle 5. Consider at present only that part of the tie-up within the dotted lines and marked Group II.

In order to find the white threads to be raised it is necessary to refer to treadle No. 3. It is found that the lowest white thread, Figure 457, was last raised. Treadle 5 must leave this white thread down. When all the blacks or whites in a certain group are used all the others are left down.

Treadle No. 6 carries a black thread. All the white threads in Group II are left down, all the others outside the group are raised. Every other black thread within the group and also those outside the group are raised as indicated on treadle 6.

Treadle 7 carries a white thread.

All the blacks within the group are raised. All blacks outside the group are left down. Half the whites within and outside the group are raised.

Treadle No. 8 carries a black thread; therefore all the whites in Group II must be down. All the other whites must be raised. Every other black, both within and outside the group must be raised.

It is now evident that the treadles in Group II when

repeated over and over will produce the second change in the pattern.

The Loom

The loom used for double weaving should be equipped with the double set of lams and the overhead fixtures, as shown in Figs. 262, 263 and 264.

By this arrangement no part of the harness remains stationary, but is pulled either up or down, thus producing a good shed. One great difficulty in having but one set of lams is that the heddles do not return to their original position after being pulled down.

This is specially true when the harness consists of eight or more heddles.

Other Materials

In most of the old-time double woven counterpanes the colored warp is of wool while the white is cotton. It has been found practical to make the entire warp of cotton, using the desired colors. The colored woof may be of wool.

If both wool and cotton are used there should be two distinct warps, the one of wool being placed on one warp beam and the one of cotton placed on another beam. The beams may be placed as shown in Fig. 458. An extra pair of warp beam brackets is placed below the pair already on the loom. Pegs are used just above the ends of the lower beam to prevent it from being drawn upward as the warp is tightened. See A, Fig. 458.

The two beams are absolutely necessary unless the

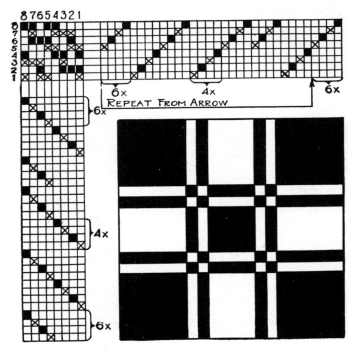

Fig. 459

wool used has a very hard twist, thus preventing it from stretching.

The separate beams make it possible to tighten the wool beam to meet the tension of the white warp.

When two beams are used it is best to place the warp

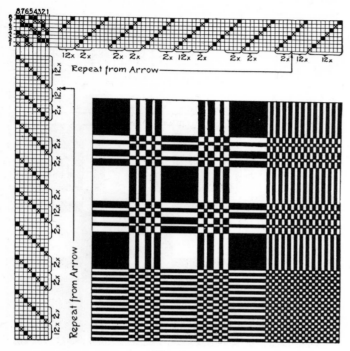

Fig. 460

12 or 15, may be purchased of the Western Thread Company, Elgin, Illinois.

This thread may be had either bleached or unbleached.

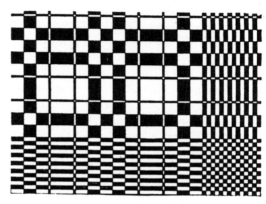

Fig. 461

of wool on the upper beam. Separate lease rods are used and ends of the white warp are carried right over the blue warp beam.

When threading, a thread is first taken from the blue and then from the white beam. A very superior thread for double weaving, known as Swiss Tidy cotton, number

Figure 459 shows a very simple eight heddle pattern. The threading draft is written above the pattern and the treadling draft is written at the left. The tie-up is shown to the left of the threading draft. The black squares and crosses show the number of black and the number of white heddles tied to each treadle.

Figure 460 shows another interesting eight heddle double weave. The entire threading and also the treadling drafts are written in the condensed form.

It will be observed that the first part of each treadling draft takes care of the front border.

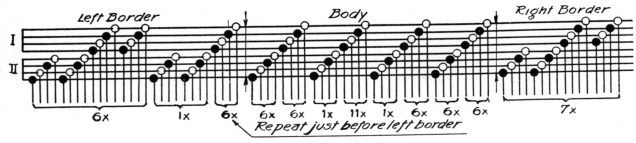

Fig. 462—Double Weave Draft

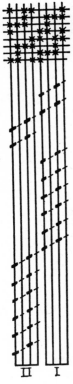

If a pillow top is desired the border must be repeated around the entire center.

The borders at the sides must be cared for in the threading. The front and back borders are made by following the treadling draft. When two strips are to be sewed together, it is necessary to care for the border along one side only.

Figure 461 shows another interesting series of squares and oblongs arranged so as to form a pleasing pattern.

Material

Use a No. 12 Swiss Tidy Cotton in blue and white, forty threads to the inch, twenty of which are white and twenty blue.

Use blue wool for the filler (woof) and white cotton the same as was used in the warp.

Threading the Reed

Use a number 20 reed, drawing a blue and a white thread through each dent.

The threading in this draft is indicated by white and black disks placed on the lines representing the different heddles.

The Tie-Up

The tie-up is indicated by stars placed where the lines representing the heddles and those representing the treadles cross. Fig. 462.

Treadling

The light and heavy dashes on the vertical lines indicate the order of treadling. Fig. 462.

Fig. 462 also tells the weaver that when a treadle on which a light dash appears is pressed down, a white thread passes through the shed. A heavy dash indicates that a blue thread passes through the shed.

In weaving, two shuttles are required, one with a bobbin of blue and the other with a bobbin of unbleached Swiss Tidy Cotton.

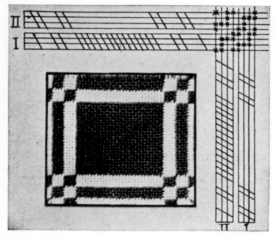

Fig. 463

The first treadle to the right in group I is pressed down and a white thread passes through the shed. The second treadle is pressed down and a blue wool thread is passed through the shed. The third treadle is pressed and a white thread passes through. The fourth treadle is pressed and a blue thread passes through. The next treadle pressed down is the first.

The front border is made by repeating the first two changes in the treadling draft.

The weaver must use his own judgment in the number of wool threads to use.

Figure 463 shows the Danish way of writing an eight heddle draft for double weaving. The threading resembles that of the Damask weave.

Double Weaving with More Than Two Changes

Figure 464 shows a double woven pattern, involving four changes.

Analysis of Pattern

The process of analyzing a double woven piece of cloth is more simple than that of the ordinary four-harness patterns.

The changes are very definitely marked, and the draft more easily written. The fact that it requires double the number of harnesses makes the weaving a little more difficult.

Until the weaver becomes familiar with the various steps in analysis, it is well to draw out the pattern to be analyzed on paper, as shown in Fig. 464. Draw the vertical lines that mark each change as shown below the pattern. Since there are four changes, draw horizontal lines which cross the vertical lines at right angles. Within the spaces thus formed write the number of threads in each change. It must be remembered that there are always double the number of threads than appear on either the

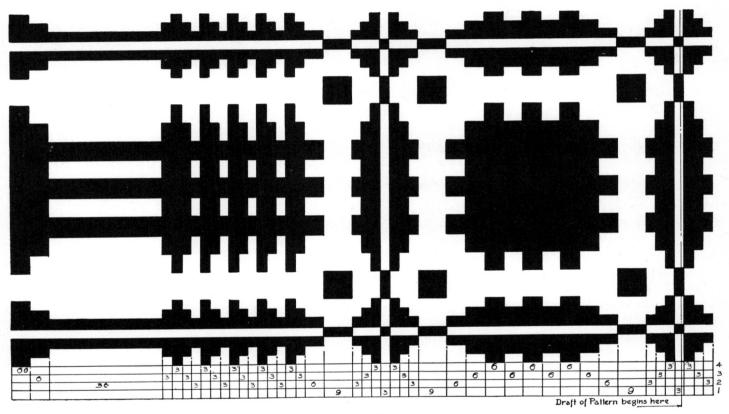

Fig. 464

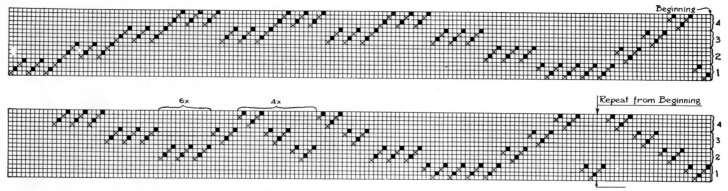

Fig. 465—Completed Draft. A Pattern Analysis

upper or under surface.   For example—the first square is recorded as having three threads, this means that there are three threads of another color in the same square of the under surface.

It has already been stated, and the weaver should have experienced the fact by this time, that four heddles or harnesses are required for each change, two for the white and two for the blue.   As a matter of convenience divide the checked paper on which the draft is written into sections and mark one, two, three and four, as indicated in Fig. 465.

If each change in the pattern is lettered, the number of threads recorded, and the checked paper marked off into sections, there will be no difficulty in writing the draft for any particular square.

That part of the draft between the arrows shows the unit that is to be repeated.   The place of beginning is marked in Fig. 464.

After the pattern or unit has been repeated the desired number of times, the border which follows is threaded. This places the border along the left edge only, and is woven with the understanding that two strips are to be sewed together.   If the woven piece is to be a pillow top, the border should be threaded at the beginning as well as the end, thus making a border around the entire weaving. Figure 465 is the completed sixteen-harness draft.

The No. 14 Swiss Tidy Cotton makes a very good warp. It has been suggested that the entire warp, in both white and blue be made of cotton.   The colored filler or woof may be of wool and the white filler of cotton.   If wool is

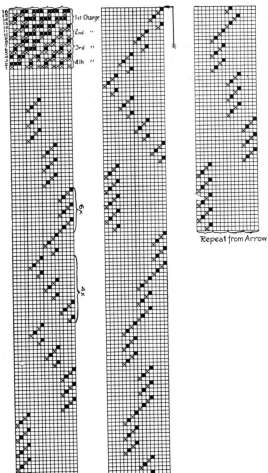

Fig. 466—Treadling Draft

used in the warp, it should have a very hard twist to avoid stretching as much as possible.

The Reed

A number 20 reed is used. Two threads, one white and one blue, are drawn through each dent. (Reeds may be purchased of R. R. Street, 543 W. Washington Blvd., Chicago.)

The Treadling

There are sixteen treadles. As a convenience the treadles may be divided into sections or groups, to correspond with the division shown in the harness, Fig. 466. It requires four treadles for each change in the pattern. The weaver soon learns the particular four treadles that will operate that portion of the harness which will produce any one change of the pattern.

The complete treadling draft is shown in Fig. 466. Counting from the right it is the third set of four treadles that produces the first part of the pattern. Each time that a treadle marked by the dark square is pressed down, a blue thread passes through the shed thus formed, and each time a treadle marked by a cross is pressed down a white thread passes through the shed thus formed.

This series of treadles is pressed down three times in succession. The second change in the pattern is formed by pressing down the second four treadles from the right. The third change is produced by the first four treadles and is repeated as many times as the figure before the brace

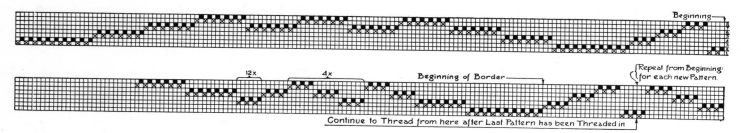

Fig. 467—Threading Draft for Two Harnesses

indicates. The entire treadling draft is followed as above described. The double set of lams is used in the tie-up. A better shed is produced if the lams and treadles are lengthened. This is easily accomplished by placing brackets to the side of the loom thus allowing the lams to extend beyond the loom as far as the brackets will permit. This extension of the lams gives the treadles at the left a greater leverage and thus produces a better shed.

The Treadles

Brackets may be cut and screwed to the floor to hold the lengthened treadles.

Warp Beam

Lengthened brackets may also be placed at the back to hold the warp beam, thus giving a greater distance between the warp beam and the harness.

Double Weaving with Two Harnesses

A great advance was made in the weaving of patterns when the idea occurred of passing the warp threads through two sets of heddles, each set having its own separate function to perform, such as making the ground, forming the pattern, or binding a portion of the design separately, as is sometimes necessary.

A good example of the action of two separate harnesses working together is afforded by the double cloth pattern, Fig. 464. The making of plain double cloth has been fully described at the beginning of this chapter.

Advantage of Two Harnesses

Fig. 467 shows the threading draft when two harnesses are used for the pattern shown in Fig. 464.

It will be observed that for each change in the pattern there are but two heddles instead of four, thus reducing the number to one-half the number of heddles.

Pattern Harness

The pattern harness for Fig. 464 consists of eight

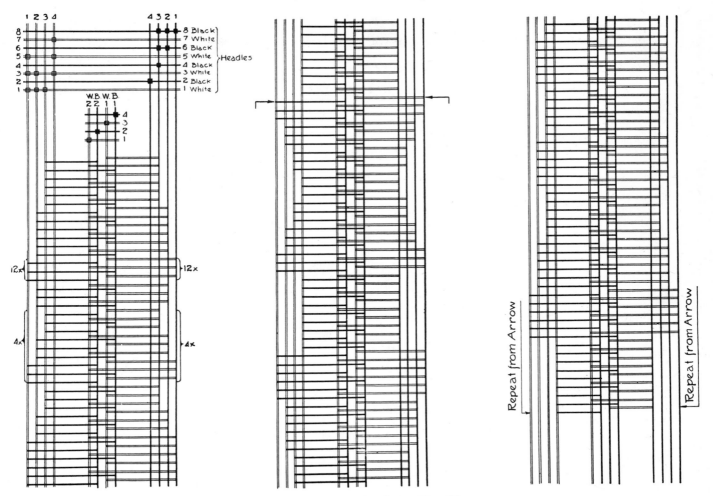

Fig. 468—Treadling Draft for Fig. 464

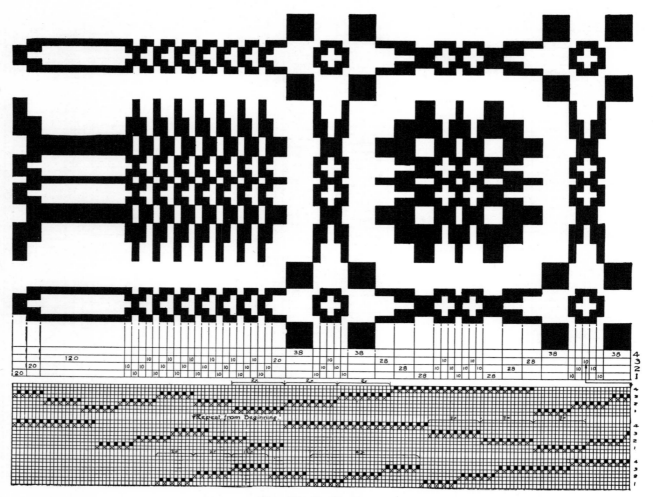

Fig. 469—Double Pattern

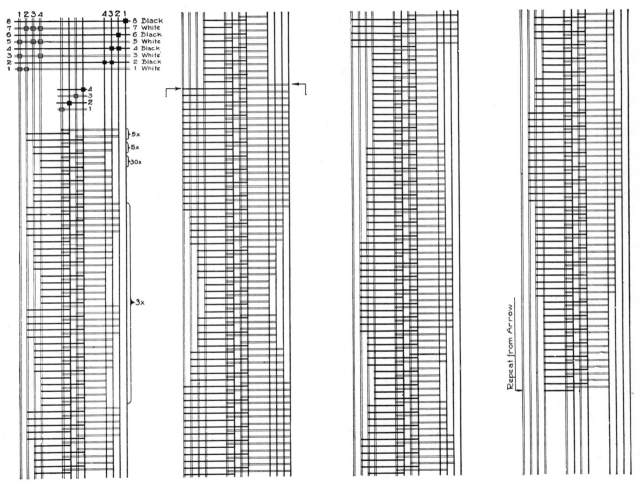

Fig. 470—Treadling Draft for Fig. 469

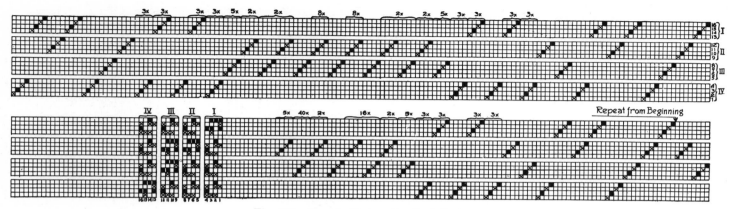

Fig. 471—Lover's Chain.   Draft of Pattern

heddles, two for each change in the pattern. These heddles should be at least twelve inches long, having small eyes through which the pattern threads are drawn.

The entire pattern is threaded following the threading draft, Fig. 467.

The Tabby Harness

The tabby harness, consisting of four heddles, is hung in front of the pattern harness.   The tabby heddles are of the same length as the pattern, but the eyes are about four and one-half inches in length.

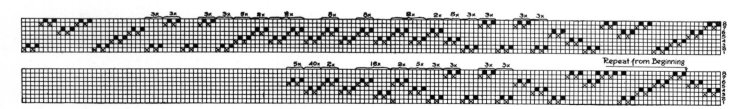

Fig. 472—Threading Draft for Double Harness, Lover's Chain

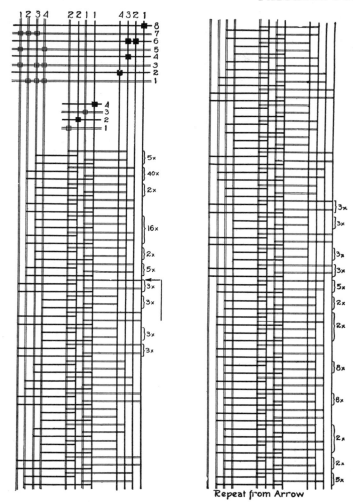

Fig. 473—Treadling Draft for the Lover's Chain

Repeat from Arrow

Fig. 474—Lover's Chain

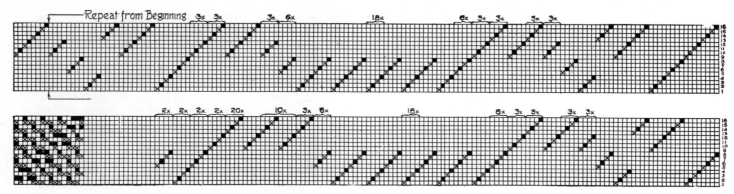

Fig. 475—Draft for Lover's Knot Pattern

Each pattern thread now passes through an eye of the tabby harness. The threading is done through the tabby harness the same as for plain double cloth.

The long eyes of the tabby harness allow the pattern threads to work up and down freely.

The Work of the Figure Harness

The province of the figure harness is to form the design in large without regard to the binding or weaving of it together.

If only the figure harness were used, the design would be formed, but the threads of both warp and weft would only interlace where the black takes the place of the white or the white that of the black.

The plan, tie-up and treadling of the double harness

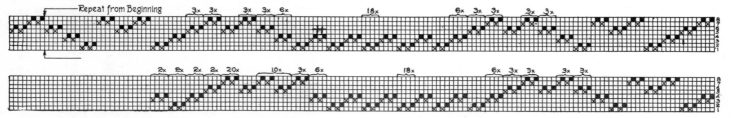

Fig. 476—Threading Draft for the Lover's Knot—Two Harness

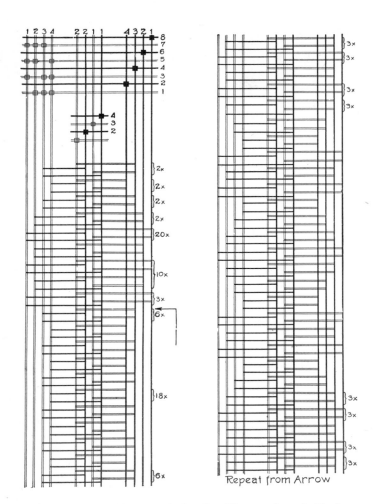

Fig. 477—Treadling Draft for Two-Harness Lover's Knot

Fig. 478—Lover's Knot

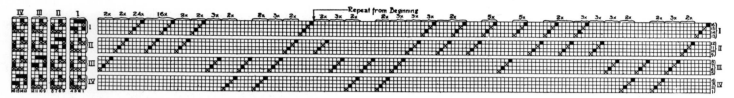

Fig. 479—Threading Draft, Mosaic Pattern—Single Harness

method for the pattern shown in Fig. 464 is given in Fig. 468.

Explanation of Tie-Up

The tabby treadles are in the middle, the treadles carrying the white are at the left and the black at the right.

The tie-up complete, the third black treadle is pressed down and at the same time the first white treadle in the tabby. This is indicatd by the double line drawn from the third black pattern to the first white tabby. A white thread is passed through the shed thus formed. The second shed is formed by pressing down the third white treadle and the second black of the tabby at the same time. This is indicated by the single continuous line drawn from the third white pattern to the second black tabby. A black thread is passed through the shed.

The third shed is made by pressing down the third black pattern treadle and the second white tabby, and a white thread passed through the shed.

By carefully following the treadling draft the weaver cannot go astray.

All solid black lines indicate colored threads while the double lines indicate white. All lines within brackets indicate the number of times a series of threads is to be repeated.

It is well to arrange the shuttles so that when the right white tabby treadle is pressed down the white shuttle is thrown from the right and when the right black tabby treadle is pressed down the shuttle carrying the black or blue thread is thrown through the shed.

When the left white tabby is pressed down the shuttle carrying the white is thrown from the left. By following the above order it greatly simplifies the handling of the shuttles.

Fig. 480—Threading Draft for Double Harness, Mosaic Pattern

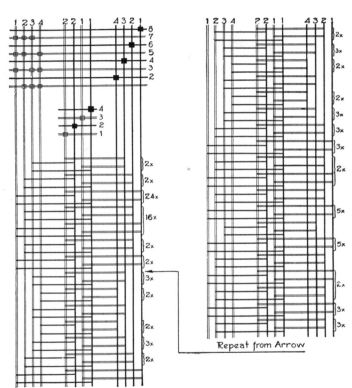

Fig. 481—Treadling Draft for the Mosaic Pattern

Fig. 482—Mosaic Pattern

Fig. 483—Counterpane Pattern

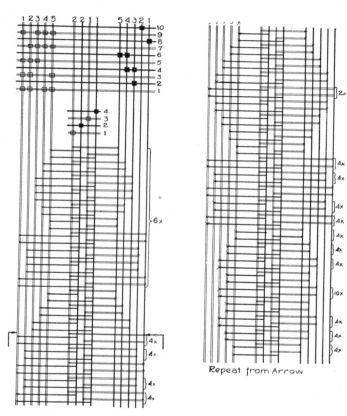

Fig. 484—Treadling Draft for Counterpane Pattern

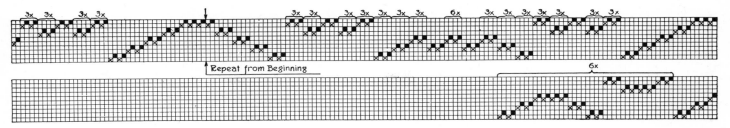

Fig. 485—Threading Draft for Counterpane

The treadling draft, Fig. 468, is a key to all the other drafts.

Figure 469 shows a most attractive double pattern. The treadling draft is shown in Fig. 470, and is followed the same as in Fig. 468.

Figure 474 shows what is known as Lover's Chain. Upon inspection it is found to contain but four changes. The draft is written in two ways. Fig. 471 shows the threading draft and tie-up without the tabby draft. The pattern is threaded from the beginning to the arrow as many times as desired. The part of the draft following the arrow is the border and is threaded only once. The threading draft becomes the treadling draft in the double weaving just as it does in the four harness weaving.

When weaving, the treadles in group I are pressed down first. Groups II, III and IV follow in their regular order. The treadling then goes back to groups I and II and then down to group IV.

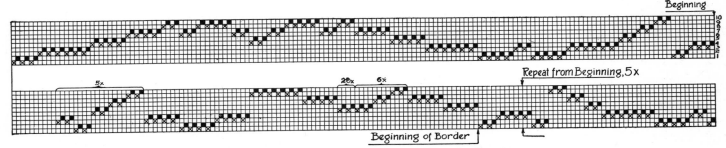

Fig. 486—Threading Draft for Pattern Shown in Fig. 488

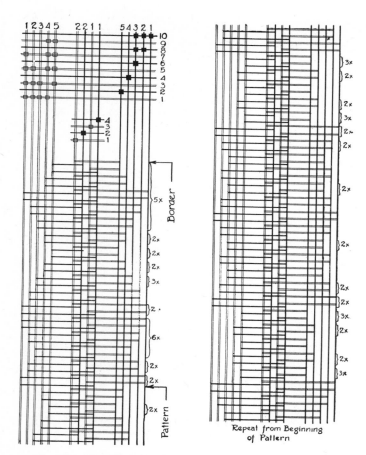

Fig. 487—Treadling Draft for Pattern Shown in Fig. 488

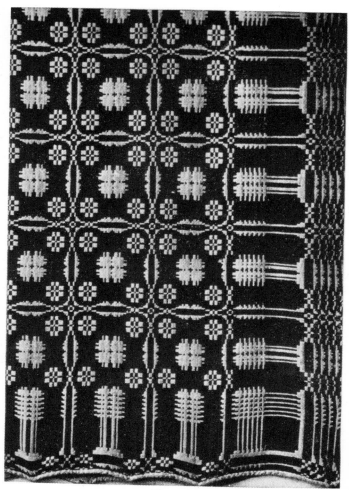

Fig. 488

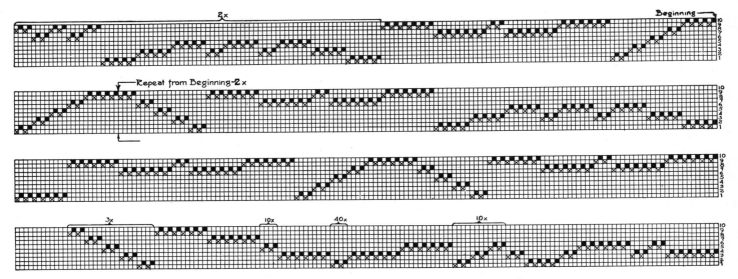

Fig. 489—Threading Draft for Counterpane (See Fig. 491)

Repeat any particular group as many times as is indicated by the bracket and figure.

Figure 472 shows the threading draft for Lover's Chain when the double harness is used.

Figure 473 shows the treadling draft for Lover's Chain when the double harness is used.

Another well known double weave is shown in Fig. 478.

The draft is written both ways.

Figure 475 shows the four changes written by using sixteen harnesses.

The threading draft becomes the treadling draft as previously described.

The tie-up is shown at the end of the draft.

It is well to remember that the part of the draft which follows the arrow, is the border.

Figure 476 shows the threading draft when two harnesses are used.

Figure 477 gives the treadling draft for the two harnesses.

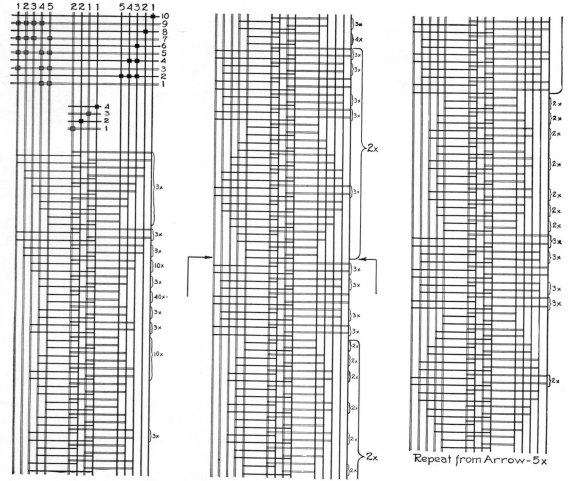

Fig. 490—Treadling Draft for Counterpane (See Fig. 491)

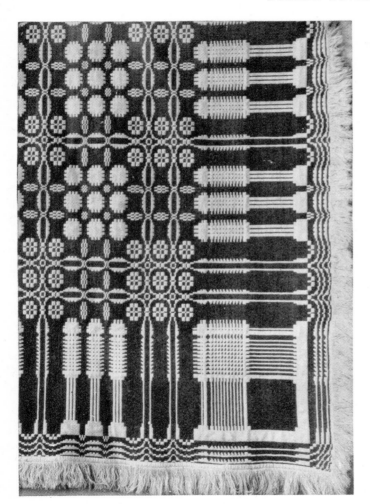

Fig. 491—Double Woven Counterpane

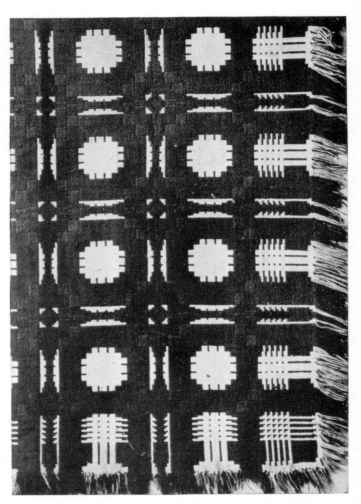

Fig. 492—Counterpane in Blue, Green and White

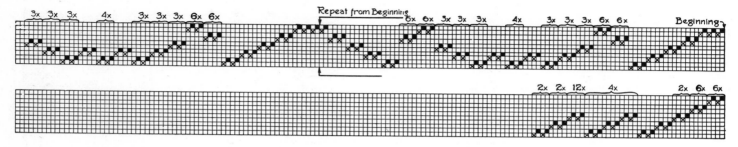

Fig. 493—Threading Draft for Counterpane (Fig. 492)

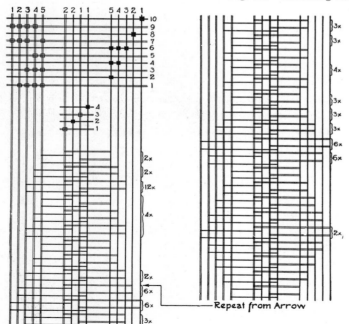

Fig. 494—Treadling Draft for Counterpane Illustrated in Fig. 492

Figure 482 gives the completed pattern for what is known as Mosaic.

Figure 479 shows the threading draft when only the single harness is used. Fig. 480 shows the pattern draft for the double harness method.

Figure 481 gives the order of treadling the double harness.

The weaver will find the double harness method very practical, and through its use most complicated patterns may be reproduced.

It must be remembered that the double harness threading is the same as threading the entire pattern twice. First the pattern is threaded and then the tabby harness is threaded by drawing these same threads through the long eyes of the tabby harness. The order in this threading is simply 4, 3, 2, 1, every other thread being colored.

Figure 483 shows an interesting counterpane pattern, involving five changes.

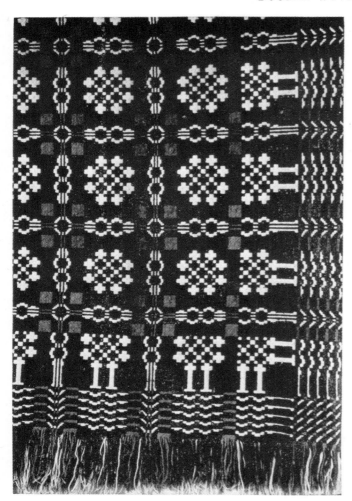

Fig. 495—A Pattern in Three Colors

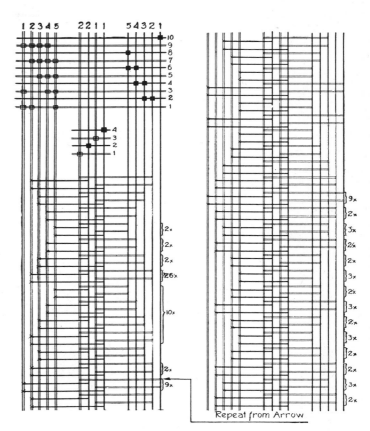

Fig. 496—Treadling Draft

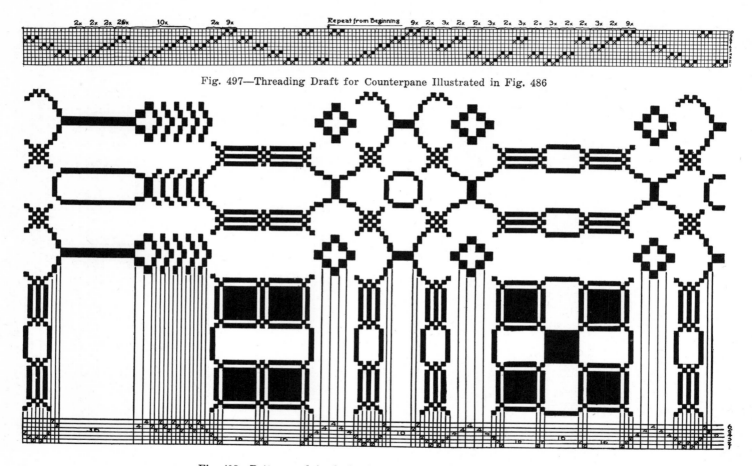

Fig. 497—Threading Draft for Counterpane Illustrated in Fig. 486

Fig. 498—Pattern and Analysis of Counterpane Illustrated in Fig. 501

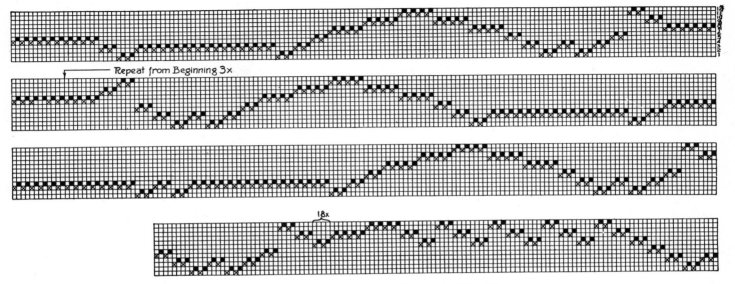

Fig. 499—Threading Draft for Pattern in Fig. 498

If the threading draft was written for the single harness it would require twenty heddles. By using the double harness it requires ten heddles for the pattern and four for the tabby.

Figure 485 gives the threading for the pattern, while Fig. 484 gives the order of treadling. Since this is the same as for the four-change patterns which have already been described, it will not be necessary to give further detail.

Figure 488 is a pattern involving five changes. Fig. 486 is the threading draft for the pattern and Fig. 487 gives the treadling draft.

It must be remembered that the threading of the tabby harness is always the same regardless of the number of changes in a pattern.

Figure 491 shows a double woven counterpane that came originally from the State of New York. The name is unknown to the author.

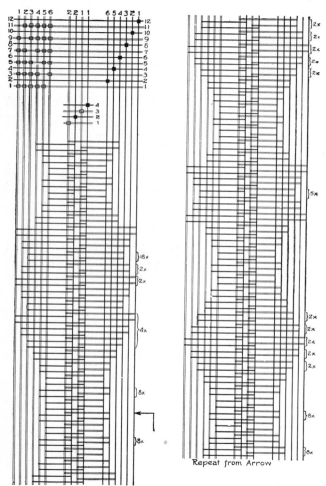

Fig. 500—Draft for Treadling (See Fig. 501)

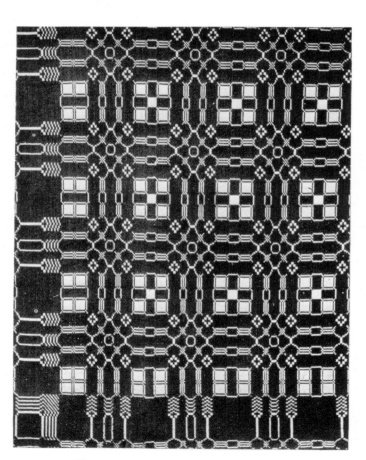

Fig. 501—Counterpane in Blue and White

Fig. 502—Pattern and Analysis of Counterpane Shown in Fig. 496

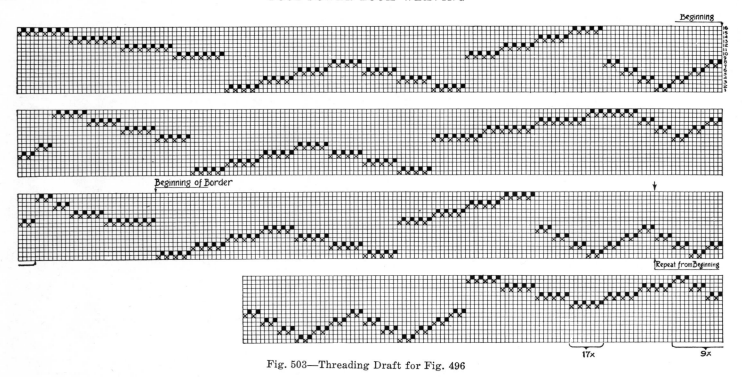

Fig. 503—Threading Draft for Fig. 496

The pattern threading draft, Fig. 489, shows five changes. Attention is again called to the threading of the pattern which is threaded from the place marked "beginning" to the arrow.

The part of the draft which follows the arrow is the border.

To find the number of threads necessary for any particular draft, count the threads in a repeat and then multiply by the number of times the pattern is to be repeated. The border is threaded but once. Forty threads are usually used to the inch, twenty blue and twenty white. A number twenty reed is used, a blue and a white thread

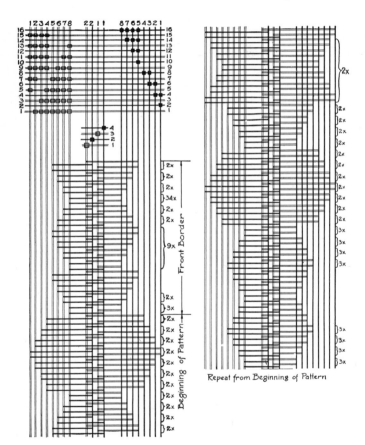

Fig. 504—Treadling Draft for Counterpane

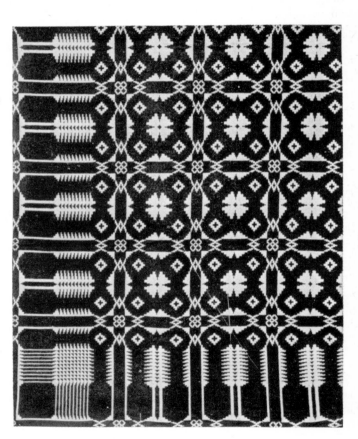

Fig. 505—Counterpane

drawn through each dent.   Each pattern is written so that two strips may be sewed together, the seam coming through the center of the unit.

It must be remembered that the two harness plan of weaving the double counterpanes is the same as threading two distinct looms.   The pattern draft is threaded through the small eyes.   These pattern threads after being drawn through the small eyes are all again threaded through the long eyes of the tabby harness, which hangs directly behind the batten or beater, as it is sometimes called.

Figure 490 gives a detailed treadling draft which when accurately followed produces the finished pattern shown in Fig. 491.

Figure 492 shows a finished counterpane into which a third color has been introduced.   The prevailing background is blue, the small squares are of green and the centers and border are of white.

When reeling the warp for three color weaving, care must be taken that the green and blue are reeled together to produce the green squares on a blue background.   If the green squares are to appear on a white background the white and green must be reeled together.

The pattern threading draft for Fig. 492 is given in Fig. 493.   No draft is given for the tabby because of the fact that it is always the same for all patterns.   The threading is the same as for the plain double weave; namely, 4, 3, 2, 1.

Figure 494 gives a detailed treadling draft for the draft Fig. 493.

Fig. 495 gives another five change pattern in which a third color is introduced.   In this case the small squares are of a madder red.   If the red squares are to appear on a white background the red is warped with the white.   In this particular pattern the red squares appear on a blue background, so the red is warped with the blue.

In the threading and treadling drafts a slight variation has been made from the pattern given in Fig. 495. Instead of giving the border as shown in 495 a pine tree border has been substituted.

If the weaver will carefully follow the threading draft shown in Fig. 497 and the treadling draft shown in Fig. 496 the pattern shown in 495 will be produced with a pine tree border.   All the patterns in this chapter are for counterpanes and are written in such a way that the two strips necessary for a counterpane may be sewed together.

Figure 498 shows a pattern in which six changes appear.   The detailed analysis is given by drawing the vertical and horizontal lines indicating the changes.   The number of threads in each change is placed in its proper place, directly below the spots in the pattern.

The threading pattern fully written out is shown in Fig. 499.

If the single harness plan of weaving were used in this particular pattern it would require a harness of 24 heddles. By using the double harness plan, however, only sixteen harnesses are required, twelve for the pattern and four for the tabby.

Figure 501 shows the completed counterpane in two colors, blue and white.

Figure 502 shows an interesting pattern in which eight changes appear. The entire analysis is given to aid in understanding the writing of the pattern draft.

To weave this pattern, using the single harness, would require a harness of 32 heddles. By using the double harness only 20 heddles are necessary, 16 for the pattern and 4 for the tabby.

Figure 503 shows the pattern threading draft. Fig. 504 gives the treadling draft and Fig. 505 shows the complete pattern and border in a counterpane.

CHAPTER X
Textiles and Wood

Applications to Furniture

Heretofore very little has been done in the combination of hand-woven textiles and wood, yet there is no combination of materials that gives such a large variety of artistic effects as this one. The different ways in which this material may be used, in combination with wood, are too numerous to mention; therefore, we shall take only those simple problems which are within the capabilities of even a sixth, seventh, or eighth-grade boy.

Foot Stool

The first problem that we suggest is that of a small foot stool, upholstered in hand-woven material. Fig. 506 shows the working drawing of a unique, but simple, little foot stool showing the wide possibilities for individual design. Here is a problem that a whole class may construct, and no two made alike. We have given a few suggestions as to how the design of the legs of the stool may be altered or enlarged upon. The size of the stool itself may be changed with pleasing results by making it longer, lower, or narrower, so that there are any number of ways of changing the design of this stool without losing any of its artistic qualities. It is a most flexible problem.

After the stool is constructed, upholster it with a piece of hand-woven material. This may be either woven by the boy himself or by the girls in the weaving class of the school. Here again are more possibilities for making each piece individual, since each piece of material may be of a different pattern, yet all may be woven from the same threading on the same loom.

Hand woven material might be used to upholster a great variety of household furniture with most pleasing and beautiful results. A little touch of hand-woven material gives to any article upon which it is used a most subtle appearance.

Figure 507 shows the completed stool made from the working drawing shown in Fig. 506. The design used for weaving the material is one of the adaptations of the Rose Path pattern.

Waste Basket

Figure 509 shows the working drawing of a very simple waste basket that any sixth-grade boy could build without much difficulty. The only difficulty is in boring the holes at the proper angle.

Two pieces of cloth are woven the length of two sides and the bottom. Hems are sewed at both ends so that

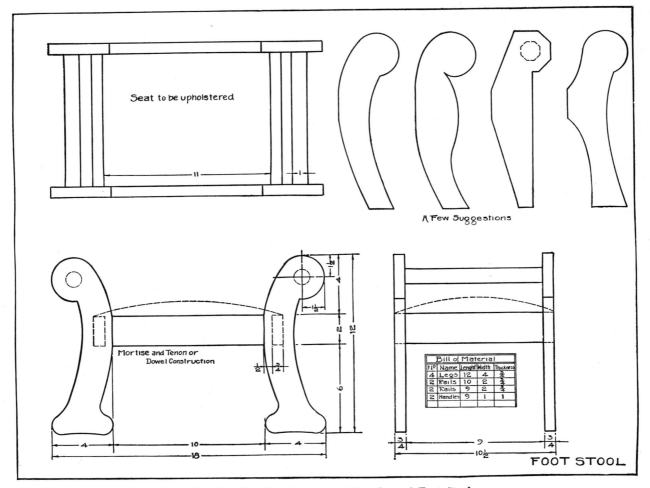

Fig. 506—Working Drawing of Upholstered Foot Stool

Fig. 508—Finished Waste Basket

when the dowel rods are placed through the hems and then put in place, the cloth will hold the basket together. It is necessary to have the cloth stretched very tightly in order to have the basket rigid.

Figure 508 shows the finished waste basket. The border around the top of the cloth is woven with the Rose Path pattern.

If the tapering of the sides of the waste basket seems too difficult, a straight sided sewing basket may be constructed as shown in Fig. 510. The construction is the same as for the waste basket. The design of the hand-woven cloth used on the sewing basket shows another possibility of the Rose Path pattern.

Screens

There is no article of furniture in which hand-woven cloth may be used so effectively as a screen. Fig. 511 shows the working drawing of a screen in which the panels are of hand-woven material.

The inner sides of each frame are grooved the same as for a wooden panel; a key is made to fit loosely into this groove. The cloth is placed over the groove, the key placed on top the cloth over the grooves, and then forced down

Fig. 507—Finished Foot Stool

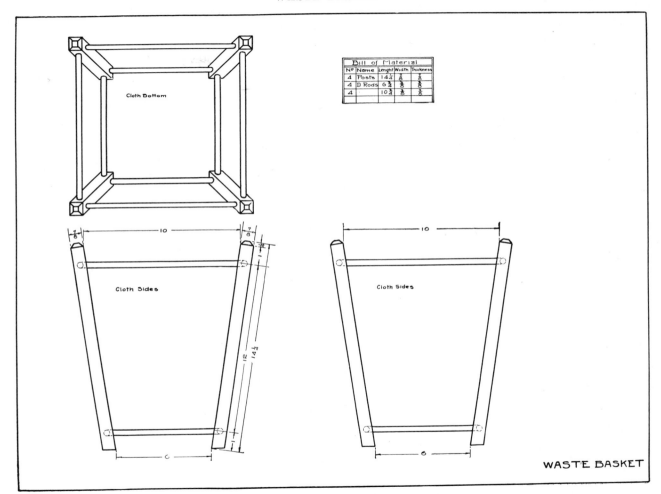

Fig. 509—Working Drawing of Waste Basket

into it. This makes a very good way of fastening the cloth to the frames. A few finishing nails may be driven through the key into the frame to hold the key in place.

That this combination makes a beautiful as well as useful piece of furniture may be seen from the photograph shown in Fig. 512. The cloth is woven from the Orange Peel pattern, a border being woven at the top and bottom to break up the space.

Though the construction of this screen is simple, it should be made as a group problem rather than an individual one; the boys to make the frame, and the girls to weave the cloth.

Figure 513 shows the working drawing of another very attractive screen of different construction from the first one mentioned. In this screen build the inside frames as shown, of any lumber, then cover both front and back with the cloth, tacking it along the outside edges of the frames. Make the grooved strips as shown, and tack them on the outside edges of the frame, covering up the edges upon which the cloth has been tacked. This gives a very neat and effective finish to the screen, since all of the frame that shows is the little grooved moulding on the outside edges.

Figure 514 shows how attractive this kind of a screen can be made to look by just using strips of hand-woven cloth, embroidered with rope silk. Observe how beautifully the panels are broken by skillful designing.

Fig. 510—Finished Sewing Basket

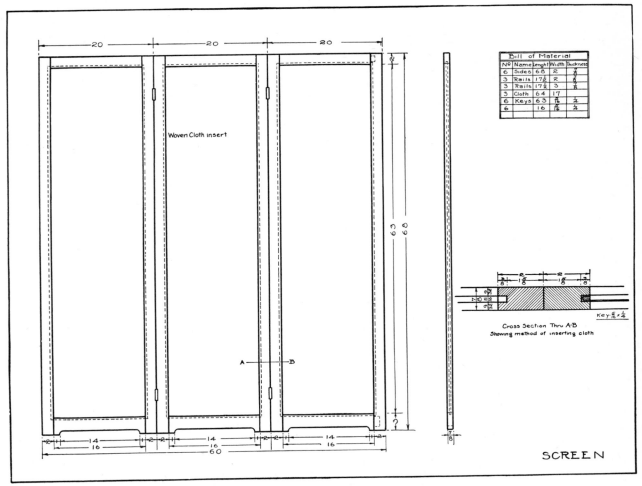

Fig. 511—Working Drawing of Screen

Fig. 512—Finished Screen

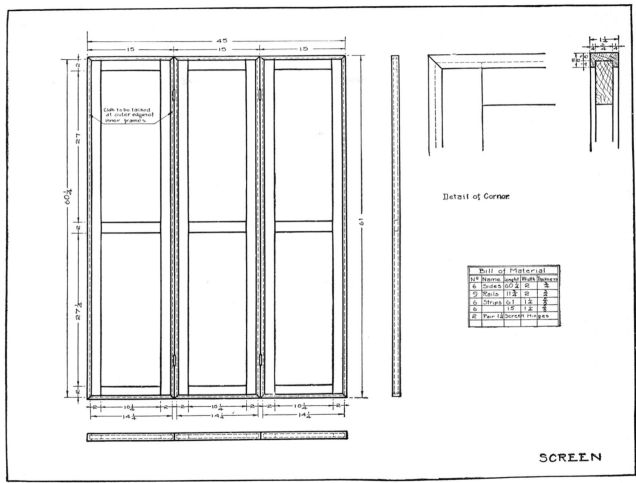

Fig. 513—Working Drawing of Screen

Fig. 514—Finished Screen

CHAPTER XI

The Design and Construction of Looms

Danish Loom

The following cuts show the working drawings for both the Danish and Swedish looms. If light work only is desired then the Danish loom shown in Fig. 515 is the loom to construct. Fig. 516 shows the front working drawing. Fig. 517 shows the side and Fig. 518 shows the detail drawings of the various parts.

Swedish Loom

Figure 519 shows the completed Swedish loom. If space is available this is the loom to have. On this loom may be woven very fine articles as well as the Colonial rugs. On the Danish loom only the lighter work can be successfully woven. Fig. 520 shows the working drawing for the front of Sweedish loom. Fig. 521 shows the side, and Fig. 522 shows the detail drawings of the beater, warp beam, heddle sticks and other movable parts.

Fly Shuttle

The detailed drawing, Fig. 523, is that of a fly-shuttle loom. The batten or beater of any loom may be made into that of a fly-shuttle.

The fly-shuttle arrangement is especially practical in the weaving of materials that require but one shuttle. The necessary materials may be purchased of R. R. Street, 543 West Washington street, Chicago.

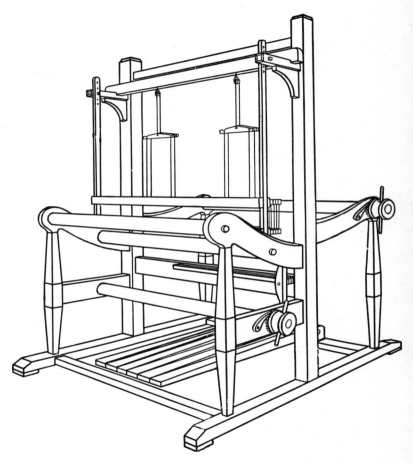

Fig. 515—Sketch of Danish Loom

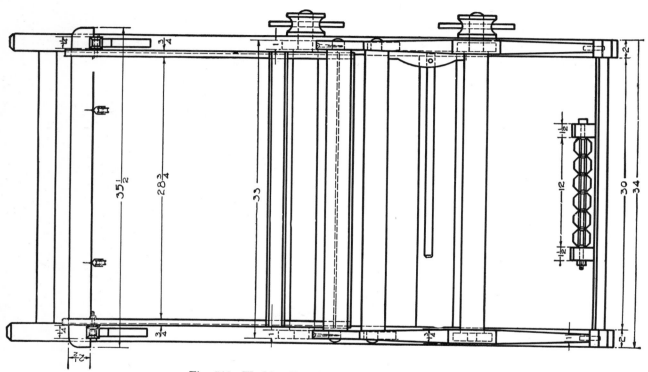

Fig. 516—Working Drawing of Loom—Front View

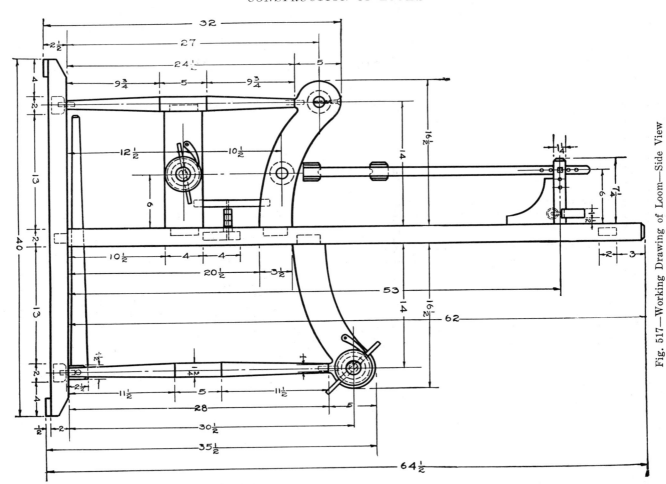

Fig. 517—Working Drawing of Loom—Side View

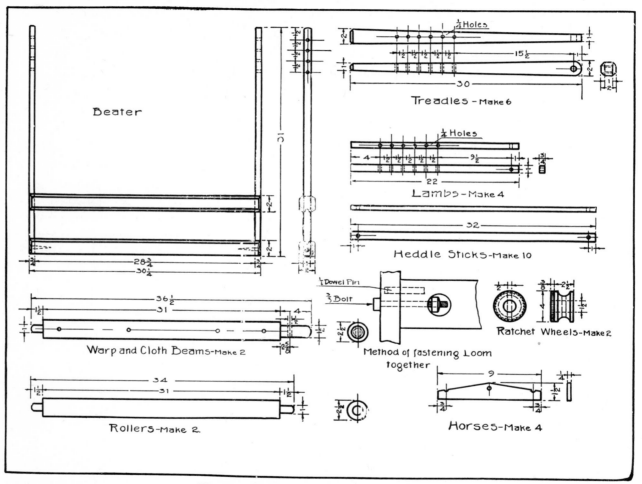

Fig. 518—Working Drawing of Loom—Details

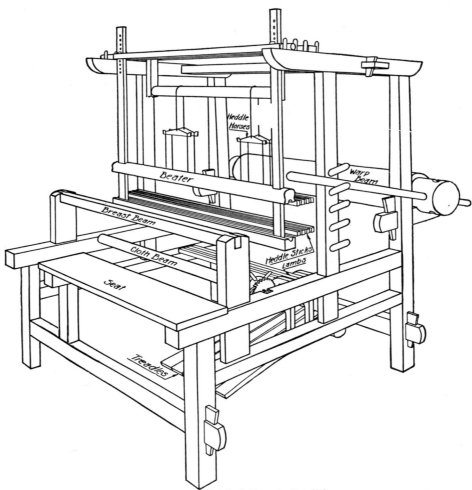

Fig. 519—Finished Loom—Swedish

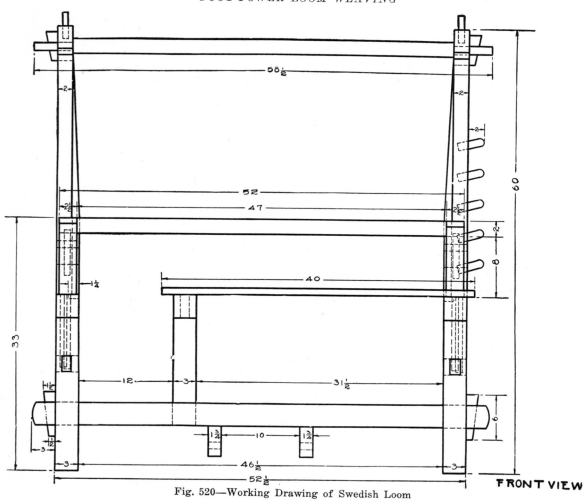

Fig. 520—Working Drawing of Swedish Loom

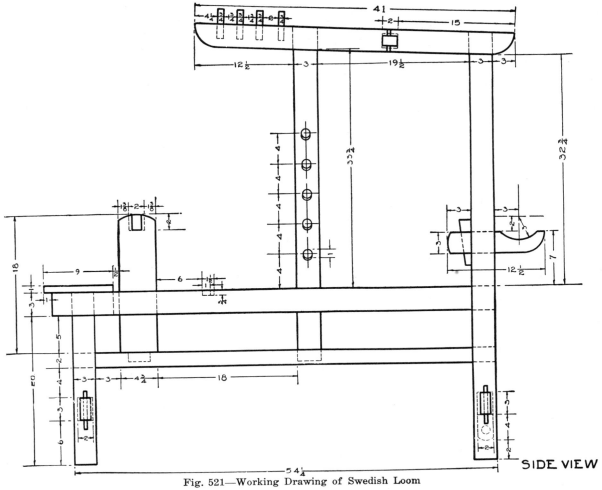

Fig. 521—Working Drawing of Swedish Loom

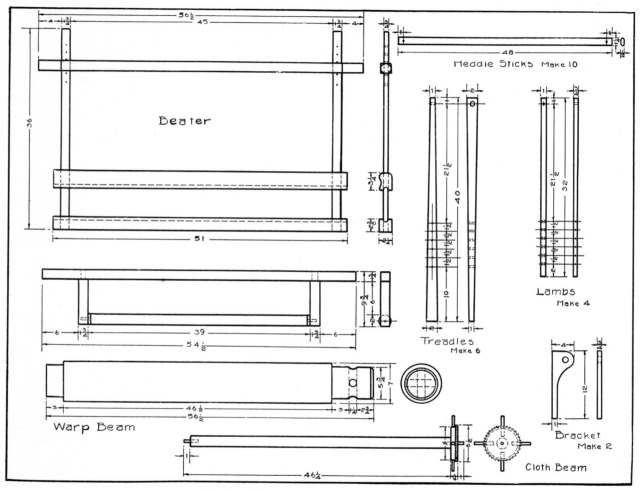

Fig. 522—Working Drawing of Swedish Loom—Details

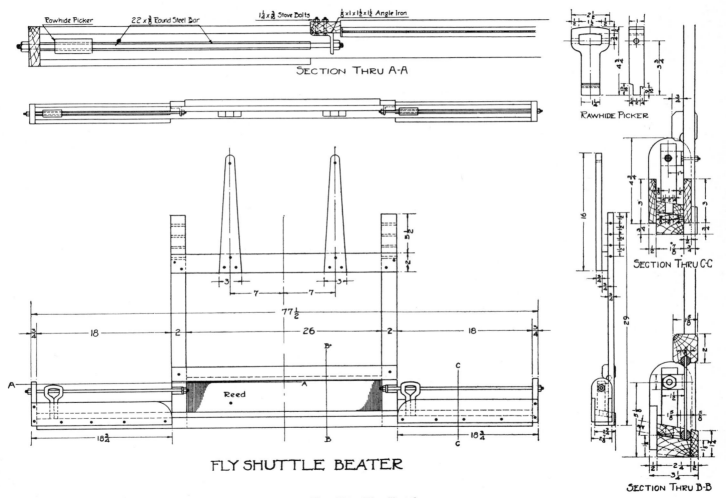

SECTION THRU A-A

FLY SHUTTLE BEATER

Fig. 523—Fly Shuttle

CHAPTER XII

Dyes and Dyeing

When we come to the coloring of materials to be used in textile work, a field is entered that has been only partially explored.

It is true that vegetable dyes may be duller and that they do not run through such a lengthy, diverse, and brilliant gamut as the various branches of aniline. But, they are apt to be more permanent and they are so softened by the mellowing touch of time, that they gain, with age, an exquisite combinaton of color values which is altogether inimitable.

It is claimed that the Shah of Persia punishes with death, the man who brings aniline dyes into his kingdom. Vegetable dyeing is a fascinating part of textile work. When one is interested he is led to make many new discoveries.

Utensils Used

Copper kettles are the best and when possible should be used in vegetable dyeing. Tin is good for bright colors but is affected by acids. Iron is good for certain plants but is very hard to keep clean. Brass may be used but is not so good as any of the other above named utensils. Enameled ware may be used but should never be used for food purposes after dyeing.

Cleaning of Utensils

The untinned copper kettles are best cleaned with fine sand and a little sulphuric acid. Vinegar or sour milk may also be used.

Washing of Wool

All materials to be dyed must be thoroughly clean.

Wool is usually washed but very little before spinning. To obtain the best results the skeins of yarn must not be too thick. Ordinarily 80 grams in weight to the hank is quite sufficient. The finer the yarn, however, the less there should be to the hank. It must be remembered that to obtain definite results care must be taken to weigh all materials to be dyed and to hold to definite measurements.

Water Used in Washing

Rain water is the best for washing purposes. All newly spun and unwashed wool must be washed three times in lukewarm water.

The first washing is done in eight parts of water containing 200 gr. of soda.

The second washing is done in 10 parts of water to 100 gr. of soda and 200 grams of good soap equal in quality to Ivory soap.

The third washing is done in 10 parts of water and 110 grams of soap only.

Care should be taken not to wash too large a quantity of wool at one time. From 2 to 5 kilograms in the bath at one time is quite sufficient.

If the wool is very dirty wash it in two solutions of soda and water and then proceed as above directed.

The washed material is first rinsed in lukewarm water and then in several cold waters.

Mordant

All material is mordanted before dyeing. Sometimes the mordant is placed in the dye itself but more often the material itself is mordanted before placing in the dye. Alum is a useful mordant for most vegetable dyes. When alum is used it must be boiled in order to become thoroughly dissolved. All goods must be wet before entering the mordant.

If vitriols are used in mordanting they must be placed in lukewarm water only. Mordant materials from one to two hours.

When mordanting the material should be well covered with water.

Formulae for Dyeing

The following recipes have been successfully tried out and are offered to those who are interested enough to not only use what is here suggested but to make further investigation in the broad field of vegetable dyes.

Yellows

1. *Wax Yellow*

   Yarn ....250 gr.
   Alum (mordant)...... 32 gr.
   Fresh bayberry leaves..500 gr.

   Mordant before dyeing, boil the leaves one hour, drain, add material and boil one hour.

2. *Greenish Yellow*

   Yarn ....250 gr.
   Alum (mordant)...... 35 gr.
   Fresh wild parsley..... 1 kg.

   Boil the parsley one hour, drain, add the alum, stir well until alum has dissolved. Boil material in solution from ½ to 1 hr.

3. *Greenish Yellow*

   Yarn ....250 gr.
   Alum (mordant)...... 32 gr.
   Fresh alder........... 1 kg.

   Mordant the material first. Boil the leaves 1 hr., drain, add mordanted material and boil ½ to 1 hr.

4. *Strong Greenish Yellow*

   Yarn ....250 gr.
   Alum (mordant)...... 40 gr.
   Bayberry leaves.......500 gr.

Mordant the material first. Boil the fresh leaves 2 hr., drain and add mordanted yarn, boil from 1 to 2 hr., according to darkness of color desired.

5. *Greenish Yellow*

Yarn ....250 gr.
Alum (mordant)...... 32 gr.
Dry birch leaves.......500 gr.

Soak the leaves the day before using.

Boil the soaked leaves for one hour and stain. Add the alum to this solution and boil yarn in it from ½ to 1 hr.

If the yarn is dried without rinsing and then placed in a weak birch ash lye, the color becomes a reddish yellow.

6. *Reddish Yellow*

Yarn ....250 gr.
Alum (mordant)...... 40 gr.
Dry Apple bark........250 gr.

The material is first mordanted in the alum water.

Cut the bark into small pieces and soak the day before using. It is then boiled two hours and strained.

Boil the mordanted yarn in the bark liquid from ½ to 1 hr.

By using more bark and boiling longer a darker yellow is obtained.

This color fades a little if it is not very dark.

7. *Gray Yellow*

Yarn ....250 gr.
Alum (mordant)...... 40 gr.
Kinnikinnic .... 1 kg.

Chop the kinnikinnic fine and boil for 3 hr. Drain and boil the mordanted material in the liquid from ½ to **1 hr.**

8. *Brownish Yellow*

Yarn ....250 gr.
Alum (Mordant)...... 32 gr.
Alder bark............ 2 kg.

Mordant the yarn in the usual way. Chop the alder bark fine, and soak the day before using. Boil from 2 to 3 hr., drain and boil the yarn in the liquid 1 hr. or longer according to the depth of color desired.

Reds

9. *Dark Red*

Yarn ....250 gr.
Cream of tartar....... 16 gr. ⎫
Alum .... 65 gr. ⎬ Mordant
Madder ....250 gr. ⎭

Mordant the yarn for two hours and let it remain in the liquid till cool, then rinse in lukewarm water.

The yarn may be allowed to dry after removing from

the mordant; then it is rinsed in warm water before it is put in the madder liquid.

The madder is put to soak the day before it is to be used in enough cold water to make a very thin solution.

If there are hard lumps they must be rubbed apart in order to thoroughly soak. When ready to dye the soaked madder mass is put in clean cold water and when luke-warm the mordanted yarn is added.

This is heated slowly to 60 degrees or 70 degrees Centi-grade, or hot enough to burn one's fingers. Stir the yarn constantly and keep the solution at the same temperature as long as the yarn is in it. It *must not boil*. If the yarn is not stirred it becomes spotted as that part of the madder liquid that heats the quickest gives a stronger color than the other. The red coloring matter in the madder dissolves without boiling, but with boiling the other ingredients in the madder are also dissolved and these cause the red color to lose its brightness and change it to brown. When the yarn has been in the madder liquid for the required time it is allowed to remain in the solution until cool. Keep stirring until cool.

It is then rinsed and washed in several waters to remove the loose madder.

When the yarn is allowed to dry after being mor-danted, the red color becomes a little darker. All dark madder colors are absolutely fast. The lighter ones fade a little as the years go by.

10. *Medium Madder Red*

Yarn ....250 gr.
Cream of tartar....... 16 gr. }
Alum .... 40 gr. } Mordant
Madder ....175 gr.

Treat the same as No. 9.

11. *Light Madder*

Yarn ....250 gr.
Alum (mordant)...... 40 gr.
Madder ....125 gr.

Mordant the yarn one hour and keep it in the warm color liquid from ½ to 1 hr.

12. *Light Yellowish Red*

Yarn ....250 gr.
Alum (mordant)...... 40 gr.
Madder .... 75 gr.

Mordant as in No. 11 but keep the yarn in the color liquid only ½ hr.

13. *Pale Red*

Yarn ....250 gr.
Alum (mordant)...... 32 gr.
Madder .... 25 gr.

Treat as in No. 12.

14. *Rose Red*

Yarn ....250 gr.

Alum (mordant)...... 40 gr.

Madder .... 50 gr.

Mordant the yarn as usual; when cool wrap the wet material in a cloth so it does not dry out. Allow it to lie in this way from 6 to 8 days. It is then treated with madder as above mentioned.

The yarn should be squeezed in a little lukewarm water before putting it in the color liquid.

15. *Terra Cotta*

Yarn ....250 gr.

Cream of tartar....... 16 gr. ⎫

Alum .... 48 gr. ⎬ Mordant

Madder ....125 gr. ⎭

Oak Gall .... 13 gr.

Mordant the yarn as usual.

When the madder liquid is lukewarm add the yarn and heat slowly, allow it to boil ½ hr. Remove the yarn and to the liquid add the finely powdered oak galls.

The yarn is again placed in the color liquid and boiled for ½ hr., when it is removed and allowed to dry.

If more color is used the yarn will be darker, and if from 3 to 10 gr. of iron vitriol is added it becomes browner.

How to Add Vitriol: When this vitriol is to be added, the yarn is first removed and the vitriol is allowed to melt in the boiling liquid. This is cooled by adding a little cold water. The yarn is now returned and boiled for a few minutes, then it is removed, cooled and rinsed.

The lighter madder color may be had by coloring the mordanted yarn in the cool liquid left in No. 9, 10 or 11. These colors are somewhat more of a yellowish color than when fresh madder is used.

By using stronger or weaker mordants and more or less madder many colors not mentioned in these recipes may be made.

It must always be remembered that a strong mordant is used when a dark color is desired.

16. *Cardinal*

Yarn ....250 gr.

Tin .... 4 gr. ⎫

Nitric acid .... 50 gr. ⎬ Mordant

Water ....150 to 200 gr. ⎭

Cream of tartar....... 50 gr.

Cochineal ....100 gr.

The cream of tartar and the cochineal are soaked. When the water for the coloring is boiling, add the cochineal and cream of tartar and boil for ten minutes. Keep the liquid well skimmed. After the scum has been removed add the yellowish solution of tin, water, and acid and stir well. Put in the dry yarn, turning it quickly around and later more slowly. Boil from 1 to 1½ hr., according to darkness of color desired. Remove, cool, and dry.

17. *Purple Red*

Yarn ....250 gr.

Tin .... 4 gr. ⎫

Nitric acid .... 25 gr. ⎬ Mordant

Water ....75 to 100 gr. ⎭

```
Cream of tartar....... 50 gr.
Cochineal ........... 50 gr.
```
Treat the same as in No. 16.

18. *Bright Red*

```
Yarn ................250 gr.
Tin ................. 8 gr.  ⎫
Nitric acid .......... 50 gr. ⎬ Mordant
Water ........150 to 200 gr. ⎭
Cream of tartar....... 50 gr.
Cochineal ........... 25 gr.
```

When the water for the coloring comes to a boil, put in the cream of tartar and let it dissolve; add the cochineal. Boil for 10 minutes, keeping the scum skimmed from the surface of the boiling mixture.

Add the yellowish tin solution as in No. 17 and put the dry yarn into the boiling mixture, turning it quickly around and later a little more slowly.   Boil 1 hr.

19. *Flag Color*

```
Yarn ................250 gr.
Tin ................. 8 gr.  ⎫
Nitric acid .......... 50 gr. ⎬ Mordant
Water ........150 to 200 gr. ⎭
Cream of tartar....... 50 gr.
Cochineal ........... 50 gr.
```
Treat the same as in No. 18.

20. *Dark Carmine.*

```
Yarn ................250 gr.
Cream of tartar....... 16 gr. ⎫
Alum ................ 8 gr. ⎬ Mordant
Cochineal ........... 16 gr. ⎭
```
Mordant the yarn for 2 hrs. and cool. Put the powdered and soaked cochineal in fresh water and boil for 15 minutes.

Add the yarn and boil for 2 hrs., after which it is ready to be taken out and dried.

21. *Carmine*

```
Yarn ................250 gr.
Alum (mordant)...... 40 gr.
```
Mordant the yarn as usual.

Boil the yarn for ½ hr. in the solution left from 16 or 17.   The color becomes lighter after the use of No. 17 than after No. 16.

22. *Light Carmine*

```
Yarn ................250 gr.
Alum ................ 32 gr. ⎫
Cream of tartar....... 32 gr. ⎬ Mordant
Starch ............. 32 gr. ⎭
Cochineal ........... 15 gr.
Cream of tartar....... 6 gr.
```
Mordant the yarn 1 hr.

The starch must be mixed with a little cold water before it is added to the mordant.

Boil the soaked cochineal and cream of tartar in fresh water for 15 minutes.

The mordanted yarn is boiled in this from ½ to 1 hr.

23. *Dull Carmine*

Yarn	250 gr.
Alum	50 gr.
Cream of tartar	32 gr.
Cochineal	25 gr.
Madder	20 gr.
Starch	13 gr.

(Alum, Cream of tartar) } Mordant

Mordant as usual.

Soak the cochineal and the madder together and boil for 10 minutes.

Dissolve the starch in cold water and put it in before the yarn is added to the cold solution. Boil from ½ to 1 hr.

24. *Rose Red*

Yarn	250 gr.
Alum (mordant)	32 gr.

Boil ½ hr. in mordant.

Boil ½ hr. in solution left from 17. If the color is to be of a light shade double the amount of yarn, or throw away half the color solution and add clear water.

25. *Salmon Red*

Yarn	250 gr.

The dry unmordanted yarn is boiled from ¼ to ½ hr. in the solution left from No. 18 or No. 19. If more yarn is taken the color becomes lighter; it is also lighter when using No. 18 than when using No. 19.

26. *Red from Brazil Wood*

Yarn	250 gr.
Alum	40 gr.
Cream of tartar	16 gr.
Madder	40 gr.
Brazil Wood	40 gr.
Potash	7 gr.

(Alum, Cream of tartar) } Mordant

Mordant as usual, after which the yarn is placed in the madder solution described in No. 9 and allowed to remain 1 hr. The Brazil wood which has been soaked is placed in a bag and this is boiled in clean water ½ hr. The bag is now removed and the madder colored yarn is then boiled in the solution from ½ to 1 hr. Let it lie in the solution till cooled a little. Then it is taken out and the potash, which has been well dissolved, is added to the solution and the yarn is put in again and left for 10 or 15 minutes. Allow the yarn to remain in the solution till cool, and then wash in strong soap suds. This is an inexpensive red blue color but it is not so pretty as the Salmon Red.

27. *Red*

Yarn	250 gr.
Alum	40 gr.
Cream of tartar	16 gr.
Bed straw roots	250 gr.

(Alum, Cream of tartar) } Mordant

Mordant the yarn from 1 to 2 hrs.

The dry roots are ground or chopped fine and put to soak.

During the dyeing the yarn is treated the same as was described in No. 9 for madder coloring, except that the yarn is boiled a little toward the end.

28. *Dark Red*

      Yarn ....250 gr.
      Ground pine (mordant).250 gr.
      Madder or bed straw...250 gr.

Mordant the yarn in ground pine in the following way:

The ground pine is chopped fine and soaked in as much water as is needed for the dyeing. This mixture is heated every day and must remain in a warm place where it can be kept lukewarm. After 3 or 4 days it acquires a sour smell. Boil well and strain. As it boils, add a little water. In this strained solution put the wet yarn and heat every day for three or four days and let it stand in a warm place. The last day boil well.

The yarn will then have a light yellowish, green gray color and a sour smell.

The yarn is now rinsed and allowed to dry before it is colored red.

The madder is prepared as described in No. 9. Before the yarn is put into the red dye it must be well squeezed in warm water.

The Preparation of Olium

The Norwegians succeed in getting most beautiful shades of blue through the use of what they call Olium. This is made in the following way:

Indigo is dissolved with sulphuric acid by mixing 15 gr. powdered indigo with 125 gr. of smoking sulphuric acid. Put about 10 gr. of sulphuric acid and a little indigo—say 2gr.—in a glass jar or bottle with a well fitting stopper. Stir this till it is smooth with a glass rod, or a hardwood stick. Metal must not be used. After this, put a little of each into the jar and stir, and so continue until all has been used. Stopper the bottle firmly, allow the mixture to stand at least 24 hours before using.

When using, weigh or measure the Olium in a dry glass and pour carefully into cold water before placing in the dye. *Never* pour water into the Olium, as it effervesces and may injure the eyes. When the Olium is kept in an air tight bottle, it may be kept for a long time.

All the recipes for blue which follow, are based on Olium measured in a graduated glass. If weighed, take double as many grams. If the sulphuric acid is poor, the indigo will not dissolve, and the color will run. To prove that the indigo is well dissolved, take a few drops of the Olium, mix with water, and strain through a filtering paper. If the filtered dye is still blue, then the indigo has been properly dissolved, but if not, the dye will be white or light blue.

When Olium is to be used in dyeing, it should be measured or weighed in a dry glass, as before described, and dropped or poured slowly into the lukewarm water and well stirred.

If the color is too light, more Olium may be added, but some of the boiling dye liquid must be thrown away, and the remainder mixed with cold water before the Olium is added. If the liquid is too warm, when the goods is put in, it becomes streaked or clouded, even though it has been dyed previously. As soon as the yarn has been boiled in the dye, it will be seen whether it is too light as by that time all dye will have been drawn into the goods. If in the heating, it is getting too dark, a part of the liquid is thrown out and the remainder lightened with water before continuing the dyeing. When dyeing with Olium, the liquid must only be lukewarm when the goods is put in and it must be quickly stirred and kept in constant motion until it boils.

By using more or less Olium, many color shades and tints in blue may be obtained from the following recipes.

Blue Dyes

29. *Dark Soldier Blue*

> Yarn ....250 gr.
> Alum (mordant)...... 50 gr.
> Olium ....20 to 30 gr.

The yarn is mordanted as usual, and is then dyed red in the used liquid remaining after dyeing cochineal red. Dry the yarn. Add 10 gr. Olium to clear lukewarm water, and stir well. Add the red dyed yarn which has first been dipped in warm water, and heat, stirring constantly. Boil

for ½ hr. and dry. When dry, it is again wrung in warm water so that it becomes thoroughly wet. To the new lukewarm water, is added 10 gr. Olium and the yarn is again dyed as at first. Boil 1 hr. and dry. If one desires the yarn still darker, the dyeing must be repeated with 10 gr. Olium. When the dyeing is completed, it must be dried before washing.

If there is no red liquid which has been used, the yarn must be mordanted as No. 21, and a dye liquid made of cochineal (10 to 15 gr.) For the rest, handle as above.

The darker the blue that is wanted, the darker must be the red of the under dye, with a corresponding amount of Olium added.

30. *Light Soldier Blue*

> Yarn ....250 gr.
> Alum .... 75 gr. ⎫
> Olium .... 15 gr. ⎬ Mordant
> Madder .... 5 gr. ⎭
> Olium .... 10 gr.

The yarn is mordanted as usual. Fresh water is added to the soaked madder, and in this the yarn is dyed red as in No. 23, and then dried.

The Olium is added to lukewarm water and well stirred. The red dyed yarn is added. (The yarn must first be wrung out of warm water.) It is then heated slowly, stirred constantly and boiled 1 hr. Handle as above.

It may also be dyed red in *used* madder liquid.

31. *Greenish Blue*

             Yarn ....250 gr.
             Alum (mordant)...... 40 gr.
             Olium .... 8 gr.

When the yarn has been mordanted, it is dyed light yellow in one of the used yellow dye liquids. It is then wrung out of this and dyed blue as above. If a paler dye is wanted, add 5 gr. of iron sulphate after it has been dyed blue, and boil 10 to 15 minutes. It may now be washed without first drying.

Goods dyed with iron sulphate must be left well covered by the dye until cool, unless they are constantly stirred in the dye. This liquid forms a crust on the surface in the cooling which spots the goods or yarn near the surface.

32. *Dull Medium Blue*

             Olium .... 8 gr.
             Alum (mordant)...... 40 gr.
             Madder .... 15 gr.

The yarn is mordanted as usual. Some of the mordant water is thrown away and enough cold water is added to make the liquid lukewarm. Add the Olium, stir well, put in the yarn and heat slowly, stirring constantly.

Boil ½ hr. and take out. Add enough cold water to the liquid to make it lukewarm and add the dissolved madder and stir well. Add the yarn and heat slowly, stirring constantly and evenly. Boil ½ hr., then cool, rinse and wash.

33. *Bright Medium Blue*

             Yarn ....250 gr.
             Alum (mordant)...... 40 gr.
             Olium .... 5 gr.

The yarn is mordanted and dyed as above. When it is thoroughly boiling in the dye liquid the yarn is cooled, rinsed and washed.

34. *Light Blue*

             Yarn ....250 gr.
             Alum (mordant)...... 30 gr.

Handle the same as above.

35. *Water Blue*

             Yarn ....250 gr.
             Alum (mordant)...... 30 gr.
             Olium ....5 to 10 drops

Handle as above.

The lighter colors with Olium are not absolutely fast. They become slightly greenish after being used and cannot be washed in soda water.

36. *Dark Blue with Ground Pine*

             Yarn ....250 gr.
             Ground pine ....250 gr.
             Logwood ....100 gr.

The ground pine is chopped fine and soaked in as much water as is needed for the dyeing. The whole is heated daily and is placed where it can be kept lukewarm. When after three or four days it has acquired a sourish odor, it should be well boiled and strained. The water will diminish in the boiling, therefore sufficient water must be added so that there is enough for dyeing. When the ground pine has been strained, the wet yarn is placed in the liquid and heated every day for three or four days and kept in a warm place. The last day it is boiled; the yarn should then have a light, yellowish, green gray color and a sour odor.

The logwood, which was put to soak the day before, is placed in a bag and boiled in clear water 1 hr. and then removed. The yarn is now wrung out of the ground pine liquid and boiled in the logwood liquid ½ to 1 hr. It is then taken out and dried. When dry, place it for several hours in a weak birch ash lye and wash. The lye is made by putting the ashes in warm water.

With more logwood, a darker color is obtained.

This color is fast for covers, but should not be used for finer covers or rugs. In time it becomes slightly grayish in color.

37. *Dark Blue with Chickweed*

Yarn ....250 gr.
Fresh chickweed....... 1 pail
Alum (mordant)...... 32 gr.
Logwood .... 50 gr.

The chickweed is boiled 1 hr. and drained. The alum is added to the liquid, and well stirred. The wet unmordanted yarn is taken, and added to the liquid and boiled 1 hr. and taken out. A small bag filled with the soaked logwood is boiled in the liquid ½ hr.

Add the yarn and let it boil 1 hr. with the logwood bag.

Allow the yarn to remain in the liquid until cold.

If a darker dye is wanted, use more logwood.

Green Dyes

The pure green colors are always composed of a yellow and blue dye stuff. These are mostly made by first dyeing the goods blue, and then boiling it in a yellow dye. To obtain a dark green the blue foundation must be made dark enough the first time. No amount of boiling in the yellow dye will make the goods darker. By adding madder or iron sulphate, the green will become darker but it is another tone, gray or brownish.

Certain plants give a green dye without using blue. The yellow dye in these plants will, by the addition of an iron or copper salt, become green, but the yarn will have a shade of gray or brown.

Green with Birch Leaves

For these dyes, both fresh and dried leaves may be used. Three kg. fresh leaves make 1kg. dried leaves.

We must therefore count on using three times as much fresh leaves as dried in the dyeing. The recipes are made on the basis of dried leaves. The leaves are soaked the day before and are boiled in enough water to make the necessary dye liquid and are then strained. The boiling is done so that all dye material in the leaves may be had. After straining, the leaves are rinsed with a little clear water, and this is added to the liquid which is cooled while one is dyeing the yarn blue.

The yarn is mordanted with the amount of alum called for in the recipe.

When dyeing blue, throw out half the mordant water and add clear cold water and the proper amount of Olium.

Olium is measured in a dry graduated glass, or is dropped (counting the drops) carefully into the water which has been heated to about 20° C, and is well stirred. The wet, well wrung yarn, already mordanted, is placed immediately in the lukewarm blue liquid. It is stirred and turned quickly around with a stick. This is kept up constantly while the liquid is slowly boiling. By that time, all the dye-stuff will have been absorbed by the yarn and it may be left to boil slowly ½ hr.

Unless one is exceedingly careful in the blue dyeing, the yarn becomes clouded and this cannot be corrected later, but becomes more noticeable when dyed green.

When the yarn has been dyed, it is cooled in the liquid before it is taken out. It is then well wrung, put again on the stick and placed in the milk-warm, (about 30° C,) birch-leaf liquid. It is constantly turned and kept in slow motion until the liquid is boiling. The longer it is kept in the birch-leaf liquid, the stronger the green color. It should not boil more than 1 hr. If the yarn is not dark enough, due to poor leaves, it must be boiled for half an hour, in new birch-leaf dye after having been dried. It must be thoroughly wet in warm water before being placed in the new dye. The goods is allowed to lie in the dye until cold unless the color is becoming too strong. In that case, it is taken up at once and cooled. The color is intensified by having the material lie in the warm dye until it is cold.

If there are to be several dyes in green, these can well be boiled in the same birch-leaf dye. It is necessary to calculate in advance the proper amount of leaves and to make up separately the blue dyes.

If the birch-leaf dye is to be used for after-dyeing, it must be cooled before new yarn can be placed in it.

The dull blue green dyes may also be boiled in the same birch-leaf dye that the light fresh green colors were boiled.

For the light after-dyes, add to the cooled dye 1 to 5 drops Olium, if only light colors have been boiled in it and it contains no blue.

Whenever dark dyed blue has been boiled in the birch leaf, some of the blue remains.

Yarn and cloth are handled in the same way, with the exception that wool is to be boiled slowly, while cloth is boiled quickly and kept in constant motion.

Variations of the birch-leaf dyeing are endless.

38.   *Dark Blue Green No. 1*

Yarn ....250 gr.
Alum (mordant)...... 40 gr.
Olium (blue dye)...... 5 gr.
Birch leaves .... 1 kg.

Boil in birch-leaf liquid ½ to 1 hr. according as a more or less blue-green color is desired.

39. *Dark Blue Green No. 2*

        Yarn . . . . .250 gr.
        Alum (mordant) . . . . . . 40 gr.
        Olium (blue dye) . . . . . . 3 gr.
        Birch leaves . . . . 1 kg.
Boil in birch-leaf liquid 1 hr.

40. *Medium Blue Green*

        Yarn . . . . .250 gr.
        Alum (mordant) . . . . . . 40 gr.
        Olium (blue dye) . . . . . . 2 gr.
        Birch leaves . . . . .750 gr.
Boil in birch-leaf dye 1 hr.

41. *Light Blue Green*

        Yarn . . . . .250 gr.
        Alum (mordant) . . . . . . 40 gr.
        Olium (blue dye) . . . . . . 1 gr.
        Birch leaves . . . . .500 gr.
Boil in birch-leaf dye ½ to 1 hr.

42. *Dark Strong Green*

        Yarn . . . . .250 gr.
        Alum (mordant) . . . . . . 50 gr.
        Olium (blue dye) . . . . . . 3 gr.
        Birch leaves . . . . .1½ kg.
Boil in birch-leaf dye 1 hr.

If the dye is not green enough, dry the yarn and boil again in a new strong birch-leaf dye ½ to 1 hr.

43. *Bright Medium Green*

        Yarn . . . . .250 gr.
        Alum (mordant) . . . . . . 40 gr.
        Olium (blue dye) . . . . . . 1 gr.
        Birch leaves . . . . 1 kg.
Boil in birch-leaf dye ½ to 1 hr.

44. *Light Green*

        Yarn . . . . .250 gr.
        Alum (mordant) . . . . . . 40 gr.
        Olium (blue dye) . . . . . . 1 gr.
        Birch leaves . . . . 1 kg.
Boil in birch-leaf dye ½ to 1 hr.

45. *Yellow Green*

        Yarn . . . . .250 gr.
        Alum (mordant) . . . . . . 30 gr.
        Olium (blue dye) . . . . . . 15 drops
        Birch leaves . . . . 1 kg.
Boil in birch-leaf dye ½ to 1 hr.

46. *Dull Grass Green*

        Yarn . . . . .250 gr.
        Alum (mordant) . . . . . . 40 gr.
        Olium (blue dye) . . . . . .1½ gr.
        Birch leaves . . . . 1 kg.
        Iron sulphate . . . . . . .2 to 5 gr.
Boil in birch-leaf dye 1 hr.

When the yarn has boiled in the birch-leaf dye, it is taken out of the liquid and the iron sulphate is added and stirred well. The liquid is cooled with a little cold water, the green dyed yarn put in again and is boiled, stirring constantly for 10 or 15 minutes.

The yarn must not lie in this liquid, but must be taken out as soon as boiled.

47. *Gray Green*

        Yarn ....250 gr.
        Olium (blue dye) ...... 2 gr.
        Birch leaves.......... 1 kg.
        Common madder ...... 25 gr.
        Iron sulphate vitriol ... 4 gr.

Boil in birch-leaf 1 hr. and then take out. Cool the liquid and add the 25 gr. soaked madder. Place the yarn in the cooled liquid and let it boil ¼ hr. Take it out, add the iron sulphate, cool, put in the yarn, and boil ¼ hr.

Handle as described in 46.

48. *Pale Blue Green*

        Yarn ....250 gr.
        Alum (mordant) ...... 30 gr.

The mordanted yarn is placed in the cooled after-dye of No. 50, and slowly heated to the boiling point. Boil ½ to 1 hr.

49. *Pale Yellow Green*

        Yarn ....250 gr.
        Alum (mordant) ...... 30 gr.

Boil in the same manner as suggested in No. 40, 42 and 43.

50. *Olive Green with Heather.*

        Yarn ....250 gr.
        Alum (mordant) ...... 40 gr.
        Fresh heather tops.. 1 to 2 kg.

Chop the heather and soak and then boil 4 hrs. in a polished iron kettle. When the liquid is put back, the yarn is boiled slowly 1 to 2 hrs. according to the darkness of color desired. Let it lie in the dye till cool, but it must be stirred occasionally. If the liquid is allowed to form a crust, this will spot the yarn.

51. *Gray Green with Bayberry*

        Yarn ....250 gr.
        Alum (mordant) ...... 40 gr.
        Dried bayberry leaves..500 gr.
        Iron sulphate.....10 to 20 gr.

Soak the bayberry leaves and boil 2 hrs. The mordanted yarn is boiled in the strained liquid for 1 hr. and is then taken out. Add the iron sulphate and when this is dissolved add a little cold water. Place the yellow dyed yarn in the cooled liquid, heat slowly, stirring constantly and let it boil 5 to 10 minutes. Take it out and cool.

52. *Myrtle Green*

        Yarn ....250 gr.
        Potassium chromate.... 4 gr. } Mordant
        Cream of tartar....... 4 gr.
        Mulberry wood........ 90 gr.
        Logwood .... 25 gr.

The potassium chromate and the cream of tartar are dissolved in boiling water, and enough cold water added to make the liquid lukewarm. Place the wet yarn in this and heat slowly, stir, boil one hour and let it lie in this mordant until cold. Rinse in clear water before placing in the dye. The mulberry and logwood are put to soak the day previous. They are put in a bag and boiled in clear water 2 hrs. Take out the bag and boil the wet mordanted yarn in this dye 2 hrs. If there is room in the kettle, time may be saved by boiling the yarn with the bag the last hour. If more logwood is used, the color will be darker—less logwood makes it lighter.

53. *Dark Grass Green*

        Yarn ....250 gr.
        Alum (mordant)...... 40 gr.
        Mulberry .... 80 gr.
        Olium .... 10 gr.

The mulberry wood is put to soak the day before, boiled 1 hr. and strained. In the strained liquid, dissolve the alum and when the liquid is milk warm, add the Olium. It is all well stirred. The wet mordanted yarn is put in and stirred constantly. Heat slowly and boil 1 hr. The yarn is left in the dye until cold.

54. *Olive Green*

        Yarn ....250 gr.
        Alum (mordant)...... 40 gr.
        Olium (blue dye)...... 5 gr.
        Mulberry .... 62 gr.

        Tameric Acid......... 40 gr.
        Madder .... 13 gr.
        Iron sulphate .... 3 gr.

The yarn is mordanted and dyed blue, just as is done in birch-leaf dyeing. The mulberry having been soaked, is put in a bag and boiled in clear water 1 hr.

Take out the bag and add the tameric. Boil before putting in the blue-dyed yarn, which must not be cooled too much. When it has boiled 1 hr. in the yellowish liquid, it is taken out. The dye is cooled with cold water to about 40° C., and the soaked madder is added. Put the yarn in again and slowly heat to boiling. Boil ½ hr.

Dissolve the iron sulphate and add it to the cooled liquid, after taking out the yarn. Stir well. Put yarn back and boil for ¼ to ½ hr. Take out immediately and cool.

With more madder, the color becomes browner, with less, more green. More iron sulphate makes it duller. If the madder is omitted, the color becomes a pure green.

These colors are not durable. In time they become brown or grayish.

Violet Dyes

Violet dyes are compounded of blue and red. As a rule, indigo, cochineal and madder are used. The colors made by these dye stuffs are fast when they are not too light in color.

With cochineal, the color becomes a pure violet, with more or less red according to the proportion of blue and red dye. With madder and cochineal, the color is more brownish or plum color. The depth of the color is much affected by the quality of the wool according as it is coarse or fine. The latter becomes the darker.

Light violet dyes become dull and are not satisfactory in coarse or hard cloth. The finer dye shades require soft wool.

By using different kinds of mordant, violet shades may be obtained from the blue dye in logwood.

These colors are not as pretty or fast as the others above mentioned.

Violet with Cochineal

For violet, the yarn must first be dyed blue, then red.

The yarn is done in the same manner as for green. When the yarn has been boiled in the blue dye, it is dried without rinsing.

Cochineal is powdered fine and put to soak the day before doing the red dyeing. It is then put in clear water, boiled for ten minutes and well skimmed. Lay the dry blue-dyed yarn in the boiling dye, turn it around quickly so that it gets wet, and boil, stirring constantly for the required time; then take it out and cool before washing.

If the color does not seem to be red enough, the yarn may be left in the dye until cold. This will help with colors which have a very dark blue ground. In that case, add a little more soaked cochineal and let the yarn boil longer.

If the color is redder than desired, boil the yarn a shorter time in the red dye, but not less than half an hour.

If the foundation blue color is too light, this cannot be remedied after the yarn has been in the cochineal dye.

Among the following recipes are many possibilities by varying the relation between Olium and cochineal.

55. *Dark Black Violet*
Yarn ....250 gr.
Alum (mordant)...... 50 gr.
Olium (blue dye)...... 10 gr.
Cochineal .... 50 gr.

Mordant the yarn as usual and dye blue. When dry, boil 1 hr. in cochineal dye.

56. *Dark Blue Violet*
Yarn ....250 gr.
Alum (mordant)...... 50 gr.
Olium (blue dye)...... 5 gr.
Cochineal .... 25 gr.

Handle as No. 55.

57. *Medium Blue Violet*
Yarn ....250 gr.
Alum (mordant)...... 50 gr.
Olium (blue dye)...... 3 gr.
Cochineal .... 15 gr.

Handle as above but boil ½ to 1 hr.

58. *Blue Violet*
Yarn ....250 gr.
Alum (mordant)...... 40 gr.
Olium (blue dye)...... 50 drops
Cochineal .... 5 gr.

Handle as above.

59. *Light Blue Violet*

    Yarn ....250 gr.
    Alum (mordant)...... 32 gr.

When the yarn has been mordanted, boil for ½ hr. in the after color of No. 56.

60. *Dark Red Violet*

    Yarn ....250 gr.
    Alum (mordant)...... 50 gr.
    Olium (blue dye)...... 4 gr.
    Cochineal .... 40 gr.

The yarn is mordanted and dyed blue as the former have been and is boiled in the red dye ½ to 1 hr. according to the redness required.

61. *Indian Red Violet*

    Yarn ....250 gr.
    Alum (mordant)...... 50 gr.
    Olium (blue dye)...... 2 gr.
    Cochineal .... 20 gr.

Handle as above.

62. *Bright Red Violet*

    Yarn ....250 gr.
    Alum (mordant)...... 40 gr.
    Olium (blue dye)...... 30 drops
    Cochineal .... 10 gr.

Handle as above.

63. *Light Red Violet*

    Yarn ....250 gr.
    Alum (mordant)...... 32 gr.

Handle as No. 59 and boil in the red after-dye of No. 60 or 61.

Violet with Cochineal or Madder

When madder is to be used with cochineal for red dyeing of violet, both ingredients must be soaked separately.

Cochineal is boiled as usual 10 minutes, and the liquid is cooled with cold water and the madder is added.

The dry blue yarn must first be squeezed in warm water so that it is wet before it is placed in the milk-warm red dye. In this it is heated and kept near the boiling point, 80° to 90° C, for 1 hr.

If the color is wanted more brown, let the yarn boil in the red dye.

64. *Very Dark Brown Violet*

    Yarn ....250 gr.
    Alum (mordant)...... 50 gr.
    Olium (blue dye)...... 8 gr.
    Cochineal .... 5 gr.
    Madder .... 25 gr.

Mordant the yarn as usual, and dye blue as in the case of former blue violet dyes.

65. *Plum Color*

    Yarn ....250 gr.
    Alum (mordant)...... 50 gr.
    Olium (blue dye)...... 3 gr.
    Cochineal .... 5 gr.
    Madder .... 20 gr.

Handle as above described.

66. *Light Brown Violet*

    Yarn . . . . .250 gr.
    Alum (mordant) . . . . . . 40 gr.
    Olium (blue dye) . . . . . . 1 gr.
    Cochineal . . . . 2 gr.
    Madder . . . . 15 gr.

Handle as before.

In all these red after-dyes, many violet shades may be dyed according as the liquid is dark or light, more or less red or blue. A little of the blue dye will always be left in the red dye.

The yarn for these after-dyes is mordanted as usual and is boiled in the cooled red liquid. It may also be dyed light blue so that the red becomes the chief color.

67. *Blue Violet with Ground Pine*

    Yarn . . . . .250 gr.
    Ground pine. . . . . .250 gr.
    Logwood . . . . 50 gr.

Mordant and dye as No. 36.

68. *Blue Violet with Chickweed*

    Yarn . . . . .250 gr.
    Chickweed . . . . 1 pail
    Logwood . . . . 30 gr.
    Alum (mordant) . . . . . . 32 gr.

Mordant and dye as No. 37.

Brown Dyes

Brown is obtained by mixing yellow, red and black dyestuffs.

Several brown dyestuffs are found complete in certain barks and roots and in a number of lichens. From herbs and leaves, brown is seldom obtained.

To bring out the brown colors, a copper or iron salt must often be added to the yellow or red dyestuff. When these salts, such as iron or copper vitriol, are added, they must be well dissolved and the dye must be cooled before the goods are put back into the liquid.

In all dye to which iron or copper vitriol is added, the goods must not lie still after it is through boiling. It is best to take it out immediately, cool quickly and rinse in clean water until it is washed.

A dark scum will always form on the dye when it cools and this will spot the goods. The same effect will be produced if the dyestuff is allowed to run down a part of the goods after being hung up.

69. *Yellow Brown with Bayberry Leaves*

    Yarn . . . . .250 gr.
    Alum (mordant) . . . . . . 40 gr.
    Bayberry leaves (dried).750 gr.

The yarn is mordanted and dyed as for yellow (see No. 4) and is taken out and 15 to 30 gr. copper sulphate is added. Boil the yarn ¼ to 1 hr.

If a very dark color is desired, let it boil again in the same or a new dye. The yarn must be dried between each dyeing just as in the heather dyeing. This is a very fast color.

70. *Yellow Brown with Alder Bark*
>   Yarn ....250 gr.
>   Alum (mordant)...... 32 gr.
>   Alder bark (dry)...... 5 kg.

The yarn is mordanted and dyed like the yellow with alder bark (see No. 8). But it is boiled in the liquid 1 to 2 hrs. and left until cold. If wanted still darker it may be dried and boiled again in new alder bark dye. This color darkens in time.

71. *Bronze Brown with Buckthorn Bark*
>   Yarn ....250 gr.
>   Alum (mordant)...... 35 gr.
>   Dry bark ....500 gr.

Chop the bark fine, soak and boil 3 hrs. To the strained liquid, add the alum and when it is dissolved, the dry unmordanted yarn is laid in the boiling dye. Boil in this 1 to 2 hrs., and let it remain until cold.

72. *Bronze Brown with Walnut Leaves*
>   Yarn ....250 gr.
>   Alum (mordant)...... 40 gr.
>   Fresh walnut leaves.... 1 kg.

Boil leaves 1 hr. and strain.

The mordanted yarn boils in the dye 1 to 2 hrs. and is left till cold.

73. *Olive Brown with Juniper Berries*
>   Yarn ....250 gr.

Alum .... 32 gr.	
Cream of tartar....... 18 gr.	Mordant
Copper sulphate....... 18 gr.	
Ammonia chloride...... 13 gr.	
Juniper berries......1 to 2 liter	
Copper acetate........ 16 gr.	

The mordants are dissolved in boiling water and stirred. Put in the yarn and boil one hour and leave until cold.

The dry, ripe berries are broken, put to soak and boiled one hour in clear water. Put in the mordanted yarn and let it boil with the berries 1 to 2 hrs. and then take out. Strain the liquid and add the copper acetate. Boil the yarn again $\frac{1}{4}$ to $\frac{1}{2}$ hr.

74. *Light Red-Brown with Gray Stone Lichens*
>   Yarn ....250 gr.
>   Dry lichens .... 1 kg.

Crush fine the lichens and soak over night, and then boil in a copper kettle in a reasonable amount of water. Boil the unmordanted yarn in this $\frac{1}{2}$ to 2 hrs. As this dye becomes very thick, the yarn must be stirred constantly. The hanks must be hung far apart and be well shaken. This color becomes clouded easily unless this is done.

A fast brown color is the result.

75. *Dark Reddish Brown with Stone Lichens*
>   Yarn ....250 gr.
>   Lichens ....1 to 1$\frac{1}{2}$ kg.

Crush fine the stone lichens and strew well between the yarn which is laid in layers with the lichens in an iron kettle. The yarn must be well covered and some large pieces of lichens placed between each layer of yarn. The yarn must be wet when laid down. Pour on cold water. Let it soak a few hours before boiling. Boil slowly and evenly 2 to 6 hrs.

If the yarn is to be very dark, it must be treated again with new lichens and in the same manner. If one has some used madder dye, this may be used instead of water. Wool may be dyed in the same manner. This is more easily dyed but the yarn is apt to be clouded unless one is very careful. It must have plenty of room.

76. *Dark Greenish Brown with Tree Lichens or Moss*

    Yarn ....250 gr.
    Lichens ....1 to 1½ kg.

This color is handled as above.

77. *Light Brown with Iceland Moss*

    Yarn ....250 gr.
    Moss ....250 gr.

Clean, rinse and chop the moss fine. This is placed between the layers of yarn in a kettle. The yarn must be well covered with moss. Pour on water and boil 1 to 2 hrs., or longer. The yarn may also be hung on sticks and boiled with the moss like the light yellow brown with stone lichens.

78. *Dark Brown with Iceland Moss*

    Yarn ....250 gr.

    Moss ....500 to 750 gr.
    Cooking salt .... 50 gr.

The moss is handled as above and laid in layers with the yarn in an iron kettle.

Strew the salt between, and pour on water and keep warm and boil for 48 hrs. It may stand in an oven or on a heating stove.

Handle afterwards like the other lichen colors. If one has not enough lichens, the color may be darkened by adding iron sulphate to the dye. But the yarn must first be taken out. This brown color will be a little more grayish if lichens only are used. All these dyes are absolutely fast.

79. *Sandal Brown (Gray Brown)*

    Yarn ....250 gr.
    Santalic acid .... 50 gr.
    Madder .... 50 gr.
    Mulberry .... 50 gr.
    Oak gall .... 15 gr.
    Iron sulphate .....10 to 15 gr.

Madder, santalic acid, mulberry and oak gall are pounded fine, put in a bag and boiled ¾ hr. The yarn is put dry into the liquid and boiled with the bag ½ hr. and then both are taken out. Add the iron sulphate and cool, and then boil the yarn 5 to 10 minutes.

If wanted darker, use more iron sulphate.

80. *Dark Red-Brown with Madder*

    Yarn ....250 gr.

```
Alum ........ ....... 45 gr. ⎫
Cream of tartar....... 16 gr. ⎬ Mordant
Madder ..............125 gr. ⎭
Oak gall ............. 12 gr.
Iron sulphate ......... 10 gr.
```

Mordant the yarn as usual 1 hr. Put the soaked madder in clear water. When the liquid is milk warm, add the wet mordanted yarn. Heat and boil, keeping in even motion 1/4 hr. and then take out. Add the crushed oak galls and stir. Boil the yarn in this 1/2 hr. Take out, add iron sulphate, cool a little and put yarn back. Boil, stirring evenly for 1/4 hr.

Gray Dyes

All plants that contain tannic acid, will make gray dyes.

Many kinds of bark contain much tannic acid from which, by adding iron salts, gray to black dyes may be obtained.

Boil the plants and the material first in this dye, which will give it a yellow, red or greenish color. Remove the goods and add the iron sulphate, which will change the color to gray. This gray will always have a tone of the foundation color which the plant alone gives; but the more iron sulphate that is added, the darker and more gray the color will become.

It is necessary always to maintain accurate proportions between the strength of the dye and the amount of iron sulphate. In a weak dye, a dark gray dye cannot be obtained, however much iron sulphate is added.

81. *Gray Brown with Alder Bark*
```
Yarn .................250 gr.
Alum (mordant)...... 32 gr.
Alder bark ........... 4 kg.
Iron sulphate.....10 to 30 gr.
```
Mordant the yarn and dye yellow with alder bark, as in No. 17. When it has boiled one hour in the alder bark, add the iron sulphate (see No. 54) and boil the yarn again 1/4 to 1/2 hr.

82. *Gray Violet with Birch Bark*
```
Yarn .................250 gr.
Dry birch bark .......600 gr.
Iron sulphate .....10 to 20 gr.
```
The bark is put to soak the day previous and is boiled 1 hr. Strain and boil the unmordanted yarn in the liquid 1 hr. Add the iron sulphate and boil the yarn 1/4 hr.

83. *Gray Reddish with Mountain Ash Bark*
```
Yarn .................250 gr.
Alum (mordant)...... 40 gr.
Dry bark ............. 2 kg.
Iron sulphate.....30 to 50 gr.
```
Boil the bark 1 to 2 hrs.—strain. Boil yarn in this dye 1 hr. Add iron sulphate and treat as described in No. 54.

84. *Blue Gray with Kinnikinnic*
```
Yarn .................250 gr.
```

Kinnikinnic ....1 to 2 kg.

Iron sulphate......5 to 20 gr.

The yarn is mordanted and dyed as for yellow (see No. 16). When boiled, add iron sulphate and boil yarn ¼ to ½ hr.

85. *Green Gray with Lady's Mantle*

Yarn ....250 gr.

Alum ....260 gr. ⎫

Cream of tartar....... 16 gr. ⎬ Mordant

Fresh lady's mantle.½ to 1 kg. ⎭

Iron sulphate......5 to 30 gr.

The yarn is mordanted as usual.

Boil the lady's mantle 1 hr. and strain. Boil the mordanted yarn in this liquid 1 hr. Remove this. Add the iron sulphate. Boil the yarn in the liquid until the color is dark enough.

86. *Green Gray with Sorrel*

Yarn ....250 gr.

When in the sorrel dye, yarn has been dyed black (see No. 89); from the after-dye one can get a gray green after color. The wet unmordanted yarn is boiled ½ to 1 hr. or longer in this liquid. The liquid may easily stand 1 to 2 days in an iron kettle.

87. *Gray with Sumac*

Yarn ....250 gr.

Mulberry wood .... 10 gr.

Sumac .... 25 gr.

Oak gall .... 10 gr.

Iron sulphate .... 10 gr.

The mulberry wood, which has been soaked, is boiled ½ hr., and then the sumac and oak gall are added and boiled. The yarn is placed dry in the boiling dye, and boiled ½ to 1 hr. Iron sulphate as usual is added (see No. 54) and the yarn is again well boiled.

88. *Light Gray*

Yarn ....250 gr.

Oak gall .... 3 gr.

Mulberry wood ....1½ gr.

Madder .... ½ gr.

Iron sulphate .... 3 gr.

The oak gall, mulberry wood, and madder is boiled ½ hr. The dry, unmordanted yarn is put in the boiling dye and boiled ½ hr. The yarn is taken out and the iron sulphate added. The yarn is again put back and boiled ½ hr.

By taking more or less of the different dyestuffs, the color will have a yellowish, reddish or violet tone. More iron sulphate darkens it.

Black Dyes

Black dyes can, like the gray, be made with the aid of iron salts from the plants containing tannic acid. But they can also be obtained from the blue dye-stuff in logwood. This latter is now most generally used. Although the dye-stuff in logwood is blue, black may be obtained from it by using different sorts of mordants. In order that the black shall not be too bluish, a little yellow dye should be added to the logwood.

For black dyes, an iron kettle is best. Untinned copper may be used, but not tinned copper kettles.

Logwood is always put in a bag to be boiled and, to save time, the goods may be boiled at the same time as the bag. But it must have plenty of room in the kettle.

Goods dyed black must be dried immediately after dyeing and then washed well in strong soap water and rinsed in clean water until it is absolutely clear. When the black dyes are well boiled and properly handled, they do not crock, but are absolutely fast.

89. *Black with Sorrel*

        Yarn ....250 gr.
        Fresh sorrel.......1 to 1½ kg.
        Logwood ....175 gr.
        Birch ashes ....250 gr.

Boil the sorrel 1 to 2 hrs. in a clean scrubbed iron kettle. Strain, scour the kettle before putting the dye back. In this the wet unmordanted yarn is boiled 2 hrs. and lies in the liquid until cold. The yarn should be a dark gray green. Put to soak the logwood, the day before dyeing, and boil in clear water 2 hrs. and take the bag out.

The mordanted yarn which has been squeezed out of the sorrel dye and rinsed in lukewarm water is put in the logwood liquid and boiled 2 hrs. When the logwood dye is nearly cold, it is mixed with 1 to 2 liters of lye which is made by pouring boiling water on the birch ashes, stirred and let stand till cold and clear. Let the yarn lie in this lye for 12 hrs. and then dry. Wash later.

Further Use of Used Dye Liquids

When yellow or red dyes have been made, the after liquid will always contain enough dye so that they may be used again to dye woolens and cotton goods—goods that do not require a decided color. These after-dyes are more or less fast, but are very pretty. The most are fast as regards washing and can be used for articles that are not much exposed to sunshine.

The goods are mordanted and handled the same as previously described. If one is dyeing rags and such common things, the mordant, if it be alum or cream of tartar, may be put in the after-dye direct.

Yellow After-Dyes

Different yellow after-dyes may be mixed together and the alum added at once. With after-dye of heather, cotton and linen may both be dyed yellow. This is a pretty color for the warp in simple rugs and carpets.

In the after-dye of ground pine, wool and cotton may be dyed. If they be re-boiled in used log-wood dye, a good blue gray color is obtained both in wool and cotton. It may be used for warp and carpet rags.

Red After-Dyes

Madder dye may be used to the last drop. Wool, rags and cotton yarn may be dyed in it. It must boil and the goods will become a light brownish red. Cotton and linen dye very light and fade in the sun, but the color is very pretty and may be used for warp where white is not wanted. The after-dye may also be used as the foundation color for darker red and brown shades. A little dye-stuff may be saved for this.

Cochineal dye may be used until there is only the clear water left. The light red almost colorless dye makes pretty light tints for old pure wool, white dresses and blouses, and a large amount of woolen sweater yarn may be dyed light red in such liquid.

If salmon color is desired, a tin solution is added, and the clean dry goods is allowed to boil in the liquid ¼ to ½ hr. The amount of tin solution is regulated by the weight of the goods. For 250 gr. goods use 50 to 100 gr. prepared clear yellow tin solution.

If a more bluish red is wanted, mordant the goods first in alum and then boil without the tin.

Madder and cochineal dyes may be mixed.

Blue After-Dyes

Indigo gives no after-dyes, as the goods always draws all the color into itself. In logwood dye, however, light gray blue after-dye is found.

Violet After-Dyes

The same is true of these dyes, as for the red after-dyes, where madder or cochineal has been used.

Green After-Dyes

Green after-dyes are not worth while using. They only give a dirty, undecided color.

Brown, gray and black after-dyes will give lighter shades. The gray after-dyes may be quite dainty and pretty.

From black logwood after-dyes, gray blue is obtained.

Dyeing of Old Goods

If one wishes to dye old, faded goods, it must first be well washed and then boiled ¼ hr. in soda water (which must not be strong enough to injure the goods) so that as much of the original dye is removed as possible. Then rinse it well. After that handle as the white.

When old goods is to be dyed, a darker color than the original must be chosen. For success a great deal depends on the foundation color, as the new must be dark enough to cover the old.

Only pale yellow or pink may be dyed yellow.

Pale yellow, pale violet, light gray, light brown, very pale green and red may be dyed red.

Pale yellow, pale green, violet, blue gray and light brown may be dyed blue. With ground pine and chick-weed dyes, pretty blues may be obtained.

Blue and red may be dyed violet.

All other light colors may be dyed brown.

All colors, light or dark may be dyed black.

It must be understood that with re-dyeing, the new color, unless it is very light, will always have a tone of the old ground color.

Unless one knows what dyes were used originally, it is best to dye a sample especially if the goods be of value, as the result may prove to be a different color than the one planned for. The old color is dissolved, so to say, by the new, and forms an entirely new compound.

Bleaching of Woolen Goods

No matter how well woolen goods are washed and how thoroughly the fats removed, it will never be perfectly white. If one wishes chalk white yarn or woolen cloth, it must be bleached. A peculiar odor will be noticed from these goods if boiling water be poured over them.

In the bleaching of woolen goods sulphur is used. This bleaching may easily be done at home by using sulphur in a tightly closed room where the damp woolen goods have been hung.

For bleaching, a large tight box or barrel with cover may be used. On one side, and quite near the floor, cut out a piece large enough to admit a fairly good sized iron kettle. The hole must be provided with a cover. At the top of the barrel or box, on the inside, strips of wood must be nailed on which the stick, holding the yarn, may be rested. Sometimes the wool is hung from a large spool or placed loosely in a net.

After the yarn has been thoroughly washed and rinsed it is allowed to dry enough so that the water does not drop from it. It must be evenly wet, without dry spots. It is hung in the barrel or box, and the top is well covered.

Glowing charcoal is placed in the iron kettle or dish. A handful of coarsely powdered sulphur is placed on the glowing coals and the opening is quickly closed.

There must be a large enough opening near the bottom to allow draft enough to burn the sulphur. The yarn or other goods is left in the box or barrel about 12 hrs. If it is white enough, it is rinsed in cold water and dried. If not, bleach again. Care should be taken not to hang the goods too near the kettle.

It is not necessary to bleach woolen goods which are to be dyed with plants. As a rule it is not done, but if one does not object to the work, certain light, dainty colors become cleaner when bleached. Some, however, are duller and not as pretty as when using the bleached yarn.

Hand Measures

25 gr. soda—1 handful.
100 gr. greensoap—1 heaping wood spoon.
25 gr. madder—1 heaping tablespoon.
20 gr. mulberry—1 heaping tablespoon.
15 gr. logwood—1 heaping tablespoon.
20 gr. cochineal—1 heaping tablespoon.
8 gr. pulverized alum—1 heaping teaspoon.
8 gr. coarsely powdered cream of tartar—1 heaping tablespoon.
12 gr. coarsely powdered potassium chromate—1 heaping teaspoon.
10 gr. iron sulphate—1 heaping teaspoon.
10 gr. coarsely pounded copper sulphate—1 heaping teaspoon.
1 gr. olium—5 drops.

INDEX

Abbreviations: (w. d.), working drawing; (ill.), illustration; (pat.), pattern; (dr.), draft.

INDEX — Concluded